Living with Intensity

Understanding the Sensitivity, Excitability, and Emotional Development of Gifted Children, Adolescents, and Adults

Susan Daniels, Ph.D. and Michael M. Piechowski, Ph.D.
Editors

Great Potential Press™

Living with Intensity: Understanding the Sensitivity, Excitability, and Emotional Development of Gifted Children, Adolescents, and Adults

Cover design: Huchinson-Frey
Interior design: The Printed Page
Copy Editor: Jennifer Ault

Published by Great Potential Press, Inc.
P.O. Box 5057
Scottsdale, AZ 85261

Printed on recycled paper

© **2008 Great Potential Press**

10 09 08 07 06   5 4 3 2 1

Library of Congress Cataloging-in-Publication Data

Living with intensity : emotional development of gifted children, adolescents, and adults / Susan Daniels and Michael Piechowski, editors.
    p. cm.
  Includes index.
  ISBN-13: 978-0-910707-89-3
  ISBN-10: 0-910707-89-8
1. Gifted persons. 2. Emotions. I. Daniels, Susan. II. Piechowski, Michael M. (Michael Marian)
  BF412.L58 2008
  152.4087'9—dc22
                    2008037615

Dedication

For Devin—
With love. S.D.

For Eva—
With gratitude. M.M.P.

Acknowledgments

Many voices have contributed to this volume—all of our authors, of course, but also many whose names do not appear in the Table of Contents. Sharon Lind was an early collaborator and guiding voice in the planning of this work. Numerous conferences and workshops brought the authors herein together over many years. Jane Piirto initially brought a group together to explore the work of Kazimierz Dabrowski and its applications with the gifted when she hosted three workshops in the early 1990s at Ashland University. Robert Clasen, at the University of Wisconsin – Madison, provided a venue over several consecutive summers for many of us to meet and further this work in the mid 1990s. At the Wisconsin summer conferences, numerous ideas for further collaborations were generated, including the development of the OEQ-II and ultimately planning for the OEQ-2C. Other colleagues from Wisconsin were incredibly supportive during this time as well, including Cynthia Clark, Tim Connell, Karen Fiske, and Julie Seaborg. Thanks to all who collaborated at those Midwest gatherings.

Most recently, Wendy Zinn has been a valued friend, sounding board, and project assistant, spending countless hours listening, reading, and making suggestions and late night runs for coffee as this book emerged.

Finally, working closely with Great Potential Press has been a pleasure, and particularly working with Jim Webb and Jan Gore, as each iteration led to yet another—patient and insightful until the finish. Thank you.

Contents

List of Tables

Foreword

Sal Mendaglio, Ph.D.
Division of Teacher Preparation
Graduate Division of Educational Research and
Centre for Gifted Education, University of Calgary

Living with Intensity: Understanding the Sensitivity, Excitability, and Emotional Development of Gifted Children, Adolescents, and Adults represents a unique contribution to the social and emotional domain of giftedness. The distinctiveness of this book rests in its in-depth treatment of the emotional development of gifted individuals and the particular lens through which it is seen. Numerous citations in the literature attest to the importance of emotional development in our current approach to giftedness and gifted education. In *Living with Intensity*, Susan Daniels and Michael Piechowski provide us with a comprehensive discussion of various aspects of emotional development authored by an array of contributors, including practitioners and researchers, all of whom are established experts in the area. The compendium of information contained in this book will be of great interest to parents, teachers, researchers, and gifted individuals themselves.

Of particular interest to me is the Dabrowskian lens through which the chapter topics are viewed. Dabrowski's theory of positive disintegration is, without doubt, the most influential theory in the study of giftedness. Readers unfamiliar with the theory need not worry, because the authors explain Dabrowski in the course of discussing their topics.

Kazimierz Dabrowski proposed a theory of personality that is analogous to Freud's theory of psychoanalysis in scope—but that is where the similarity with other personality theory ends. Dabrowski's theory is a unique approach to personality, replete with apparently oxymoronic phrases that compel readers to re-assess their explicit and tacit assumptions regarding human development. Until recently, the breadth and complexity of the theory were not widely known in the field of gifted education because the focus was on only one of Dabrowski's numerous concepts, *overexcitability*, so much so that it seemed to me that "theory of overexcitability" was a more suitable label than "theory of positive disintegration." As a result, Dabrowski's true genius was masked. Daniels and Piechowski's book contributes significantly to a movement in the field to represent the theory of positive disintegration as Dabrowski himself presented it.

That the representation of Dabrowski's theory in *Living with Intensity* goes beyond the emphasis on overexcitability is not surprising, given several of the contributors to the book. The book includes chapters by authors who were instrumental in the initial application of Dabrowski's theory to gifted education. These pioneers include Linda Silverman, Nancy Miller, and Frank Falk. The most notable pioneer, however, is Michael Piechowski, who collaborated with Dabrowski and who introduced the theory to gifted education. Michael is unique because he knows the theory as a result of discussions and debates that he and Dabrowski had in Polish. Piechowski, Silverman, Miller, and Falk have a history of productive collaboration regarding the theory, including development of instruments to assess overexcitability. This group of pioneers has a rich knowledge of the theory, and they have worked hard to apply it to broaden our understanding of giftedness. The remaining contributors all have a long-standing interest in the theory and have used it to understand various phenomena associated with giftedness, including giftedness itself.

In addition to using Dabrowski's theory as an appropriate conceptual framework for the topic, I see a practical advantage accruing to Daniels and Piechowski's use of the theory: it provides a theme that unites the various chapters. Edited books, unlike authored ones, run the risk of simply being a disparate collection of chapters. The contributors' use of Dabrowski's theory as a common thread has reduced this possibility, as has the logical organization of the book.

The book begins by providing a solid foundation in the theory as it relates to giftedness, and subsequent chapters provide a lifespan progression. Another notable feature of the book is the illustrative material provided by the authors, which is particularly useful when describing Dabrowskian concepts. Many of his concepts are counterintuitive, and examples provide great assistance to the reader. Further, the authors provide strategies for enhancing the emotional development of gifted individuals, which will also be appreciated by parents, educators, and practitioners.

I congratulate Susan and Michael for their illuminating chapters and for recruiting a stellar array of contributors. Through their own work and shepherding the works of their expert authors, they have produced a resource that will serve our field well for many years to come.

Part One

Kazimierz Dabrowski, Overexcitability, Giftedness, and Developmental Potential

Chapter 1

Embracing Intensity: Overexcitability, Sensitivity, and the Developmental Potential of the Gifted

Susan Daniels, Ph.D., and Michael M. Piechowski, Ph.D.

"She is never satisfied!"

As a small child, I heard these words a thousand times....
Long before I understood what these words meant, I made
them into a family, much like my stuffed animals. Their
family name was "Un." They were the "Uns," and each of
them had the same ability to put a surprised or worried look
on my mother's face.... I created a family tree for them. The
great-grandfather of the words was Uncontrollable.

After Uncontrollable, there came quite often Unsat-
isfied. Then Unmanageable. Or Impossible. Undisciplined.
Insatiable. Insubordinate.... Unadaptable. Unpredictable.
(Grimaud, 2006, pp. 1-2)

Hélène Grimaud, who wrote the above recollection of her childhood trials, became a concert pianist, settling in upper New York state, where she created a Wolf Conservation Center inhabited by wild wolves. Her memoir of her growing up years, *Wild Harmonies: A Life of Music and Wolves*, offers profound insight into the rocky path of a highly gifted and passionate person growing up in a world that doesn't always understand or appreciate such energy and passion.

Emotional Intensity of Gifted Children

The emotional intensity and high level of energy of a gifted child cannot be ignored because they disturb the routine and the order of things set before the arrival of the little Energizer. Gifted children take in information from the world around them; they react and respond more quickly and intensely than other children. They are stimulated both by what's going on around them and by what moves them from within.

Because they can be so greatly stimulated, and because they perceive and process things differently, gifted children are often misunderstood. Their excitement is viewed as excessive, their high energy as hyperactivity, their persistence as nagging, their questioning as undermining authority, their imagination as not paying attention, their passion as being disruptive, their strong emotions and sensitivity as immaturity, their creativity and self-directedness as oppositional. They stand out from the norm. But then, what is normal?

It is of course unfortunate that something exceptional, something that is outside of the norm, is often looked upon as being abnormal, and that "abnormal" usually means annoying or bad, whereas "normal" means mostly acceptable or good. We forget that these notions come from a statistical convention, the bell curve, which does not tell us what is good and what is bad.

In statistics, what is average constitutes the norm. The norm has a defined range that includes the majority of cases. The average income is normal because that's what the majority of people earn, yet is it a good income? Many consider it insufficient—and therefore inadequate. It is an example of something that is normal and yet it is not quite good enough. What we value as good income is above the norm. A similar case can be made for intelligence. The majority of people are within the normal range of intelligence, but this is not sufficient for all situations or circumstances. For example, average intelligence does not guarantee acceptance or success in graduate school. Statistical norms are a poor guide to what is good.

Psychology, in its origin, based its models on physics as an ideal. Had psychology chosen life science as its model—after all, people are living beings—the concept of what is normal would not be the average, but rather what is well-functioning—that is, in good health. Optimal, in life sciences, is often quite different from statistically average or normal, yet optimal functioning is what we hope people will strive for. Such optimal functioning is a major thrust of this book. We can put it like this:

Statistical norm: normal = average; average income and average intelligence are normal

Life science norm: normal = well-functioning or healthy; a healthy organ, a healthy organism are normal but are not necessarily average

optimal = well-developed through training and/or by having a higher natural endowment

Suppose that 67% of adult males in Chicago have some form of heart disease. This would be normal from the statistical point of view but certainly not desirable or optimal, and it would even be abnormal from the life science point of view, because the norm is a healthy heart. Good health is above average, and unquestionably it is better.

Abraham Maslow (1970) was one psychologist who understood the life science norm. He set out to find people in robust psychological health because he realized that the average represents a stunted norm. An ordinary or average person was, in his mind, a full human being whose powers and capacities have been somewhat dampened and inhibited. When he found men and women who were examples of robust psychological health, he saw them as ordinary people with nothing taken away and thus fully capable to realize their potential. Maslow called these individuals *self-actualizing.* Albert Schweitzer is an example of someone who was self-actualizing. He was a talented musician and doctor, and then, wanting still more challenge and to help people in need, he left the comforts of civilization to go to Africa and build a hospital. He found a mission that extended beyond himself.

A Change in Perspective: Dabrowski's Theory

A gifted child, rich in intensities and sensitivities, cannot be brought down to the "normal" range, as Hélène Grimaud so eloquently expressed. Gifted children should not be pressed to "fit in" with all of the other children the same age. Rather, their capacity for intense experiencing is an asset that deserves to be understood and affirmed instead of squashed.

We owe this positive perspective about gifted young people to Kazimierz Dabrowski (1902-1980), a Polish psychiatrist and psychologist who also held a Master's degree in Education. Dabrowski had a strong interest in the emotional development of intellectually and artistically gifted youth. He was struck by their intensity, sensitivity, and tendency toward emotional extremes. He didn't see these traits as abnormal but as part and parcel of their talented, creative selves. In their intensified experiencing, feeling, thinking, and imagining, he perceived potential for further growth (Dabrowski, 1967, 1972). He saw inner forces at work that on the one hand generated overstimulation, conflict, and pain, but on the other hand, these factors provoked individuals to search for a way through the pain, strife, and disharmony. Dabrowski's life work embraced the heightened excitability of individuals, their drive, curiosity, and their urge to challenge conformity, complacency, and smug self-satisfaction.

Major life experiences undoubtedly influenced his work and his quest to understand human nature. Dabrowski lived through both World Wars. As an adolescent, he witnessed the brutalities of World War I, literally in his own backyard. In World War II, during the German occupation of Poland, he helped Jews to hide, and he suffered imprisonment by the Nazis himself. After the war, he was imprisoned again, this time by the Communists, because he spoke out strongly for individual self-determination and against subjugation of the individual by the state.

As a clinician in Warsaw, he counseled talented artists, writers, actors, and members of religious orders. In many psychological frameworks of the 20th century, creative visions and ecstatic experiences were considered immature and neurotic, even delusional (Hall, Lindzey, & Campbell, 1997), but Dabrowski discerned deep seeking in those having these experiences and saw a potential in them for advanced development.

Dabrowski built his theory over many years and called it a theory of positive disintegration. "What can be positive about disintegration?" one might ask. Disintegration means breakdown, collapse, ruin, but it also means dismantling as a prelude to construction and subsequent creation at a higher level. If we think of the self as having many parts working together, we are relying on a concept of order or structure. Things can and do change in the self, as they do everywhere else in life. As a result of great loss, grief, and despair, one may experience an inner fragmentation, a collapse, even a breakdown. That's the disintegration part. For example, when the girlfriend whom a boy loves passionately leaves the young man and breaks off the relationship, he may become so upset that life for him loses meaning, thereby triggering a process of psychic crumbling. Such a breakdown, if he feels no hope, may proceed to a full disintegration. But once he starts to question himself and realize that others have lived through similar experiences, that one cannot make another person responsible for one's happiness, he is on the way out of the disintegration. Inner growth begins, and it is positive—a process of emotional development within the broader context of personality development.

We tend to think of human development as following the stages of life that all of us go through—infancy, childhood, adolescence, adulthood, old age. Dabrowski viewed human development in completely different terms—that is, as powered by the tension between the higher and the lower, the good and the bad, experienced within the self. For Dabrowski, the drama of inner seeking, figuring out the world, feeling anguish, questioning the meaning of human existence, testing one's values and ideals, growing in empathy and understanding of others—these are the elements that encompass the striving for optimal human development. For Dabrowski, human development was characterized by reflection, self-evaluation, and the urge for inner transformation.

Bold New Concepts

Two concepts lie at the foundation of Dabrowski's theory: (1) developmental potential, and (2) multilevelness. Developmental potential refers to the initial endowment that is different for each individual. The stronger the endowment, the greater the potential for advanced development. How it will be fulfilled depends on the life conditions that either assist or block personal growth. Potential is a concept that says only what is possible; it does not predetermine how a life will unfold. Weaker endowment means that the potential is limited, yet if conditions are favorable, they will nurture a person's development into a decent human being (Piechowski, 2008).

Multilevelness presents the bold idea that human experience varies according to level or type of development. Human emotions, motivations, values, desires, and behaviors are expressed in strikingly different ways. For example, joy could be experienced as feeling superior, defeating an opponent, succeeding by cunning, or from the feeling of power when cleverly manipulating others. But to many people, such joy would be offensive because of its disregard for others. A different kind of joy would be the joy that the name of a loved one brings, the joy of overcoming bad habits, the joy of self-discovery, the joy of a creative moment and inspiration, the joy of being able to help another. In the first case, the experiences of joy are egocentric, self-serving, self-protecting, and power-seeking. In the second case, they arise from love and empathy toward others, from positive changes in oneself, and from expansive feelings of a higher order. The first case represents joy at a low emotional level; the second case represents joy on a high emotional level.

This comparison can be extended to all emotions and behaviors. Emotional level, in Dabrowski's theory, means inner growth rather than the usual age-related maturation through the lifespan. In this model, then, it is quite possible for a young person to operate on a higher emotional level than a so-called mature adult.

In this way, expressions of emotions and behaviors vary according to developmental level. Dabrowski described five such levels, which will be discussed in Chapter 2.

Developmental Potential

Dabrowski's concept of developmental potential is of particular interest because its components overlap with characteristics frequently found in both gifted children and adults. Talents, specific abilities, and high general intelligence constitute the initial and most obvious component. Overexcitabilities constitute the second component. These aspects of Dabrowski's theory have been readily embraced by the field of gifted education because heightened excitability and hyperstimulation are frequently observed in gifted children. The sensitivity and capacity to be intensely stimulated, and to stay stimulated, provide fuel for the development of gifted children and adults.

Another component of Dabrowski's concept of development, called the *third factor*, refers to the capacity for self-directed emotional growth, self-determination, and autonomy. This component may not be present in some people.

Five Overexcitabilities

Overexcitability is an innate tendency to respond in an intensified manner to various forms of stimuli, both external and internal (Piechowski, 1979, 1999). Overexcitability is a translation of the Polish word "nadpobudliwość," which literally means "superstimulatability." (It should have been called superexcitability.) It means that persons may require less stimulation to produce a response, as well as stronger and more lasting reactions to stimuli. Another way of looking at it is of being *spirited*—"more intense, sensitive, perceptive, persistent, energetic" (Kurcinka, 1991).

There are five forms of overexcitability in Dabrowski's theory: psychomotor, sensual, intellectual, imaginational, and emotional. Each can have a wide range of expressions (see Table 1.1). The forms of overexcitability appear to be the necessary—but not sufficient—raw material for advanced, multilevel development.

Overexcitability means that life is experienced in a manner that is deeper, more vivid, and more acutely sensed. This does not just mean that one experiences more curiosity, sensory enjoyment, imagination, and emotion, but also that the experience is of a different kind, having a more complex and more richly textured quality.

Overexcitabilities impart an intense aliveness to those who experience them. They may be thought of as distinct modes of experiencing or as channels through which flow the color tones, textures, insights, visions, emotional currents, and energies of experience. An analogy is often made to having a cable connection that pulls in many streams of information from far and near, in contrast to the old rabbit ears antenna limited to local channels only.

Behaviors and characteristics that frequently typify the five forms of overexcitability (OE) can be described briefly as follows:

- *Psychomotor*—movement, restlessness, drivenness, an augmented capacity for being active and energetic

- *Sensual*—enhanced refinement and aliveness of sensual experience

- *Intellectual*—thirst for knowledge, discovery, questioning, love of ideas and theoretical analysis, search for truth

- *Imaginational*—vividness of imagery, richness of association, facility for dreams, fantasies, and inventions, endowing toys and other objects with personality (animism), preference for the unusual and unique

- *Emotional*—great depth and intensity of emotional life expressed in a wide range of feelings, great happiness to profound sadness or despair, compassion, responsibility, self-examination

Table 1.1. Forms and Expressions of Overexcitability
(Piechowski, 1999)

PSYCHOMOTOR

Surplus of energy

rapid speech, marked excitation, intense physical activity (e.g., fast games and sports), pressure for action (e.g., organizing), marked competitiveness

Psychomotor expression of emotional tension

compulsive talking and chattering, impulsive actions, nervous habits (tics, nail biting), workaholism, acting out

SENSUAL

Enhanced sensory and aesthetic pleasure

seeing, smelling, tasting, touching, hearing, delight in beautiful objects, sounds of words, music, form, color, balance

Sensual expression of emotional tension

overeating, sexual overindulgence, buying sprees, wanting to be in the limelight

INTELLECTUAL

Intensified activity of the mind

curiosity, concentration, capacity for sustained intellectual effort, avid reading, keen observation, detailed visual recall, detailed planning

Penchant for probing questions and problem solving

search for truth and understanding, forming new concepts, tenacity in problem solving

Reflective thought

thinking about thinking, love of theory and analysis, preoccupation with logic, moral thinking, introspection (but without self-judgment), conceptual and intuitive integration, independence of thought (sometimes very critical)

IMAGINATIONAL

Free play of the imagination

frequent use of image and metaphor, facility for invention and fantasy, facility for detailed visualization, poetic and dramatic perception, animistic and magical thinking

Capacity for living in a world of fantasy

predilection for magic and fairy tales, creation of private worlds, imaginary companions, dramatization

Spontaneous imagery as an expression of emotional tension

animistic imagery, mixing truth and fiction, elaborate dreams, illusions

Low tolerance of boredom

need for novelty and variety

EMOTIONAL

Feelings and emotions intensified

positive feelings, negative feelings, extremes of emotion, complex emotions and feelings, identification with others' feelings, awareness of a whole range of feelings

Strong somatic expressions

tense stomach, sinking heart, blushing, flushing, pounding heart, sweaty palms

Strong affective expressions

inhibition (timidity, shyness), enthusiasm, ecstasy, euphoria, pride, strong affective memory, shame, feelings of unreality, fears and anxieties, feelings of guilt, concern with death, depressive and suicidal moods

Capacity for strong attachments, deep relationships

strong emotional ties and attachments to persons, living things, places, attachments to animals, difficulty adjusting to new environments, compassion, responsiveness to others, sensitivity in relationships, loneliness

Well-differentiated feelings toward self

inner dialogue and self-judgment

Some authors have referred to the overexcitabilities as *original equipment* (OE). Similar to aspects of temperament, overexcitabilities are often noticed quite early in life. For example, gifted children tend to be more active and more alert than most children and display a higher energy level, whether physical, intellectual, or emotional. Their intensity is greater than average, sometimes extreme, and an overabundance of energy enhances their experience. For example, a student described a personal reservoir of energy: "I get filled with energy when I need that energy. And, of course, I release it by doing the thing that got me excited in the first place" (see Piechowski, 2006, p. 40, for many more examples). This surplus of energy, or *psychomotor* overexcitability, has to be discharged through action.

Sensory experience for gifted children tends to be of a much richer quality because so much more detail, texture, contrast, and distinction come into awareness. Liking with passion what is pleasant and disliking intensely what is unpleasant characterizes *sensual* overexcitability. As one adolescent said, "I seem to notice more smells more acutely than a lot of other people. I love dark, musty smells and earthy smells, herbs and things like that. I love the smell of clean air in spring and tree blossoms and things and the smell of clean bodies, especially hair" (see Piechowski, 2006, p. 48, for more examples). Sensual and emotional overexcitability often combine together, making the individual's experience richer and more meaningful. In an intimate relationship, sensual and emotional elements often blend together.

Intellectual overexcitability is the characteristic most often associated with gifted children and adults. Janneke Frank (2006) wrote that intelligence is about the ability to solve problems, but overexcitability is about the *passion* for solving them. When emotional and mental energies meet, the mind supplies the intellectual power of concentration, while emotional energy drives the interest and the passion in pursuing them. "I read stories deeper, read into questions, find catchy puns or mistakes of words in people's writings, etc. If something has no meaning, I try to give it some. If it means something, I wonder why. I usually find when given a topic to write about, for example, I usually have a completely different approach to the same topic than does the rest of the class" (see Piechowski, 2006, p. 54, for many additional examples).

Gifted children and adults tend to have excitable *imagination*, but highly creative individuals display their imagination in especially rich and surprising ways; think of Albert Einstein, Walt Disney, or J. K. Rowling. Imagination is a vast concept encompassing activity and application in wide and diverse areas—literature, the arts, science, technology, culture, and interpersonal relationships. Creativity depends on imagination completely to enable the inspiration, invention, and construction of new possibilities. Boredom is anathema; the need for novelty is absolute. "Once in a while I try to hypnotize my plants. And I even tried to put a rock in a trance, but I think that day I was desperate for something to do" (see Piechowski, 2006, p. 81, for other examples, plus four additional chapters on imagination).

Emotional overexcitability finds expression in a wide range of emotions and feelings. It can reach extremes of sensitivity and intensity, as it does in many gifted children and adults. Compassion, caring, and responsibility are prominent. Empathy can work as a way of knowing. Emotional intensity becomes evident early and tends to stay with a person for life; it is also quite independent of what actually evoked the intense emotional response. "Sometimes after talking to someone, being alone watching the animals at sunrise, I feel as if I should conquer the world, do anything and everything. I feel like I am a bird who can soar with…just me, the wind, and the sun" (Piechowski, 2006, p. 134). In contrast, people who are unemotional, whose feelings and emotions tend to stay on an even keel, do not change much in this respect, even though they may be intellectually gifted (Larsen & Diener, 1987).

It would be hard to find a person of talent who shows little evidence of any of the five overexcitabilities. They are the underlying dimensions of thinking outside the box, the urge to create beauty, the push for stark realism, the unrelenting striving for truth and justice (Piechowski, 1979, 1999). Unfortunately, the stronger these overexcitabilities are, the less peers and teachers welcome them. Developing understanding that this is the child's or adult's innate makeup facilitates tolerance and acceptance—and, one hopes, even an appreciation of these fertile qualities.

The picture of superexcitability painted above assumes that these intensities and sensitivities are more or less on the surface, easy to notice. However, as Jackson and Moyle point out (Chapter 7), they are sometimes deeply hidden and therefore hard to notice. In fact, some gifted children protect themselves and try to hide their extreme sensitivity so that they give the mistaken impression of being unemotional, impassive or indifferent, and unresponsive to social cues.

When adults encounter high levels of sensitivity and intensity in children, they may not know how to respond to assist those children. Yet the challenges are even more acute for young gifted children who may not understand their own sensitivity and intensity. Who, for instance, could understand the extreme emotions that Hélène Grimaud (the pianist at the beginning of our chapter) experienced:

> *"Make her play some sports!"*
>
> *No doubt, someone had diagnosed an excessive amount of energy, an overabundance of vitality that could be released through martial arts or tennis. I did both; I took dance as well, but I was found to be completely unfit. What I hated about ballet was not just the physical discipline: the costume disgusted me too. Nothing about it pleased me, not the leotard, the tutu, the slippers, or the pink satin. I looked appallingly like the dolls that, on several unfortunate occasions, were given me at Christmas. I furiously smashed them all against the wall. The very idea that someone would think of giving me such a thing horrified me. Imagine how I felt about looking like one! (Grimaud, 2006, p. 2)*

Children exhibiting strong overexcitabilities are often made to feel embarrassed and guilty for being "different." Here is an eloquent expression of the ever-present feeling of differentness written by a highly gifted boy living in a rural area:

> *Anywhere I go, no matter if it is school or home, there is always a little block that separates me from everybody else. The signs of it are subtle, like people not understanding a word I use, or everybody jumping to work with me in group projects, but there they are, isolating me from them, making it hard to make friends. Some people would laugh at this, saying it's nothing, but the thing they don't realize is that it isn't nothing. The barrier is there, and not being able to get past it is sometimes painful. I try to ignore it, to forget the fact that I go nowhere on weekends and don't see the few friends I have until Monday. I try, by playing video games or reading, to offset it, but it's still there, and when I think about, it hurts. It's not like a sharp stinging pain that you get from a paper cut. It's dull, almost unnoticeable, but it hurts more because it doesn't get better over time. The distance between me and other people is hidden, but still there if you know where to look. That block hurts me, and there is only one way to make it stop, and that is to spend time with a person who also has to deal with this barrier, this wall.* (D. J. Gallenberger, age 14)

Criticized and teased for what they cannot help, children like this start believing that there is something wrong with them. Disguising their intensity and trying to act "normal" may work for a time, but in the end, it means denying their own self and their own unique potential. Discouragement, depression, or a state of anxiety inevitably follow.

Emotionally intense individuals can also be very sensitive to others being hurt, to injustice, and also to criticism and their own pain. If an emotionally sensitive child is exposed to much criticism and ridicule, that child may withdraw emotionally. As a result, the child's emotional vitality is gradually lost, and enjoyment of one's successes and achievements feels hollow (Miller, 1981).

Overexcitabilities, the intensities and sensitivities of how life is experienced, on the one hand create for gifted individuals the advantages for the unfolding of talents, but on the other hand, overstimulation brings on pronounced difficulties which are compounded by the lack of acceptance from others. Overexcitability is often viewed by others as overreacting or as inappropriate behavior needing to be tempered—"for the good of the child." This is no less than tampering with the child's very self. More often than not, aspects of intensity are mistaken for indicators of potential pathology rather than as signs of strong developmental potential. What looks abnormal, as compared to more typical development, mental health professionals tend to see as something to be treated rather than as a contributor to optimal development.

Multilevelness

When developmental potential includes the capacity for inner transformation, which is the ability to consciously engage in the work of personal growth, Dabrowski called it *multilevel*. What makes it "multilevel" is a tension between what is experienced as higher versus lower in oneself.

An inner ideal of a higher level of consciousness may be sensed only dimly, yet it does exercise a pull, and with time, it tends to increase in strength. The process takes an upward direction from one's current self to one's more advanced or higher self—a process of multilevel development. For example, one adolescent boy showed this direction as he reflected on his own potential. At 15, he saw himself as someone meant to develop his talents to the fullest. At 17, when he was planning to go to medical school, he realized that there was a conflict between the cutthroat competition to get admission and the role of the physician as a healer, as someone whose duty is to build people's confidence and sense of security. He saw the admissions process as self-defeating (Piechowski, 2006). Similarly, conscientious objectors like Lt. Louis Font, during the Vietnam war, and Daniel Cobos, the first well-known resister in the Air Force, came to the realization that they could no longer serve causes that were morally wrong to them (Everett, 1986).

An individual may experience a conflict in the face of unfair and unjust actions of society and then attempt to stand up for what is right. Dabrowski called such action "positive maladjustment." The adjustment required to go along with an interest group, or a whole society, when it violated ethical principles would be something negative. Opposing this would be positive, even though a conflict ensued.

Children and adolescents who stand up for their classmates when they see them treated unfairly demonstrate positive maladjustment, something not always appreciated. Jodee Blanco (2003), a girl who was horribly bullied in high school and later wrote a book about it, was very talented but also wanted to be accepted by the popular group. Against her better judgment, she went along with the group when they staged a cruel practical joke on one of the teachers. Seeing the teacher's broken spirit as a result, she deeply regretted her part and became critical of the popular group. For this, she was bullied to the end of high school. Now, she is a successful publishing executive working with best-selling and award-winning authors, entertainers, and athletes, but the vivid memory of her mistreatment remains.

Authentic Development

Dabrowski's theory describes the process of inner growth wherein the guiding principle is to be true to oneself. The search for self-knowledge entails inner struggles, doubts, and even despair about one's emotional, psychological, and spiritual shortcomings, and yet it always leads back again to the processes of gaining greater understanding of others, ridding oneself of prejudices, and becoming more self-determined in achieving one's inner ideal. Self-knowledge, as Eleanor Roosevelt (1960) observed, is not easily won. She wrote that it takes courage to face oneself and to truthfully examine one's motives. The protective veiling that hangs there is not easily removed to uncover things in ourselves that are likely to make us wince. Attaining self-knowledge requires patience, determination, and courage. Inner growth of this nature, once it starts, does not stop. Inner forces at work push for new challenges and further development.

For Dabrowski, authentic development, or multilevel development, means going beyond our innate constitution and environmental constraints. It requires making a commitment to one's own particular inner truth in harmony with the needs and values of others and their inner truths.

Lifespan Development

Dabrowski was clear that personality development does not take place in stages that correspond to childhood, adolescence, and adulthood. The theory is not an age-based stage theory, and thus it can be applied to individuals without regard to previous stages or chronological age. Since gifted children often exhibit behaviors and understanding more typical of adults than of their peers, this theory helps to guide gifted education and counseling where other paradigms fall short. We see early indicators of developmental potential, particularly high levels of overexcitability, intensity, sensitivity, moral and ethical awareness, and tendencies toward perfection, in even very young gifted children, as well as in gifted adolescents and young adults.

From this perspective, it becomes clear that our children must be reared and educated in an environment of mutual compassion, under-standing, and positive adjustment—not simply adjustment to the changing material conditions of life. We must also recognize that our potential for growth does not end with childhood. The evolution of one's personality is an individual, autonomous process of perceiving, feeling, intuiting, and striving for that which is higher and truer in oneself throughout one's life.

Chapter 2

Dabrowski's Levels and the Process of Development

Susan Daniels, Ph.D., and Michael M. Piechowski, Ph.D.

Dabrowski's theory is not an age- or stage-based theory of development, but a theory of personal growth that may be likened to scaling a mountain. One faces risks and danger, tests of courage, and the necessity to persevere. This image suggests that not everyone has the strength or the capacity to climb up. Not everyone will have an interest in mountain climbing, and some may prefer or be satisfied to stay below in the valley where it is more familiar and predictable. A person with limited potential for the endeavor may start and not get very far before returning, while another may choose to stay indoors and not even venture out. Some will strive forward determined to reach the summit, enduring the inclement weather and rough terrain but reaping the reward of breathtaking vistas along the way (Piechowski, 2009).

Types as Levels of Development

Dabrowski examined types of development, which he arranged as levels (see Table 2.1). In his view, he saw a psychological inner environment analogous to the physiological internal environment. He saw the dynamic events of felt experience as taking place in that inner space, which he called an *inner psychic milieu*. This inner space of private, subjective experience, according to Dabrowski, begins to form when the gaze is directed inward and a person experiences a tension within oneself—an inner conflict. The conflict he had in mind is of a special nature; it is not like deciding between different jobs or careers, but rather it is experiencing a tension between what a person feels to be higher and lower qualities of oneself. A self-evaluation is involved, a judgment as to the gap between the person one is and the person one feels one can become. Experience of this gap comes on with great intensity and often evokes considerable self-criticism.

The negative aspects of oneself are judged to be lower, something to get rid of or to change radically. The positive aspects of oneself are intuitively felt as higher and holding the potential for personal growth and inner transformation. In Dabrowski's vision, this process has many inwardly experienced levels, so he called it *multilevel*. Consequently, in the sense that he gave it in his theory, true personal growth is multilevel. And the rocky path leads through a difficult but positive disintegration.[1]

Table 2.1. Levels of Development and Developmental Processes

UNILEVEL PROCESS: Levels I and II

<u>Level I</u>: Primary Integration – No Inner Growth

(1) There is no development, little introspection, and little inner conflict.

(2) A crisis may precipitate a breakdown; this is a unilevel disintegration.

<u>Level II</u>: Unilevel Disintegration – Unilevel Development

(1) The individual's problems are recycled with no upward direction of development.

(2) Experiencing a developmental milestone or following a breakdown of trust in authority, development moves toward a sense of self. If developmental potential has no multilevel elements and no vertical tension, re-integration at a lower level or a negative disintegration will result.

(3) When developmental potential has multilevel elements, development may take the upward direction.

MULTILEVEL PROCESS: Levels III, IV, and V

<u>Level III</u>: Spontaneous Multilevel Disintegration – Multilevel Development

Formation of inner psychic milieu emerges. Strong vertical tension between the higher ("what ought to be") and the lower ("what is") in oneself triggers positive disintegration, multilevel development, and the process of inner transformation.

---

1 Since it is not possible to give more than an outline of Dabrowski's theory here, the reader is directed to *Dabrowski's Theory of Positive Disintegration*, a volume edited by S. Mendaglio (2008).

<u>Level IV</u>: Organized Multilevel Disintegration – Advanced Multilevel Development

When a sense of mission in life enables a person to act on his or her own ideals, it diminishes the prior vertical tension; now "what ought to be" is enacted consistently. Self-actualization takes place.

<u>Level V</u>: Secondary Integration – Highly Advanced Multilevel Development

A person of great inner knowing and depth of consciousness—a connection to something larger than us and in which we can trust—who works for the benefit of humanity, whether on a large or a small scale. Such a person may have achieved true inner peace.

To know the distinguishing elements of emotional development is essential in parenting and counseling young people, as well as understanding one's own development. For example, Dabrowski's theory provides a structure for helping teenagers in the grips of crisis—conflict of identity, conflict of values, conflict over what it means to be gifted, depression, existential anxiety, or the sense of total isolation. Jackson and Moyle (Chapter 7) discuss the invisible intensity of a gifted introvert undergoing a profound multilevel positive disintegration. They show that a young person undergoing a multilevel crisis requires a different understanding than one in grips of a unilevel crisis, which lacks the felt sense of tension between the higher and the lower in oneself.

Each level is a large universe in which a number of developmental patterns are possible (Piechowski, 2008). It is important to keep in mind that levels are abstract categories that were codified for the purposes of research. With the exception of Level I, each outlines the nature of the developmental process taking place. Beginning with Level III, they are quite complex.

As we consider the qualities of each level, it is important that we do not attempt to categorize and put people into levels, but rather that we try to understand the nature of their striving. People are far too complex to be so neatly pigeonholed. There are levels within levels, and an individual's development may span more than one level.

Level I: Primary Integration—No Inner Growth

Dabrowski designated the absence of inner growth as Level I. In this level, where there is little introspection and little inner conflict, inner growth is limited. Concern for the well-being of others tends to be limited or gives place to exploiting them. Goals tend to be geared toward material success and power over others. Focus on survival and success, often at the expense of others, makes for competitive behavior. This picture reflects lives shaped by the pressures of our society in which the worth of persons is measured in money and status or achievements. It is also a picture of very limited developmental potential and often a life of underlying fear (Piechowski, 2003).

Relationships are marked by possessiveness. Major setbacks may precipitate a crisis, a disintegration process of the unilevel type—not oriented toward growth and improvement of the self, but tied to the frustration and crisis of the moment. Resolution of the crisis usually ends with return to the previous way of life. In other words, problems are recycled—for example, quarreling over the same issue with different people, or marrying in succession a similar type of person, for instance, codependents, abusers, addicts, or philanderers.

However—and this may appear surprising—limited developmental potential does not inevitably determine this kind of life. Very much depends on how a child is raised. If the life of the family is based on mutual trust and maintains a consistent rhythm, children in such a family are capable of growing up as fair-minded, happy, and positively contributing members of society (Piechowski, 2008). Such stable environments may, however, limit self-reflection and introspection. Lack of self-examination constrains inner growth, and so development, in Dabrowski's sense, does not start here.

Level II: Unilevel Disintegration—Unilevel Development

Unilevel disintegration (Level II) can be a difficult concept to grasp, yet its importance should not be underestimated. "Unilevel disintegration occurs during developmental crisis such as puberty or menopause, in periods of difficulty handling some stressful external event, or under psychological...conditions such as nervousness..." (Dabrowski, 1964, p. 6). At this level, individuals begin to experience inner tensions, yet their development is typically influenced primarily by their social group and by mainstream values.

They often experience ambivalence, doubt, and dissatisfaction with themselves, yet they lack a clear set of inner values. Inner conflicts are typically horizontal in nature. "Unilevel disintegration consists of processes on a single structural and emotional level..." (Dabrowski, 1964, p. 6). A contest between equal, competing values ensues that results in a flip-flop of emotions and behavior. Development will continue in this way unless a crisis erupts in which multilevel elements are present.

If we again use the image of mountain climbing, this level is like never actually moving up the slope, but hiking around the base. Typically, unilevel development lacks the vertical tension. The solutions to one's life problems tend to be just different versions of the same old things. It all stays on the same plane, hence the term "unilevel." For instance, J. D. Salinger, author of *Catcher in the Rye*, kept trying one system of belief and practice after another, taking up in succession Kriya Yoga, Dianetics (the forerunner of Scientology), Christian Science, homeopathy, acupuncture, macrobiotics, the teachings of Edgar Cayce, fasting, vomiting to remove impurities, megadoses of vitamin C, and so on (Salinger, 2000).

The Salinger example above illustrates one kind of unilevel development in a highly gifted person. He was looking for answers outside of himself. When the self is undeveloped, the task of personal growth is to gain a sense of oneself as an individual, as one's own person. Trusting an authority above them, whether the head of a family, a political leader, or a religious figure, people typically depend on external sources for defining who they are. They derive a sense of self from the role defined for them by others. They conform to external norms and expectations and are vitally concerned with what others will think of them. Experiencing feelings of inferiority, they seek approval from others. Vacillating between self-centeredness and concerns about others' opinions, their self-concept rests on shifting sands.

A crisis may erupt when the authority is exposed as wrong, misleading, or exploitative and abusing. Feeling betrayed, people reject the authority because it has failed them. They begin to look for self-knowledge and self-definition in people like themselves, and eventually in themselves, but without self-reflection or evaluation. For instance, a woman in flux within this level writes:

> *I've never had a personality. I've always been someone's daughter, someone's wife, someone's mother. Right now I'm so busy being born, discovering who I am, that I don't know who I am. And I don't know where I'm going.* (Belenky, Clinchy, Goldberger, & Tarule, 1986, p. 82)

First comes liberation from passive acceptance of external authority, replacing it with trust in subjective knowing. Next comes the quest for self. In a radical shift, the person moves from dependence on external authority to listening to his or her own inner voice. Development may go no farther than this, but it is also possible for it to continue toward a more defined sense of self (Piechowski, 2008).

For inner growth to continue beyond Level II, multilevel elements have to be present. Dabrowski assumed that we differ in our developmental potential, which may or may not have those multilevel elements. This process of inner transformation requires an inward problem-solving approach, in which personal growth is the focus, along with a sense of responsibility toward others and their development. Individuals moving toward multilevel development do not dwell excessively on their inner conflict—the split between the higher and lower potentials within themselves. "Prolongation of unilevel disintegration often leads to reintegration on a lower level..." (Dabrowski, 1964, p. 7). If multilevel elements are indeed present, the individual will become active in solving the problems of his or her personal growth.

Level III: Spontaneous Multilevel Disintegration—Multilevel Development

Multilevel development through positive disintegration is where emotional development, as Dabrowski conceived it, begins in earnest. "Disintegration is described as positive when it enriches life, enlarges the horizon, and brings forth creativity..." (Dabrowski, 1964, p. 10). This type of inner growth requires a multilevel developmental potential. A complex inner psychic milieu forms. Reaching for "what ought to be" or "what could be" (the higher in oneself) and away from "what is" (the lower in oneself) is a process of intense ups and downs. Though there may be many setbacks, the overall trend is nevertheless upward. Here is an illustration from Eleanor Roosevelt of the inner work that she needed to do to conquer fear, as fear plagued her through much of her early life:

> *Painfully, step by step, I learned to stare down each of my fears, conquer it, attain the hard-earned courage to go on to the next. Only then I was really free. Of all the knowledge that we acquire in life this is the most difficult. But it is also the most rewarding. With each victory, no matter how great the cost or how agonizing at the time, there comes increased confidence and strength to help meet the next fear.* (Roosevelt, 1960, p. 25)

The disintegrative process starts spontaneously, either through external catalysts such as the loss of a loved one, severe illness, or a brush with death, or through an internal change in the psyche, a mystical experience, or the person's unconscious or semiconscious awareness of being ready to move forward. In this type of growth, striving to actualize what is higher and better in themselves, people may encounter experiences that are quite troubling, disorienting, and unsettling, if not outright frightening. Counseling and therapy, as long as it is oriented toward supporting the process rather than "curing" the individual, may be most beneficial here, as the individual experiences stress, anxiety, and at times, depressive episodes related to the disintegrative process.

The case of Fynn described by Jackson and Moyle (Chapter 7) illustrates how extraordinarily profound and wrenching this process can be. Fynn, a remarkably sensitive, intense, and complex young man, entered counseling after a weeklong stay in a psychiatric ward for depression and suicidal thoughts. Depression and profound anxiety interacted with a sharp faculty for analysis and insight as he worked toward a deeper understanding of his developing self. Over time, and with great support and encouragement within the therapeutic relationship, Fynn acquired greater capacities for functioning within difficult surroundings, and he developed a more authentic and realized sense of self.

Through Dabrowski's own clinical work and studies of autobiographies, he found that wherever such evidence of personality growth is found, great sadness also results from certain misfortune and loss. In Dabrowski's view, "It is characteristic that states of sadness, and frequently states of depression, are encountered whenever we find psychological transformations, misfortune, failure, loss, and breakdown taking place" (Dabrowski, 1973, pp. 156-157). Laurence Nixon (2008) found, in his studies of the lives of mystics, echoes of Dabrowski's conclusions.

Level IV: Organized Multilevel Disintegration— Advanced Multilevel Development

As development continues, the individual is more and more able to match his or her ideals with the actual living of those ideals. "What ought to be *will* be" is the banner for the self-actualizing potential experienced in this advanced type of development. In the process of inner transformation, individuals move toward becoming more compassionate, responsible, and more fully in the process of self-realization. Self-deprecation and comparison with both the inner ideal and the perceptions of others give way to self-acceptance and freedom from social convention, as well as distancing oneself from lower aspects of one's own self. Acceptance of others and compassion for oneself and others become dominant.

Dabrowski's Level IV is in many ways comparable to Maslow's conception of self-actualization (Maslow, 1970; Piechowski, 2003), although it must be noted that Maslow did not explain the process by which one attains self-actualization. His work did not encompass concepts of developmental potential, multilevelness, or positive disintegration—cornerstones of Dabrowski's theory (Piechowski, 1978; Tillier, 2008). Nonetheless, Maslow provided a rich and extensive description of the characteristics of self-actualizing people and the principles that they live by—for instance, lack of egocentrism; focusing on problems outside of themselves (problem-centering); a sense of kinship with all people (*Gemeinschaftsgefühl*); respect for every person, whether high or low (democratic character structure); and having definite moral standards. In Maslow's words, "they do right and do not do wrong."

Examples of development at this level have been gathered from both literary analyses and case study approaches with individuals in contemporary settings. Janneke Frank (2006) identified an inspirational teacher of gifted students and carried out an in-depth case study of his advanced multilevel development. Janice Witzel (1991) found examples serendipitously among never-married women who turned out to be gifted, happy, self-actualizing, and invisible. Thanks to the single qualification—"well thought of"—the women nominated for Witzel's study were outstanding in their achievement, often despite lack of support or acknowledgement in their environment, making their achievement even more amazing. They had a high level of energy, had drive for autonomy and development of their own powers, responded to opportunities and help offered, had high self-esteem, lived a deeply satisfying way of life, and were able to let go of difficult experiences without devaluing them. They were deeply engaged in altruistic pursuits through varied and far-reaching volunteer work. And despite such elevated personal qualities, they were, for the most part, unnoticed. They fit Maslow's criteria of self-actualization, which makes them good candidates for advanced multilevel growth (Witzel, 1991; Piechowski, 2008).

In keeping with the mountain-climbing metaphor presented at the beginning of the chapter, persevering to the top of the mountain brings about the full realization of a person's potential, which Dabrowski described as self-aware and self-chosen personality. The process leading to it and continuing further Dabrowski called "full dynamization of the personality ideal"—a dynamic force field within the self, as there is nothing static about it. At this point, the mountain-climbing metaphor is not as effective, since the metaphorical mountaintop is not an end to a journey. Inner growth does not stop; it continues. The top of the mountain is the ground floor of a universe of higher consciousness.

Level V: Secondary Integration— Highly Advanced Multilevel Development

Perhaps the image of a "magnetic field in the soul," which Dag Hammarskjöld experienced in his profound contemplative moments, can convey the sense of what inspires development at Level V. Another illustration comes from Peace Pilgrim, a woman who walked on foot for peace, crossing the United States from coast to coast in the years 1953 to 1981.

As a young person, Peace Pilgrim wanted the material comforts of life. After graduation from high school, she had no trouble finding a job, and she spent her money on clothes, matching shoes, and hats, a luxurious and very soft bed that her sister envied, and a flashy car. She was a popular dance partner. She also wrote plays in which she was the director, costume designer, lighting manager, and producer (Rush & Rush, 1992).

Later, she came to the realization that making money was easy, but spending it on material things was foolish. She became active in pacifist organizations, until one day she surrendered her life to God and vowed to be of service. From that moment on, her inner self-directed growth began in earnest.

She simplified her life, gave away all of her possessions, pared down to just a few clothes, and walked the whole Appalachian trail in order to test her ability to survive with very little. Although she did not know it at the time, this was her preparation to become Peace Pilgrim. Her original plan was to walk 25,000 miles over 11 years—on foot—for peace. She walked for 28 years in total.

The change in her was so radical that she was rejected by many of her friends and family because they didn't understand her. Some thought she had simply lost her mind. Others found her the most authentic person they knew; many were moved by her example.

Peace Pilgrim, whose talks were later transcribed, related how at first she experienced inner peace only at moments, like being on top of a mountain. Then one day, instead of moments, she found herself in an uninterrupted state of inner peace:

> *I could return again and again to this wonderful mountaintop, and then I could stay there for longer and longer periods of time, and just slip out occasionally. [Then came a morning when] I knew that I would never have to descend again into the valley. I knew that for me the struggle was over, that finally I had succeeded in giving my life, or finding inner peace. Again, this is a point of no return. You can never go back into the struggle. The struggle is over now because you will to do the right thing and you don't need to be pushed into it.* (Peace Pilgrim, 1983, p. 22; emphasis in the original)

Peace Pilgrim died instantly in a head-on collision, riding with someone who was taking her to her next engagement. Her life illustrates the process of inner growth as outlined by Dabrowski's theory (Peace Pilgrim, 1983; Piechowski, 1992, 2009). Peace Pilgrim's explanations of her state of inner peace, as well as the testimony of people who knew her for many years, leaves no doubt that she embodied the highest expression of Level V (secondary integration).

At this point, you may be thinking of other life stories and case examples that illustrate these profound processes of personal growth. There are many examples in the research literature—for example, Eleanor Roosevelt, Paul Robeson, Antoine de Saint-Exupéry, Etty Hillesum, and Abraham Lincoln, as well as persons still living today who have been research subjects (Piechowski, 2008). Other examples are found in Eleanor Roosevelt's letters (Lash, 1982, 1984) and her recounting of her inner growth in *You Learn by Living* (Roosevelt, 1960). Another classic account of seeking an inner transformation is Thomas Merton's *The Seven Storey Mountain* (Merton, 1948/1998).

Etty Hillesum's diaries and letters (Hillesum, 1985, 1996, 2002) are a breathtaking and amazingly detailed record of her inner growth during the war years as she struggled with her passions and her powerful hatred against the Germans to eventually reach inner peace. She became a luminous presence to the inmates of a transition camp on the way to Auschwitz. Beginning at the age of 27, she emerged from a hedonistic phase of life—one might say unilevel—and began the process of inner transformation. In the short span of about four years, Etty Hillesum went through the process of spontaneous and organized multilevel disintegration to reach Level V.

To many people, Dabrowski's concept of Level V is the most challenging. Part of the problem lies in his examples of people like Christ and Gandhi as exemplars of Level V, which sets the criterion of this level impossibly high. However, when one reads what Dabrowski had to say on the matter, one realizes that the boundary between Levels IV and V is insufficiently defined and that the concept of this boundary has not yet been adequately explored (Dabrowski, 1967, 1970, 1973). We are beginning to dimly perceive that Level V must have many levels within itself and that the minimum criterion for getting there is yet to be more clearly defined (Piechowski, 2009). Only further study of more individual cases can give us this.

Applications to the Gifted, Talented, and Creative

As the subsequent chapters in this book indicate, the issues facing gifted individuals are specific and many. These are issues of emotional development, identity, existential crisis, depression, the meaning of gifted-ness, moral crisis, and more—all of which knowledge of Dabrowski's theory helps to understand. Misdiagnosis and diagnosis that misses the gifted aspect of the child or adult forms still another set of issues (see Amend, Chapter 6).

Counseling the gifted requires experience and knowledge of gifted children and adults. Dabrowski's theory helps to understand their emotional development. It is common to think that personality development is something larger than emotional development, yet Dabrowski showed convincingly that personality without emotional development is nothing. We know today that cognition without an emotional sense to give it value, positive or negative, is sterile. The passion for learning and mastery so characteristic of the gifted is driven by a very powerful emotion: intense interest. Consequently, to assist gifted young people and adults in their development, and to counsel them, Dabrowski's theory is a tool of inestimable value.

Part Two

Understanding Intensity:
Practical Applications for Parents,
Teachers, and Counselors

Chapter 3

Nurturing the Sensitivity, Intensity, and Developmental Potential of Young Gifted Children

Susan Daniels, Ph.D., and Elizabeth Meckstroth, M.Ed., M.S.W.

> *Giftedness is asynchronous development in which advanced cognitive abilities and heightened intensity combine to create inner experiences and awareness that are qualitatively different from the norm. This asynchrony increases with higher intellectual capacity. The uniqueness of the gifted renders them vulnerable and requires modifications in parenting, teaching, and counseling in order for them to develop optimally.* (The Columbus Group, 1991, p. 1)

Parents and teachers of children who are gifted know that the experiences and abilities of these young people are different from more typically developing children. As well as having advanced intellectual abilities and special talents, these children have exceptional ways of experiencing the world—qualitatively, quantitatively, or often both. Being acutely aware of both their physical environment and their emotional life, gifted children tend to be more intense, more sensitive, and more prone to experiencing emotional extremes—whether exuberance or despair.

Yet highly intelligent and creative children vary greatly from one another as well. While the qualities of intensity and sensitivity greatly characterize gifted children's emotional development, we must also keep in mind that diversity describes and defines them. In many instances, gifted children differ from one another more than they resemble each other. If you choose any quality that might describe one gifted child, the opposite will define another. Children with similar IQs will have different interests, personalities, abilities, and temperaments.

Take, for example, Felicia and Jocelyn, ages eight and 10 respectively. They live in two different states, but both are in the highly gifted IQ range, with advanced verbal abilities and extremely strong mathematical reasoning abilities. Yet they are quite different. Felicia is somewhat introverted; she cares deeply about the environment—especially animals—and hopes to become a veterinarian one day. Jocelyn is extraverted, chatty, and highly social, with strong visual abilities as well. Interested in buildings, structures, and construction toys since she was quite young, she loves to draw, and she draws whenever she can. She has kept a journal since she was six, replete with drawings of buildings, bridges, sculptures, and other structures, and she plans to be an architect some day.

Gifted children's intellectual, physical, and social and emotional qualities develop in vastly different and asynchronous ranges. These children are intricate, contradictory, and complex, and the brain that drives them seems to intensify everything they do.

Gifted children can be exhausting, demanding, and perplexing enigmas. They often amaze, delight, and confound the adults who know, love, and teach them. Any day with a gifted child can bring a multitude of intense experiences for the adults who interact with them as well. While one child might begin her day with great joy anticipating a school art project, her day may conclude with inconsolable stress and dissatisfaction over some perceived imperfection in that same project. To be gifted is to experience emotional extremes. Yet few parents, teachers, counselors, psychologists, or physicians receive any special training in supporting these youngsters' highly charged emotional and intellectual needs (Webb, Amend, Webb, Goerss, Beljan, & Olenchak, 2005). In this chapter, we will address some of these needs and expressions through the lens of Kazimierz Dabrowski's work, and we will focus on ways to support gifted children's ability to manage their five areas of overexcitability.

Intensity, Sensitivity, and Overexcitability

Dabrowski explained the sensitivity and intensity experienced by many gifted individuals in terms of overexcitabilities—a greater capacity to be stimulated by and respond to external and internal stimuli. Overexcitability permeates a gifted person's existence. Whether it's music, language, physical sensing, kinesthetic activity, imagination, or something intellectual, an overexcitability orients and focuses them. Overexcitability gives energy to their intelligence and talents. It shapes their personality development. Like a plant turns toward light, overexcitability draws out a gifted person's thoughts and behaviors. An overexcitability is a temperamental disposition toward a class of stimuli that the gifted person notices and responds to. It is a lens that opens, widens, and deepens their perspective.

We can make an analogy between people's overexcitabilities and television channels. Most people are wired to receive, say, 10 channels. Others come equipped with a wide selection on cable. Some have a satellite dish and high definition. They receive and respond to signals that many others don't even know or can't imagine might exist. It's can be difficult to keep track of several stations, so it's easy to imagine a person being overwhelmed by trying to manage the hundreds of signal on a satellite dish.

While this analogy is helpful as a description, there is one caveat: In our modern world, we can upgrade our television service to receive cable if we don't have it. Overexcitabilities, which we call OEs, are referred to somewhat tongue-in-cheek as "original equipment." They are innate predispositions. We are born with them. Although everyone is born with basic modes of experience, persons with overexcitabilities are unusually intense in their experiences. They react to lower stimuli than others—that is, one's reactions may be higher or greater than others', but also one's threshold for reaction may be lower, and a person may react strongly to what others perceive as a non-event. Similar to other aspects of our temperament and personality, we come hard-wired with these modes of experiencing, and while their expression may change over the years, the OEs we have as our original equipment remain relatively consistent throughout our lifespan.

The five forms of overexcitability, as presented by Dabrowski, are: psychomotor, sensual, imaginational, intellectual, and emotional. (Table 1.1 in Chapter 1 presents an overview of the behaviors and characteristics of each OE.) Here we will further describe how each OE manifests for gifted children and suggest how adults may respond to a gifted child's overexcitabilities in a positive way rather than reacting with statements like, "You are just too sensitive," which could indicate to the child that he or she is not acceptable in some way. Or, as happens with teachers of young gifted children who have little understanding of traits of the gifted, "I recommend that you hold him back a year to let him mature; he's just too emotional and immature to be skipped to a higher grade, even though he's smart enough to handle the work. Socially, he's not ready."

Admittedly, we *are* often frustrated by the intensity of gifted children's behaviors, whether their intensity is emotional, intellectual, imaginational, or physical or sensing intensity. We often don't know how to respond. However, our goal should be to nurture our children's genuine self-expression—to support each individual child along his or her unique developmental path. In terms of the expression of overexcitabilities, we must guide our children to express and release their intensity and energy in safe and gratifying ways.

We will provide suggestions in this chapter for how parents and teachers might help gifted children to learn strategies to *modulate* the expression of their OEs, varying by circumstance and the child's needs. To modulate means: (1) to regulate or adjust, (2) to alter or adapt according to circumstance, (3) to change or vary the pitch. We have observed that all too often, gifted children are asked—or expected—to completely quiet or squelch expression of their OEs. This can be damaging to the gifted child's development. Instead, we hope that adults may gain new insights and learn to help the child discover choices and options for how and when he or she expresses an OE. Please keep in mind that a child may have one, several, or all of the OEs and that each OE may imbue both advantages and challenges for that child. Generally, the brighter or more creative the child, the more likely that the child's OEs and related behavior and needs will permeate and influence daily behaviors. It is helpful to remember that each OE, in some way, likely provides the energy or fuel that contributes to the development of a gifted young person's talent, along with the advantages and challenges that fundamentally shape his or her ultimate development.

Psychomotor OE

Psychomotor overexcitability is significantly correlated with high intelligence (Ackerman, 1993). Gifted children characteristically exhibit a high energy level. This energy may find expression in myriad ways. Children with heightened psychomotor intensity can appear very busy and restless. As infants, they generally require less sleep than is normal for most babies. Many young mothers of a precocious toddler received the following advice: "You must make that child sleep!"—an unlikely if not impossible task. Rather, periods of rest and participation in relaxing activities are more reasonable intermediate goals. ("Shall we read a story while swaying in the hammock?") In young gifted children, we hear rapid, seemingly excessive, almost compulsive speech. They may explain things until you beg them to stop! They may gesture with their entire body, much beyond punctuating hand gestures. Some gifted children have a voracious appetite for activity; they're always moving or "antsy."

This concept of psychomotor overexcitability has extensive implications for parents and teachers. It is essential that parents and school personnel aim to integrate gifted children's often intense, highly active physical needs within the day's confines. Our intense children need to learn appropriate and effective ways of self-management.

Psychomotor OE does not directly relate to advanced physical *ability*, but rather to *intensified* physical activity and sensitivity. Some gifted children certainly have high levels of physical abilities and talent and find outlets to express their physical energy through sports or dance. Others lack physical prowess or, as a component of asynchronous development, may even lag in physical development. With this in mind, psychomotor OE may or may not find expression and release in sports. We find that many highly intelligent children prefer individual sports rather than team sports. You can find them on track and swim teams, on a tennis court, doing gymnastics, fencing, and in the martial arts. But however released, physical activity is necessary for optimal self-expression and release of physical energy.

For some gifted children, sports are not the chosen arena for expression of psychomotor OE, and another physical activity or accommodation is necessary for optimal expression and release of physical energy. For some, psychomotor overexcitability is an outward expression of inner emotional tension. In this case, the children have a need to move as a release for their heightened emotional state. Such pent-up tension can be very difficult for a child to contain in situations in which much sitting is required—for instance, in the classroom or during long car rides. Anticipating this, providing plenty of opportunities for movement before, during, and after will help a great deal.

Often, preschool and other early childhood school experiences focus on "socializing" young students. "Rugtime" or circle times are often cornerstones of sharing time, yet they may become excruciatingly constricting to small bodies brimming with energy and urging to move about. Sometimes, with gifted students who have a great deal of psychomotor overexcitability, rugtime compliance becomes an educational goal. Paradoxically, encouraging these children to move about—as long as others are not disrupted—can facilitate their learning since they stop focusing on their aggravating constrictions.

Although we might like to cease the outward expression of gifted children's inner energy, this approach is counterproductive. What we resist persists. Rather than defying and fighting it, we can accommodate their need to be more on the move than most other children and harness their energy in constructive ways. They don't have to sit down to read; let them stand up! They can quietly twiddle with a soft and silent plaything to release energy while they are listening in a group. Many young "wired" children have found that martial arts lessons offer an attractive channel for focused mental concentration, body control training, and energy release. Children with psychomotor overexcitability should be expected, allowed, and even encouraged to move.

A common characteristic and outlet for psychomotor overexcitability is rapid speech. Not all gifted children express psychomotor OE through an obvious physical activity such as fidgeting or running around the block at top speed. Some show evidence of it through their verbalizations—running off with their mouths instead of their feet! In workshops given for parents, teachers, and other adults who work with gifted children, we often ask, "Can you imagine having Jim Carrey, Whoopi Goldberg, and Robin Williams—intense, verbally expressive stand-up comedians—as children and all in the same third-grade classroom or at the same dinner table?" An audible sigh, and sometimes a collective groan, inevitably follows. Yet this is what these children are like.

One approach for parents may be to give each child a moment of "air time" at the dinner table, of course providing time for others as well. A classroom teacher might manage blurting or excessive interrupting questions by providing "IQ sheets." These are photocopied sheets with an "I" for "Interesting Ideas" on one side and a "Q" for "Questions" on the other. Thus, intense ideas and urgent questions have a waiting place—or parking lot, if you will—to be saved for later exploration at a more opportune time.

Another helpful strategy to facilitate these children's participation in daily routines and other requirements is to teach them relaxation techniques. Some parents have found listening to music or recorded stories particularly calming for their children. If impulsiveness interferes with performance, halting or quieting techniques (take a deep breath, count to 10, smile) can gently intercede and promote self-monitoring and control.

It is sometimes difficult for children with abundant physical energy to shut down at the end of the day. To ease into bedtime, it may be helpful to do more calming activities in the evening. To accommodate endless ideas and questions at bedtime, provide your prolific youngsters with a notebook and pencil to archive their ideas until morning.

An unfortunate prejudice about parents of gifted children is that they "push" their children to achieve. However, it has been our experience in teaching and counseling gifted children and their parents that the parents are not pushing at all but are instead trying hard to keep up with these children and their questions and ideas! Some parents of gifted children are chagrined to admit that it is exhausting to keep pace with them, and they are even more embarrassed to reveal that this ordeal is a result of high intelligence. Chapter 8 addresses the need for parents of gifted children to protect their own needs for rest and recuperation.

Some parents have suggested, jokingly: "I know what my child needs. She needs a new family; there just isn't enough of me to go around," or "My husband and I have decided that we will just have to cancel our lives for the next six years to have enough energy to keep up with our kids." But parents need to remember that they should "put their own oxygen masks on first" so that they have the stamina and resources to be there for their gifted children and so that they can be happy and satisfied with their own lives.

Adults have many opportunities to model and impart to children that it is good to grow up. If adults do not demonstrate that they have needs and voice how they are meeting them for themselves, they miss conveying aspects of nurturing one's own well-being and personal integrity to their children. The following suggestions will help to nurture constructive expression of psychomotor OE and related social, physical, intellectual, and emotional development.

Psychomotor OE: Related Needs and Recommendations
Children with high psychomotor excitabilities need to hear:
- ○ "You have wonderful enthusiasm and energy."
- ○ "Your intensity can help you do many things."
- ○ "I wish I had your energy."
- ○ "You put your whole body into your learning."
- ○ "You like to be able to move and don't really like to sit still."
- ○ "Sometimes our bodies need to relax."

Strategies to encourage modulation of psychomotor OE:
- ○ Discuss the positive aspects of psychomotor OE.
- ○ Avoid activities that require sitting for a long time.

- Plan for movement opportunities before and after a long period of stillness.
- Provide for reasonable movement in a variety of settings.
- Involve the child in a physical task; send her on an errand.
- Help your child notice signs of exhaustion or need for quiet time.
- Provide for and model activities that soothe and calm.
- Teach that time-out can be a choice, not a punishment.
- Teach relaxation techniques.
- Consider physical or occupational therapy as needed.

Sensual OE

Sensual overexcitability gives children heightened experiences of seeing, smelling, tasting, touching, and hearing. As our sensually overexcitable children seek and receive heightened pleasure through their senses, they can experience intense irritation and frustration from their sensory overload encounters. Smells and tastes are more pungent to them. Sounds seem to have more depth and character.

Those with sensual overexcitability have heightened sensory awareness and with it, often, enhanced aesthetic appreciation. It is as if these children see through a different pair of glasses than do most of their age peers—their perception is acute and exquisite. Some exceptionally sensitive children view the world as if through a microscope as compared with normal vision. They sometimes see what others cannot even imagine (Webb, Meckstroth, & Tolan, 1982). They catch details and may, for example, be captivated by the beauty of a glistening drop of oil floating and swirling across a rain puddle. The sight of a sunset over water may bring a tear to the eye and hold a sensually overexcitable child captivated until the last sliver of sunlight disappears over the horizon. Some children love color as an entity unto itself and experience the range of tonal palette such that they can veritably hear, feel, and smell the colors as well. Many gifted artists have reflected on the intensity of their perceptions and their cross-modal experiences. For example, they can be deluged with visual, auditory, emotional, and concept impressions that virtually demand to be represented through a single piece of sculpture, music, or poetry.

Smells and aromas may hold deep emotional connections for these children, such as the aroma of fresh baked bread triggering an instant replay of the last family holiday gathering. Conversely, these children can have intense negative reactions to certain odors—they may not be able to bear the smell of a hard-boiled egg or grilled meat, for example. The same sensual sensitivity that could contribute to a later love of fine dining may also present as a finicky eater in their early years. Our experiences with families suggest that many gifted children are "picky eaters." Some eat no "mushy" vegetables, others only pizza, bread, and peanut butter. Finding creative ways to broaden acceptable food choices to include more variety may prove to be a challenge.

Some gifted youth crave certain music as others may crave certain foods, listening to Scheherazade or another beloved piece of music until they feel every note and measure completely. Others can gain real comfort from the sound of waves, birds, wind in the trees, or even just their parents' breathing while being tucked in at night. Some sounds, however, become excruciatingly invasive to these children. They may have extreme reactions to the smack of gum chewing or the din in a shopping mall or school cafeteria. Sensually overexcitable children may have trouble filtering out background sounds and may be equally aware of a train in the distance as the voice on the radio next to them.

Perhaps a heightened awareness of the sensation of touch is most apparent in persons with sensual overexcitability. Whenever we address audiences of parents of gifted children and mention that some of these children insist that tags be cut from the backs of their shirts or that socks be turned inside out so that the seam does not irritate their toes, many of the parents gasp, groan, and laugh in recognition! Elastic at wrists and ankles can become an intolerable bind. One young gifted boy loved sweatshirts and sweatpants but needed the ribbed band cut off the sleeves and the elastic cut off the ankles. Another parent said that it took until fourth grade before her daughter would wear jeans or any pants without a stretchy waistband.

These same children may choose a sensual mode to express their emotional tension. They just can't function until their socks are changed or turned inside out. If they are sad, they may try to console themselves with food (Heinigk, 2008). (We encourage healthy "comfort food," such as oatmeal, applesauce, yogurt, fruit, chicken soup, tea, and fresh-baked breads, rather than sweets, chips, or soda—taking food allergies into account, of course.) Some choose sensory pleasures to comfort themselves, such as stroking the cat. They may stay attached to stuffed animals or favorite blankets longer than is usual, lingering in softness and coziness. One boy, well into elementary school, finally felt ready to let go of his baby blanket but kept just a corner of it to hold onto when tucking in for the night. We have even heard of a gifted boy who took a corner of his blanket with him to college and tucked it in the back of a dresser drawer!

Considering comfort, it may be soothing to adults to let go of the notion that these overexcitable children are being ornery, manipulative, or controlling with their exaggerated complaints. In many ways, they are more tender and permeable than we may be. Although it may not be in our realm of reality to have such intense or extreme reactions, for them, these experiences and perceptions are real.

As understanding and supportive adults, we can help these children learn to mediate and modulate their experiences. We can help them develop a menu of options to cope with things that irritate and annoy them, and we can also encourage them to seek what gives them pleasure. We can let them make suitable choices and be responsible for adjusting their environment as much as is possible and appropriate, thus giving them opportunities to manage their own needs effectively. Our goal as parents and teachers is to work ourselves out of a job—to promote self-efficacy in these concerns. Rather than rescuing these children, we can become inventive and responsive in our support by encouraging them to effectively manage these aspects of their personality and development for themselves. We can support them by giving them some important coping skills.

Sensual OE: Related Needs and Recommendations

Children with high sensual excitabilities need to hear:

- ○ "You take such delight in beautiful sights, sounds, and feelings."

- ○ "You like _____ sound/textures, etc., but I notice that _____ noises/textures, etc. bother you."

- ○ "I think you know what you like and what feels good to you."

- ○ "Sometimes, it's good to try new things. Would you like to try _____?"

Strategies to encourage modulation of sensual OE:

- ○ Discuss the positive aspects of sensual OE.

- ○ Provide environments that limit offensive stimuli and maximize comforting stimuli.

- ○ Provide opportunities to dwell in delight. Take time to smell the roses or watch the sunset.

○ Co-create a pleasing and comfortable aesthetic environment.

○ As much as possible, foster control of the child's own living space and work setting (e.g., the child's room is his own room, unless mold is growing on the left-over pizza or there are other health hazards).

○ Help the child find comfortable and appropriate clothing.

○ Understand that attachments to stuffed animals and favorite blankets may run a tad longer than with other less sensually sensitive children.

Intellectual OE

Children with intellectual overexcitability have almost insatiable curiosity, as well as a voracious appetite and capacity for intellectual effort and stimulation. Almost inevitably, we receive an affirmative response when asking a parent of a highly excitable gifted child, "Does she go to bed with a flashlight under the covers?"

Mental activity in these children is usually intensified and accelerated. Driven by wide and deep interests, they relentlessly probe the unknown. Incredibly tenacious and persistent at problem solving, their seemingly endless "why" questions sometimes become annoying and tiresome to parents and teachers, who think, "Don't you ever stop and take a break?" One teacher who attended a workshop on overexcitabilities referred to this as "the perpetual toddler syndrome."

While the streaming questions can fuel ongoing intellectual pursuits, they become a challenge for a teacher with 34 students to teach in a class period of 45-50 minutes. One teacher we know responded by instituting a system of question rationing. Although it might sound harsh, the approach had many positive aspects. The teacher would announce: "Okay, today we'll take four questions," or three or 10, varying with each given day. Now a gifted child might invest a great deal of thought in how to phrase her one question to encompass many ideas, and this is a critical thinking skill in itself! For parents, this limiting technique might work at suppertime or bedtime as well. Honor the child's interest, but establish a limit if time is short.

Daydreaming in the classroom is another way in which highly excitable children engage their imaginations to fuel their voracious appetite for intellectual stimulation. "What if" questions dance in their heads. Yet when called upon, these children can be quite aware of the topic and activity in the classroom. This capacity for multi-tasking and focusing will come in quite handy over the course of a student's lifetime. However, a student who is prone to concurrently creating an alternative scenario in his mind may not be appropriately challenged and may need a more highly differentiated curriculum to fuel his ravenous intelligence. Given the choice for individual or small group explorations, the complex mental projects that these children sometimes construct for themselves can develop into endeavors to which they become strongly devoted.

Highly excitable gifted children already know much of what is new information for most of their classmates. The U.S. Department of Education's report, *National Excellence: The Case for Developing America's Talent* (1993), acknowledged: "Gifted and talented elementary school students have mastered from 35 to 50 percent of the curriculum to be offered in the five basic subjects before they begin the school year" (p. 2). How is this possible? They seem to absorb knowledge from just being in the world, picking up information from adult conversations and various forms of media. Schools have yet to recognize that these children come to school already knowing a great deal. Acknowledging these children's intellectual capabilities and accommodating their particular learning needs has enormous implications for the children, their families, and our society. If we take these children seriously, providing them with new information is a huge responsibility.

It is evident that highly excitable gifted children require substantial mental experiences and opportunities to maintain optimum cognitive and emotional running order. We can make an analogy by asking: What would be the result if we filled a high performance car with cheap fuel or allotted only 1,000 calories per day for a top marathon runner? These resources might work in some situations (for an everyday vehicle, for a person on a weight loss diet), but they would be greatly insufficient in others. Similarly, the intellectually excitable child requires access to rich and varied intellectual challenges and resources to quench her intellectual appetite and optimize her intellectual performance.

Some of this avid intellectual activity may lead to gifted individuals developing stringent standards and high expectations for their own performance. Perfectionism is a frequent trait of the gifted, with both positive and negative aspects. (For more on perfectionism, see Silverman, Chapter 9.) On the positive side, perfectionism can lead an individual to pursue excellence, but at the other extreme, it can lead one to fear, avoidance, and near-paralysis. Gifted children who are perfectionists may stay focused on a project or activity and persist until they are satisfied, or they may withdraw in deep frustration. In their minds, they have conceptualized how an activity or a project should be, and if it does not turn out "right," then it is professed to be a complete failure. We have seen first and second graders crumple one paper after another as they attempt to get their letters "perfect." We have even heard of young perfectionist children with tension headaches. This kind of perfectionism is of course something we want to avoid or re-direct to a healthier manifestation.

One approach that we've found to be effective with young children is to talk about how mistakes are a necessary part of how we learn. Learning to write (as in learning to ride a bike and many other skills) is a gradual process with certain beginning steps, then later steps, and then finally an acceptable product or performance. A teacher can talk about how every single adult who writes had to practice and practice until they learned. We can talk about how in learning to play the piano, one has to hit many wrong notes and keep trying until the right notes are automatic. Mistakes help us. Hearing adults talk about mistakes they've made and the need for practice helps gifted children understand.

It is also effective in such situations to support the child in reflecting on and responding to multiple aspects of a project or performance. Then, an all-or-nothing, perfect-or-failure vision may be modulated and channeled for further consideration and direction. Questions such as: "What part(s) of this project were you pleased with?" "What part(s) were you not pleased with?" "What might you do differently next time?" help the child view potential for progress rather than a total all-right or all-wrong response. These children may be continually striving for excellence and perfection to know and to actualize their evolving understandings and related potentials. They often have strong ideals and goals. Ideally, we can support them in meeting their goals in increments and with positive self-encouragement while also providing alternatives for responding to a harsh inner critic. (*How do you eat an elephant? One bite at a time.*)

Our highly excitable children's drive for perfect performance is where their intellectual intensity intersects with their emotional development. The field of gifted education is replete with means to accommodate children's intellectual needs, but a child's intellectual overexcitability signals a need for more holistic supportive responses from parents and teachers— ones that encompass and nurture their affective and emotional development, self-concept, self-esteem, and self-discipline as well.

For these children, their intellect can become their comfort zone and a key aspect of their emerging identity. In their little lives, they have been recognized and rewarded for displaying how much they know and how quickly they learn. Highly intelligent children are particularly vulnerable to serving some of their parents' ego needs by vicariously accomplishing what reflects pride for these well-meaning parents—the child's advanced knowledge and performance (Miller, 1982). When parents discuss a child's high performance and repeatedly take pride in it publicly, the gifted child's core social and emotional needs may go unmet. The child may think that his only worth is when he is performing or achieving, or that his only purpose in life is to get good grades and "be smart" to please his parents. Our goal as parents and teachers should be to help the child learn and achieve for himself—for his own reasons.

Perhaps readers will recognize someone who reverts to thinking or cognitive functioning when experiencing intense emotional entanglements or when there is an opportunity for aesthetic pleasure. Adults need to help these children integrate their intellectual function with the other aspects of their lives and celebrate the expanse of intellectual pursuits, but not allow their intellect to dominate. One child actually produced a self-portrait with an enormous head and a small body somersaulting down a hill. The caption read: "Sometimes, I just feel like a big head rolling around. What about the rest of me?"

Intellectual OE: Related Needs and Recommendations

Children with high intellectual excitabilities need to hear:

- ○ "Your curiosity fuels your intelligence."
- ○ "You have wide and/or deep interests."
- ○ "You have great potential to learn new things and to make changes."
- ○ "You really stick to projects that interest you."
- ○ "You defend your ideas and are open to learning different information."

Strategies to encourage modulation of intellectual OE:

- ○ Discuss the positive aspects of intellectual OE.

- ○ Honor the need to seek understanding and truth, regardless of the child's age.

○ Accept and provide for sustained effort; alter sleep patterns as necessary.

○ Help children find answers to their own questions.

○ Remember that this child is not a small adult; the gifted label does not apply to all of the child's parts!

○ Teach inquiry methods and communication skills.

○ Allow children to develop their own projects based upon individual interests.

○ Help children to develop goals and engage in self-reflection based on steps toward these goals.

○ Seek opportunities to provide interaction with intellectual peers, not necessarily age peers (chess club, multi-grade extracurricular offerings, or enrichment classes).

○ Incorporate multi-modal explorations and mind-body integration of experience whenever possible.

Imaginational OE

Michael Piechowski (2006) once said, "Tigers might not have imagination, but imaginary tigers can be made of flames"—a novel thought, and somewhat quirky, some might say. Yet this is the way of the imagination. With imagination, anything is possible. Imagination is key to creativity, from everyday creativity to the creativity of eminent individuals. When we ask, "What would I like to do today?" and think of possibilities, our imagination is engaged. When we plan a unique menu for a dinner party and think of a novel color scheme and flower arrangements, our imagination and creativity are involved. And if one has an imagination like J. K. Rowling, an entire feast hall with floating candelabras, wizards, and dragons can result.

Creative children are closely in touch with this capacity for fantasy and are less constrained by notions related to the concrete world. In the imagination, one can travel from a stormy day in the Midwestern United States to a land where scarecrows dance, lions sing, and magic red shoes transport and protect you. Imagination turns a sheet draped over two chairs into a fort, a castle, or a cave. Imagination gives birth to creating fairy tales, science fiction, poetry, murals, and amazing structures made from pasta and shaving cream.

Imagination works and plays in the everyday and contributes to daily joy and reverie, as well as to great discovery and invention. Einstein said, "Imagination is more important than knowledge." He also said, "It is a miracle that curiosity survives formal education." Picasso reflected that he spent the first half of his career learning to paint and the second half learning to be a child again. He said, "Everything you can imagine is real." The childlike quality of creative people and the imagination that comes with it are essential aspects of their personalities and important cognitive tools for their work (and play!).

In the vast variety of traits and backgrounds of creative people who later became eminent, one common childhood experience is having an imaginary companion. This is disclosed in the retrospective stories, biographies, and autobiographies of creative writers, artists, performers, inventors, and innovators across domains. At least one political figure has acknowledged the significance of imaginary companions (Piechowski, 2006). For example, Princess Margaret of Great Britain directed blame toward her imaginary companion. When her nanny found that little Margaret had done something wrong, she would say, "It wasn't me; it was Cousin Halifax" (Taylor, 1999).

Imagination creates imaginary friends, a hallmark of creativity in children and an antecedent of adult creativity. Even so, imaginary companions make some adults uncomfortable, concerned that the child may be out of touch with the real world. It may comfort these adults to know that children tend to know the difference between the contents of their imaginings and what constitutes our shared sense of what is real. For instance, as one parent tucked her six-year-old son into bed one night, he suddenly said that he knew his stuffed animals, all of whom had names and personalities, were not really alive and that they would need to stay home when he went to college.

If there is apprehension over a child's depth of imagination, exploration in fantasy, and/or close relationship with imaginary companions, we typically ask the concerned adults to consider what kinds of relationships the child has with family, teachers, or other children. Maintaining positive relations with family, teachers, or a close friend provides a reality check that indicates balance and healthy development with others, while fantasy gives our children mental practice in relating to others. In general, as long as a child can give and receive affection and can relate to others, imaginary play-mates are unlikely to indicate anything other than brightness, creativity, and imaginational OE.

Children involved in make-believe play may well know that their play comes from their imagination. However, at other times, children's imaginational experience is real to them (and also to imaginative adolescents and adults). Fairies, gnomes, angels, and other little or giant folk often appear quite real to the imaginative child.

If you suspect that a child is describing some event from his imaginings as if it were actual experience, you might help him discern the difference while still honoring his imagination. This can usually be accomplished with gentle questions: "Is this a story?" or "You have such a great imagination, don't you?" Whatever the imaginary events might be, children's accompanying feelings are real. Accepting the child's feelings and respecting the experience, whatever the source, can help keep trust in place between the two of you. This means that the child can feel safe enough to reveal more of his elaborate thoughts to you. Perhaps you remember how painful it was when you were chastised for expressing something you cared about with the words, "Oh! That's just silly stuff all in your head!"

Parents and teachers can enjoy and encourage children to engage with their imaginations like a best friend. Imagination is a safe place to mentally try out new experiences and anticipate consequences. One strategy to help children manage their fantasies is to help them think of their mind and behavior as instruments that they can direct and regulate. Rather than getting completely swept away in imagination, they can evaluate whether their thoughts are working *for* or *against* them.

It might also be helpful if children with heightened imaginations can compare their minds to television sets. First, they become aware that they always have pictures and sounds in their head. Then, they can analyze and judge whether or not these words and pictures are helpful to them. Here, they can use their consciousness to "switch channels" if they want to select a different, more helpful program to come into view!

Rich imagination, fantasy play, daydreaming, and imaginary friends are sources of reverie and delight for the young gifted and creative child. Many of us who teach, parent, and counsel gifted children have had the opportunity to meet a wide assortment of imaginary companions, as well as their pets, friends, and families. We have had delightful opportunities to share in children's imaginations, inventions, and stories.

One way that we can help children to maintain and nurture the development of their imaginations is to help them record or otherwise "save" their creative thoughts and ideas. More than one parent of a gifted child has helped to capture these creative musings in an idea or project journal. Writing for the child (until the child can write herself) will encourage the practice of giving ideas a place for safekeeping. Journaling collaboratively can be an alternative to a bedtime story, or in conjunction with one. This can also be done in the classroom, where students can keep journals or where a classroom wall of creative ideas might be posted for community sharing. Where imagination is honored, creativity will flourish.

Imaginational OE: Related Needs and Recommendations

Children with high imaginational OE need to hear:
- "You have a rich imagination."
- "You view the world in a different way."
- "You think of and tell great stories."
- "You make the mundane extraordinary."

Strategies to nurture and encourage modulation of imaginational OE:

- Discuss the positive aspects of imaginational OE.

- Cherish creative and imaginational expression.

- Encourage children to share imaginings—tell stories or draw images of imagined friends, pets, buildings, creatures, and worlds. "How would this story be told if it took place in another country or time period or world?" "Would you like to make a picture book about an imaginary pet?"

- Provide opportunities for design and invention. "What do you think cars may look like and be able to do in 2020?" "What are some possible interesting uses for recycled cardboard?"

- Provide opportunities for relaxation and channeling imagination with stories and guided imagery.

- Help children to distinguish between the imaginary and the real world.

- Provide outlets for creative pursuits—writing, drawing, acting, dancing, designing, building, etc.

○ Include opportunities for both individual and group involvement to validate and honor imaginational activities.

○ Help children use imagination to solve problems and cope with challenges.

○ Offer open-ended activities.

○ Record imaginative content and ideas in a journal.

Emotional OE

Among the five OEs that Dabrowski identified, the expressions of emotional overexcitability are the most extensive (Piechowski, 1979). Intense feelings manifest themselves in extreme, complex, positive, and sometimes negative ways. Children with these OEs seem to have extra emotional antennae, to be permeable by feelings and impacted by emotions. It is as if everything gets inside of them and they feel it. We might say that they are much more emotionally endowed.

Such endowment is often regarded as maladjustment and an interference when it comes to a productive, rational life. However, emotional overexcitability can be recognized as a form of giftedness—a finely tuned awareness. For Dabrowski, emotional overexcitability was the most important aspect of human development. It is a significant, logical component of developing a person's potential. Emotions can keep people in touch with themselves and their own needs for change, as well as connect them to the larger world and social fabric of humanity. Conversely, low emotional excitability seriously hampers people from developing their enriching affective possibilities (Piechowski, 1979).

Emotional overexcitability manifests itself in myriad ways. To define emotional overexcitability in a few written words is like depicting the Grand Canyon with a set of Tinker Toys. Emotional overexcitability is partially described as depth and breadth of feeling, an intense emotional response to the most minute nuance of language or meaning. It becomes a shrine for a lost pet, or as sadness felt for the fallen leaves that remain ungathered for the first grader's leaf collection that were later to be lovingly preserved and ironed between wax paper.

These intensely emotional children may be bearing enormous loads of feelings that accumulate from various fears and anxieties—concern about death, love, loneliness, deep caring for others, and excruciating self-scrutiny. They are exhilarated in joy and affection, and they also know

51

great sadness and compassion encompassing ecstasy and despair. When they are joyous, their radiance lights up the whole house! When they are sad or disappointed, the weight of the world is on their shoulders.

Their feelings can be complex and ambivalent. They can simultaneously experience an entire range of contradictive reactions. They may be riveted in an approach-avoidance dilemma. Excitement may draw them toward a person, project, or idea; anxiety may simultaneously create a tug of avoidance or withdrawal. Sometimes emotional overexcitability inhibits children. They feel so much that they are almost paralyzed to act for fear that they might act wrongly or get a negative reaction from someone.

Interpersonal relationships are extremely important to these children, although their most significant emotional attachments may not be with their peers. Adults may be concerned that the emotionally sensitive child has no friends. Perhaps he has reverted to find emotional connections among younger children or a compassionate great aunt. Special intergenerational bonds are not uncommon for emotionally sensitive youth. Oftentimes, compassion and understanding is more available for those who are younger; at other times, greater connection exists with older children; and sometimes a connection with elders complements high personal regard and caring.

Emotional connections with others and awareness of others' emotions is heightened in children with emotional OE. These children tend to both absorb and respond to the feelings of others. Jenise came home from second grade and told her mother that she hated math. Her mom was surprised, because the girl was doing very well in math. Then Jenise explained that other kids were having trouble learning it, and that made her very sad and even angry. Much of the time, emotionally sensitive children are protective and considerate of their peers' feelings. Yet some of them cannot conceive of the idea that other children just do not feel what they feel. Shannon, age five, said to her mother, "I understand other children better than they understand me." These emotionally astute children are perplexed about how other children can be so selfish and uncaring.

Jamal's family was quite poor when he was younger. His mother worked full time to put herself through college while raising two young boys as a single mother. Jamal, now 10, lives in a Southern California city with favorable weather and a long strip of parkway along the beachfront that includes a safe zone, where homeless individuals can come to sleep in the evening under a large tarp and receive a free meal and personal care items like soap and a razor. Tears well up in Jamal whenever they drive near that area. At first, his mother thought that he might be experiencing fear that his family's circumstances would once again become challenging. Jamal said, "Oh no, Mommy, I know we're okay now. I just want to help them. I wish I could take half of our dinner down there. We don't need it all, and you make the best chocolate cake. We could bring them a cake." After more discussion, Jamal and his mother now volunteer at the local library donating and distributing books and art supplies for children in low-income families. Highly excitable children often feel compelled to act on their empathy, concern for others, and the environment.

Emotional overexcitability extends to somatic expressions. Some children have trouble finding the words they need to describe what they are feeling, yet their feelings are expressed in their actions or through physical symptoms. They may read others' almost imperceptible body language and notice that it is incongruent with the words the person is saying. This can create stressful confusion about how to respond.

Emotional overexcitability mixed with giftedness brings with it great access to inner experience, as well as special needs for comfort, safety, and security (Roeper, 1995, 2007; Piechowski, 1997). Adults who care about these children must be the safe haven where young ones can express their deep feelings. Listen to them with your entire body, mind, and spirit as if nothing else at that moment matters as much as this child's thoughts and feelings. Listening like this conveys the message that what they have to say is important, and thus you build the child's self-esteem and self-respect. They need confidence and self-esteem to actualize some of the intricate wonders that they feel and know. Careful listening can be a lifeline in a world where others do not understand or take them seriously, which can lead them to mistrust themselves. They need adults who understand and care. Careful listening can convince children that there is someone who feels that they are valuable and worth understanding. It helps build courage, understanding, and trust such that these children can come to eventually be their own source of power, possibility, and safety.

Respond to their feelings and affirm them. Help them label those feelings. If a child can identify them, then she can do something about what her feelings are telling her. Proactive listening with critical care is especially worthwhile with gifted children because most of them are essentially introverts (Silverman, 1993b)—that is, they tend to protect their most vulnerable feelings inside themselves. What they reveal may not be nearly as significant as what they guard within.

Adults can also help children distinguish between their feelings and their behaviors. This can especially pertain to deep, angry feelings. Thinking and feeling does not mean doing. We can be angry, but we can learn to handle our anger in acceptable ways. There is a delicate balance in honoring a feeling and managing its expression. It is unfair to allow children to perpetuate socially inappropriate behaviors. They are harmed if they do not learn what actions will work *for* them versus *against* them. Young, emotionally sensitive and intense children need to know what strategies they might use to self-regulate and appropriately communicate intense feelings. What good is it to be highly skilled and talented if other people want to close you out?

Relaxation techniques and taking a personal time-out as a choice rather than a punishment are two very useful approaches to assist children in managing deep and strong feelings. And these can be useful for parents and other adults as well. Choosing and using relaxation techniques or giving ourselves a personal time-out models using these strategies for our children and can provide enough of a break for all to regroup with a different perspective.

Emotional OE: Related Needs and Recommendations

Children with high emotional OE need to hear:

- ○ "You are sensitive to others' feelings."
- ○ "You care very deeply and have deep feelings."
- ○ "You are very loyal to those you care about."
- ○ "You are very aware of joy, frustration, sadness, love, anger, and a whole world of feelings."

Strategies to encourage modulation of emotional OE:

- ○ Accept feelings and their intensity.

- ○ Teach the child to share his emotions and feelings with others in positive and productive ways—verbally, through movement, art, journaling, or music.

- ○ Teach children to be respectful of others' feelings or seeming lack thereof.

- ○ Develop a feeling vocabulary—include a continuum of feeling words. How many ways can we describe feeling "bad" (e.g., annoyed, irritated, frustrated, aggravated, uneasy, anxious, uncomfortable, bored, concerned, sad, etc.)? How many ways can we describe being

54

happy (e.g., content, glad, joyful, blessed, ecstatic, buoyant, and so on)?

○ Learn listening and responding skills. Much attention is devoted to the importance of listening and responding in *"Mellow Out," They Say* by Michael Piechowski (2006).

○ Teach children to anticipate physical and emotional experiences, and rehearse responses and strategies.

○ Teach, model, and share relaxation techniques, including deep breathing, stretching, and two minutes of quiet (a personal time-out).

○ Use journaling to express feelings.

○ Model "temperature taking." "How do I feel right now? What's my emotional temperature? Am I feeling warm? Cool? What might this mean? What are my feelings telling me?"

○ Find and choose activities that provide meaningful opportunities for empathy and social concern. Volunteer at a pet shelter, participate in a community service project, or find some other humanitarian outreach activity to give deep caring some active expression.

Awareness and Advocacy

Overexcitabilities are an integral part of the gifted child's essential self. The child's expression of overexcitabilities should not be viewed simply as worrisome behaviors, although they may present difficulties at home, school, or in a variety of other settings. Overexcitabilities are not pathologies that need therapy or a prescription for a "cure"; instead, they represent qualities of personality and emotional development that characterize each child and contribute to the total development of the child.

In creating this chapter, we tried to write descriptions of each overexcitability category and to highlight the ways in which these OEs contribute to gifted children's development. The strategies that we provide are not meant to squelch or diminish the OEs, but to help children modulate their expression. We hope that they will assist parents, teachers, and others to nurture the optimal development of the many kinds of gifted children we know, love, and support.

Although awareness and resources are essential in this process, we know that awareness and resources are not enough. We must *use* this knowledge on behalf of our gifted children and campaign for them until they have the experience and ability to advocate for themselves. Beyond awareness of gifted children's innate sensitivity and intensity, we suggest that the next step is toward advocacy and action to protect and promote your intense children's innate nature. Just as we accommodate learning differences in a wide range of identified disabilities, such as behavior disorders, dyslexia, dysgraphia, hyperactivity, allergic reactions, sensory processing disorders, and more, we must also recognize that gifted children's sensitivities and intensities contribute to unique variance in development and related learning needs.

In that regard, we're all pioneers in developing awareness and support for young gifted children. Acknowledging, accommodating, nurturing, and supporting gifted children's innate psychomotor, sensual, intellectual, imaginational, and emotional overexcitabilities is essential for their mental health and optimal self-development.

Chapter 4

Inner Awakening, Outward Journey: The Intense Gifted Child in Adolescence

P. Susan Jackson, M.A., R.C.C., and
Vicky Frankfourth Moyle, M.A., L.P.C., L.M.H.C.

Adolescence as a Disintegrative State of Being

Adolescence, as a stage in the human life cycle, is commonly known as a period of turmoil and change. Erikson (1950, 1968) described adolescence as a time of identity crisis and conflict—an internal process when an individual acquires a personal identity and seeks a place in the larger world outside of the family. Whereas puberty refers to biological, sexual maturation, adolescence—with less clear boundary definition—refers to the cultural and psychosocial transition to adulthood.

Dabrowski (1964) wrote that during times of environmental crises and/or biological change (such as puberty/adolescence and menopause), humans experience natural disintegrative states. Other acceptable, albeit usually more temporary, disintegrative states of being occur when we are asleep, fatigued, confused, ill, or in contemplation; when we are feeling strong emotions such as passion, ecstasy, confusion, and rage; when we are flushed with creative inspiration, improvising, or in a state of flow—to name just a few. A disintegrative state, then, need not be looked upon as dysfunctional. It can occur when we become temporarily a new or different person, when our sense of self in the world—or our sense of self *to* our own selves—changes or becomes suspended. A disintegrative state is a time of great potential change in a human life.

Adolescence, rife with disintegrative experience in all spheres of knowing, is a time of great expectancy. In fact, adolescents can be terror-ridden with the awareness of the possibilities of what could be or the feeling of the inevitability of what will be. In optimal circumstances, though, a disintegrative experience can be a triumphant transcendence of a young person's way of being.

Seventeen-year-old Ilia, a profoundly gifted Russian-born American young man, describes the heightened inner awareness and self-discernment common to intense gifted teens. In the following passage, he reveals a developmental prescience unique to this population, and he hints at the special kind of guidance that he seeks during this often tumultuous period of growth:

> *Yes, it is true; I have been in a state of extreme disintegration. Very much so. I am not sure I can even describe it to you: apart, disparate, disconnected, and unfeeling. That girl I was connected to has moved on. I have dropped out of University. It simply was not working.... I hope that she has found a good guy. I hope to meet him one day.... It will be easier if he is a good guy. I wish the best for her, truly. But, in truth, I can tell you I feel liberated in some way, as if something has lifted.... I am not sure we had a lot in common. I am not sure the relationship had a lot of depth. I am anticipating another disintegrative experience; it seems inevitable. I am pretty sure I will be okay, but I think I will disintegrate again before a more resolute integrative state is achieved. I am feeling much better now. Much better. But I definitely need something to do. Can you help me with that?* (personal communication, April, 2008)

Ilia's heartfelt question is an entreaty that shows humility and a "felt sense" (Gendlin, 1997) of a journey or a process, which is ultimately, for him, a quest. It is clear that Ilia is aware of his changing self and evolution to greater depth. He senses inevitability in the process that he is experiencing, and he wonders about the part he should and could play in his unfolding self.

Features of Adolescence, and Those Specific to the Gifted

For the gifted child, the period of adolescence is distinguished not only by characteristic features of typical development, but also by some uncommon experiences peculiar to the gifted. These atypical experiences are often accompanied by considerable challenge. Puberty is a stage rife with significant opportunity for personal growth. Substantive gains in cognitive capacity, shifts in social/emotional functioning, and growth in moral realization characterize this time of life. It is the time when a sense of self as an autonomous being emerges. Whereas previous psychological awareness and identification were embedded in the norms, perceptions, and sociocultural givens of childhood, these milieus are now appraised by adolescents with new eyes and emergent capacities. This so-called adolescent awareness, in our experience, may occur at uncharacteristically young ages, particularly for the exceptionally gifted child, and this finding is not ours alone (see Roeper, 1995).

The following vignette illustrates such developmental precocity:

At the airport terminal, Tiegan begs her mother for a teen magazine. Her mother declines. Tiegan challenges her mother's decision and then, in a rapid change of focus, comments on a social-political issue that she has been contemplating. In the next breath, she presents their traveling companion with a scenario rich with moral dilemma and waits, expectantly, for an answer. The rapidity of her mental processing, the scope and scale of her interests, and her predilection toward processing multiple ideas simultaneously contribute to her intense and often overwhelming profile. Her mother (a single parent) is often fatigued and at her wits' end, and her teachers find her extremely taxing as well. Buoyed by complex imaginational faculties and possessing rapid-fire verbal capacities, Tiegan is most often unsatisfied with her school experiences; the pace is too slow, the ideas limited, and her age peers do not share her interests, nor can they keep up with her capacity for moral reasoning and critical thought. She is bewildered by the rapid changes in her maturing physical body and surprised by her intense changeable moods. Tiegan is nine years old—not even a teen yet.

Gifted teens seek to discover who they are in all aspects of their being—who they might be, what they are capable of, and how they might interface with and impact the world anew. They experience an overwhelming need to affiliate—to find a place with others in a vital, life giving, and meaningful human context. Arising, too, is a not-to-be-ignored yearning to find meaning in existence—both for ultimate knowledge and for engagement in a wider and deeper sphere of contact, influence, and experience. It is a time of firsts. It is a time when all aspects of self—moral imperatives, gender identity, sexual orientation, communicative capacity, and spiritual awareness—explode with new capacities, augmented awareness, and novel experiences. Complex creative impulses and instinctive forces are energized. Hormonally driven physical and psychosexual urges begin to surface. This intense, often turbulent period of life is characterized by vital thrusts of discovery, newness, feelings of urgency, and questioning. The timing and tempo of all of these essential aspects of growth and development vary greatly (Roeper, 1995; Silverman, 1993b).

One difficulty for the gifted teen is maintaining a continuity of self amidst this evolutionary flux. This difficulty is bound up and intertwined with an overarching feeling of a primal evolutionary force (it seems to be inherent in every fiber of their being) that will thrust them toward a life outside of their current knowledge. It feels like something *beyond*, something unknown—a prescience that is ineffable and inevitable. It is as though some inborn evolutionary missive informs them that, to go *beyond* where they are, they must go *within*. And to go within means to leave behind familiar psychological moorings. Something tells them that, in order to achieve a new unity in their thinking, emotions, instincts, and behaviors, they must move *ahead*, trusting deep developmental instincts and making a commitment to an intuitively derived and fluid sense of self.

Catalyzed and changed by this "inner agenda," there arises a profound disconnection between what the world sees and what gifted teens experience in their inner lives. Attention to this inner life is not a new phenomenon for many gifted children. From their youngest years, gifted children (in varying degrees) attend to an internally derived sense of self. What is new in adolescence is an intense meta-awareness of the power and potential impact of their inborn capacity. Wedded to this awareness is an enormous sense of responsibility for the effect that such seemingly immeasurable powers might have. If the child possesses a strong and dynamic imaginative capacity, the weight of this knowledge is amplified (Roeper, 1995).

The sense of responsibility creates a paradoxical tension in the inner world of intense gifted teens. On the one hand, they are aware that they must attend to this inner force, and they feel certain that developmental emergence is unavoidable; on the other hand, they cannot be sure about the scope and nature of the capacities that will emerge. They also become aware of the existential dilemma of choice—that is, "When I make a choice, I automatically exclude all of the other choices that I might have made at this time. What if I become a concert pianist? A scientist who discovers the cure for cancer? Will I be able to have a family, too?"

At the same time, they are aware of their responsibility toward others and the interconnectedness of "all that is." They become acutely aware of the unique core of their own being and the awakening of their own unparalleled developmental agenda. Dabrowski wrote, "There is no existence without genuine essence. The condition of a truly human existence is awareness of and choice of what is quintessential, unique, and enduring in a person, without which existence itself would be valueless" (Cienin, 1972, p. 11). During the time of adolescence, this value-rich idea comes to the fore of the developmental trajectory. When it speaks and the intense gifted child heeds the call, it is inevitably met with varying degrees of support and understanding in the environment—as well as varying positive or negative outcomes.

Physical Maturation: A Key Determinant in Asynchrony

In general, physical development is an important gauge of maturation. Classical definitions of the beginning of adolescence refer to the onset of puberty as a critical signifier—the external manifestation of this phase of life. Achievement of physical maturation varies greatly: some teens mature physically at a very early age, some mature at average rates, while others are very late developers. This difference in the rate and degree of physical maturation impinges on all other aspects of growth and development. And while this is true for all teenagers, it is especially true for the gifted. There may be immense discrepancies in how aspects of the gifted child's core potential are expressed. A gifted child may have the cognitive capability of a person many years older—enclosed in an exceptional, typical, or delayed physical development and augmented by exceptional, average, or stunted social/emotional functioning. This enormous variance and asynchrony of function can feel overwhelming for the sensitive and intense gifted adolescent.

It is not uncommon, for instance, for a highly gifted eight-year-old to be extraordinarily cognitively advanced, while his physical body lags considerably behind. It is an enormous challenge to be chronologically eight years old with the physical capacity of a five-year-old, the mental maturity of a 16-year-old, and the emotional maturity that is at yet a different age.

This makeup is made even more complex by age-*less* imaginational capacities. Additionally, the lack of uncomplicated access to true peers—others who are like them intellectually, socially, emotionally—may effectively stunt social/emotional development. This is a common experience for highly gifted children. For them, easy access to like-minded peers in a variety of settings is rare, but social/emotional awareness and capacity cannot develop in a vacuum (Jackson, 2001; Jackson & Moyle, 2005). Socialization requires being with others. As the philosopher Jean Paul Sartre said: "In order to get at any truth about myself, I must have contact with another person. The other is indispensable to my own existence, as well as to my knowledge about myself."

In addition to their differences in cognitive processing speed, gifted children encounter other issues of disparity and unshared experience when they interact in the social arena—in realms both subtle and overt, including insight, humor, moral reasoning, sense of justice, passionate engagement, discernment, etc. All of these issues can cause discomfort and a feeling of being out of place.

Given their innate intra- and interpersonal differences in capacity and quality, the attainment of adolescent milestones is made more complex by the individual's attempt to incorporate aspects of awareness that are beyond the norm. Lack of environmental fit and inappropriateness of resources and context also contribute to unsatisfactory outcomes. Issues of asynchrony and social misinterpretation contribute to convoluted and deep-seated frustrations that play out on multiple levels. Gifted teens' capacities for meta-processing (awareness of their own perceptions and behaviors) only serve to augment and intensify all aspects of this emergent developmental experience.

Impacted by environmental factors, the unique nature of individual giftedness determines the degree to which the essential components of growth and development—cognitive, emotional, social, physical, moral, and spiritual—are synchronized and harmonized within any individual. Inevitable periods of disintegration are embedded in the developmental trajectory of the gifted adolescent. Dabrowski's theory, rich in dynamic concepts that describe the inner landscape, help to give a core understanding of the experiences of individuals in such a disintegrative state, promoting a positive role for conflict as a catalyst for evolutionary development.

Diving into Dabrowski Deeply

Some important concepts from Dabrowski help us understand issues of adolescent expression, development, growth, and change.

The *disposing and directing center* is a term that Dabrowski used for those aspects of mental processing, or collection of dynamisms, that organize and direct our behaviors. Its structure and function depend on the level of the individual's development. This center both transforms and is subordinated to the processes of human mental development.

In Dabrowski's view, the *inner psychic milieu*, or inner psychological environment of an individual—where a person thinks, imagines, introspects, feels, etc.—is the main factor of personality development in children and young people with "superior abilities." Those who show the greatest promise for development are those exhibiting an array of multilevel dynamisms, high degree of insight into oneself, evidence of creative ideation, striving toward improving or perfecting one's behavior, and having the ability to control and reshape one's mental cognitions. He theorized that individuals with this higher developmental potential—a synthesizing plurality of interests and abilities, combined with an intense emotional life—have a better chance of developing true personality ideals.

The *third factor* is Dabrowski's term for the uniquely human capacity to evolve one's personality beyond the circumstances of biological makeup and environmental influences. It incorporates the making of conscious choices through affirmations or negation of certain beliefs, cognitions, moods, reactions, feelings, values, trends, and behaviors. The genesis and maturation of this third, or autonomous, factor contributes to the realization of a fully authentic personality. Dabrowski called such concepts of the mental landscape *dynamisms*. The third factor interacts with other dynamisms and is the driving force that carries out the work of deciding what is to be accepted or rejected in the inner psychic milieu.

Inner conflict may appear as neurotic, ambivalent, hesitant, inhibited, or indecisive behavior. It describes an individual's dawning consciousness of his or her own differing levels of perception, motivation, behavior, and consequence. But inner conflict results when an individual becomes aware of opposition between needs, values, and interests—in the inner milieu—and he or she attempts to improve automatic behavior and to work though realizations of better actions, thoughts, and emotions. Its first appearance represents a transition of great importance in a person's development, and it benefits from positive emphasis.

Positive regression was Dabrowski's term for a temporary regression to an earlier emotional period or withdrawal from current activities in search of isolation. It allows an individual to prepare for the unfolding of his or her creative potential, to prevent mental disorders, or to preserve and develop his or her autonomy. It is common in people with emotional and imaginational overexcitability (Dabrowski, 1972).

For an adolescent, "regression" with this positive spin represents an opportunity to garner resources and revitalize one's core self on a lower level of functioning to gather strength for the work of development. It is a good thing, is temporary and restful for the individual, and should be supported quietly and without drawing overt attention to its appearance or dissipation.

Positive disintegration of an individual's self-conceptualization is the idea from Dabrowski's work that recognizes psychoneuroses—anxiety and depression—as an appropriate, natural, and necessary breakthrough for persons in accelerated development. This can occur when an individual moves from the influences of genetic endowment and cultured conditioning (determined by both biology and culture/environment) to advanced development toward a personality ideal.

We encourage adults who work with adolescents to use these ideas to help conceptualize patterns in adolescent behavior and to focus on potentially positive and growth-enhancing interpretations.

"Issues of Adolescence" Present in Younger Gifted Children

Perhaps the most important thing to remember about persons "fortified" with inner intensity (see Jackson & Moyle, Chapter 7)—who are intelligent, sensitive, and creative—is that many may exhibit adolescent-type behaviors at ages younger than expected. Such individuals may or may not have signs of physical or sexual maturation, but they do appear to experience the inner turbulence of persons in their teenage years. With cognition at the stage of abstract reasoning (Piaget's Formal Operations)—beyond the typical stage of their age peers, and coupled with enormous imaginational capacities and perhaps moments of clear perception characteristic of advanced moral and ethical development (Kohlberg's sixth stage of Universal Principles)—it is easy to understand how a young gifted person can be frustrated, confused, or even volatile. With that said, we will be referring to even these younger persons in our discussion of adolescent issues.

Helping the Adolescent to Align with His or Her "Better Self"

Possessing acute reasoning abilities, profound emotional responses, and palpable imaginational capacities can feel overwhelming to a gifted individual at any stage of life. However, when coupled with the burgeoning hormonal changes of adolescence, this combination can be unbearable. Outbursts of frustration may be followed immediately by feelings of shame and disgust at one's inability to control oneself. Some gifted adolescents may additionally cover up this embarrassment by a feeling of justification. Some, who feel justified in taking a stand, increase their obstinate stance. Others internalize their frustration in observing the hypocrisy and incongruent behavior of others, the duplicity of the world, or the lack of passion of those around them. Still others may become fatigued or hopeless in desperation of not seeming to be able to live up to an ideal standard, or they may be saddened and depressed in realizing that their behavior has hurt another person.

Helping the adolescent to develop an awareness of what Dabrowski called *subject-object* in oneself (see Chapter 7)—to regard one's own behavior critically and to reflect on the behavior of others in a non-judgmental way—is important, but this cannot be done without first creating trust and excellent rapport. Because the adolescent is struggling to establish an identity separate and unique from adults, this can be a challenging task. Nevertheless, the intense adolescent also has an overwhelming desire to inhere—to connect and to fully integrate fully—all aspects of his or her being in a deeply congruent way. Many, too, are desperate to experience communion—a deeply resonant and reciprocal connection with another—that doesn't necessarily involve physical intimacy.

However, we have found that, because most intense and highly gifted individuals have had little opportunity to experience this deep sort of friendship and sharing—and they are so *hungry* for it—it is in adolescence that this deep need *does* get tangled in urges for sexual experiences, which can lead to early commitments and unions that become problematic in complex ways. Our experiences indicate that this need for sharing and friendship can be closely linked with the observed tendency for highly gifted individuals to take on the struggles of others at their own expense, supplanting their own growth with a desire to help another. And because of the nature of the Shadow function (see Chapter 7), this can often be entirely unconscious on the part of the gifted and intense adolescent.

Additionally, when the integrative forces are thwarted and there is inadequate communion, a highly undesirable outcome may be a severe depressive state. Lacking meaningful, reciprocal, and sustaining relationships—a keystone developmental variable in adolescence—the gifted adolescent may implode. Other critical factors impact this phenomenon—degree of successful attachment relationships within the family, for instance—but the absence of rich, satisfying relationships and an appropriate arena to explore the social/emotional self are predictors of depressive states for some high-potential teens (Jackson, 1995, 1998; Jackson & Peterson, 2003).

Developmental Trends Relevant to the Adolescent Stage for Gifted Individuals

Dabrowski wrote that individuals possessing the kind of intensity that promotes advanced development are high in *developmental potential* (DP) (Dabrowski, 1977). In our practice, we have identified three trends that are particularly relevant in the development of gifted children during the adolescent stage. These trends are not exclusive of each other and may occur simultaneously—exacerbating difficulties and/or accelerating or inhibiting growth.

Precocious Development

We observe one trend in which gifted individuals reach developmental milestones at uncharacteristically young ages. This maturity may be exhibited in any one of the dozens of lines of development (Jackson, 2007; Wilber, 2000) that exceeds what would be typically expected for age norms.

Wilber (2000) identified some 24 (or more) developmental lines that, somewhat independently, determine any individual's growth. The authors' Integral Psychotherapy model and Jackson's Integral Programming for the Gifted (Jackson, 2008) incorporate these multiple aspects of development into an integrated theory, giving breadth and depth to the concept of asynchrony as identified in the gifted literature. The developmental lines include: cognitive, psychosocial, creative, kinesthetic, and moral aspects, communicative capacity, self-identity, worldview, psychosexuality, modes of time and space, and spirituality, to name a few. Inherent in each of these developmental lines are levels (stages of awareness and capacity). Each level has characteristic features, and the levels build in ascending complexity and faculty. None of these evolutionary steps can be skipped over, and each line of development operates in its own way, although they are affected by and affect all other lines. The gifted teen, then, may find him- or herself exceptionally advanced in some developmental lines at a very early age—worldview, cognitive, and moral, for instance. Again, this precocity impinges upon and affects all other aspects of development (Jackson, 2006).

Arrested Development

This observed trend occurs as a result of the exceptional sensitivity of the high DP child. Arrested development occurs when an external factor or factors cause injury and/or significant pain, resulting in fragmentation or disassociation. This could include everything from a benignly non-validating environment, where the child feels simply painfully out-of-place, to an overtly counter-validating environment, where the child experiences actual abuse. Minor incidents that occur over time can cause "lesions" in the psychic fabric of the individual. Aspects of the growing child remain fixed at that "age" or level of functionality as the result of such experiences. Typically, access to the injured site is difficult, as the individual becomes well-defended through a variety of defense mechanisms—and this is particularly the case with gifted individuals, whose levels of complexity are intertwined, sometimes quite creatively!

It cannot be emphasized enough that the external factors may seem, to others, benign, but to the child, they can be adevelopmental, noxious, debilitating, and even deadly. The factors can cause a tyrannical imbalance in the homeostasis of the growing child.

Repressed Functionality

This state of development is achieved when a child with high developmental potential does not manifest or utilize (consciously or unconsciously) certain aspects of his or her being. In this case, the aspect has not been destroyed or fragmented but remains underutilized, guarded, buried, or protected in some way. Dysfunction is created from a two-fold exacerbating process: (1) the lack of use of crucial self-aspects diminishes their vitality, and (2) the energy that is expended to protect an aspect of self robs energy, as it were, from spontaneous and healthy growth. (Repressed functionality in the gifted adolescent may also result from expending energy to protect another, including a parent or other adult. This is a crucial reason why adults responsible for the care of the gifted must attend to their own development! See Chapter 7.)

The consequences of repressed functionality can be severe and include overall diminished vitality and capacity for the individual, anxiety states, depressive conditions ranging from dysthymic depression (relatively speaking, a more minor and ongoing condition) or major depression (exceptionally debilitating and potentially fatal), and/or compromised or reduced creative, physical, or sexual energy.

Why Adolescence Is Difficult for Gifted Teens: Environmental Influences

We have identified some important factors that interact and interfere with healthy adolescent growth for gifted individuals. Many of these factors appear to be manifestations of the time in which we live. They include the following.

Segregation of the Teenage Group away from the Rest of Society

Modern high schools offer little interaction with heterogeneous age groups. Given the asynchronous nature of high-potential teens' development and the crucial importance of communion, access to intergenerational forces and multiple kinds of relationships are vital. Teens' development can be obstructed and negatively impacted in such homogeneous environments. Parents and teachers can encourage involvement in cross-age activities.

Subtle and Not-So-Subtle Pressures to Conform

There is great pressure from peers, parents, educators, media, and popular culture to conform to external standards. Although different arenas make different demands and often have competing expectations, all urge the adolescent to present in "normative" fashions, without regard for authentic unfolding and realization of uniqueness. Parents and teachers can accept unique expressions of individuality.

Lack of Awareness of Gifted Phenomenology

Healthcare professionals and educators are often untrained and unaware of the overall phenomenology of giftedness. Many are quick to diagnose all disintegrative states as negative. Often eccentricities are seen as evidence for diagnostic criteria, and authentic (but non-normative when compared to the majority of the population) behavior is dismissed as reflexively pathological (see Amend, Chapter 6).

Emphasis on External Manifestations

Adolescents are often judged based on overt, external, observable behaviors. This simplified and overt focus negates the authentic inner life of the gifted child.

Achievement Inflation

Often talent becomes emphasized, and this in turns becomes focused on performance and competition—to the detriment of wise development of all aspects of a child's capacities. This could also exacerbate imaginings of self-importance or, conversely, feelings of deep inadequacy and depression.

Vicarious Parenting

"Soccer moms" and "Helicopter" parents may become over-identified and over-involved in their offsprings' activities, thus hindering authentic development. By vicariously living through their children, they rob themselves and their children of deep engagement with others and the world.

Little or No Access to Environments that Encourage Authenticity

It is rare to find venues where it feels safe to reveal one's truest self, heartfelt desires, and deepest fears, where deep engagement with others is accepted and encouraged, and where passions can be expressed. This feels especially discouraging to the adolescent who thrives on exchange and intensity and who longs to integrate his or her sensations and cognitions.

Adult Preoccupation with Providing Ideal or Optimal Circumstances

This preoccupation is nearly always pre-arranged and pre-determined, having little room for flexibility or regard for unique individuation. It originates in a desire to help ensure "success"—but removes the authentic struggle and unpredictability from childhood experiences, robbing experiences of vitality. This generation of parents, armed with heightened knowledge and more comfortable lifestyles, are often in search of the most advantageous circumstances for their offspring and may inadvertently subvert the necessary struggles, challenges, and trials that are grist for the developmental mill.

Why Adolescence Is Difficult for Gifted Teens: Inner Space

From the perspective of the inner world of a gifted adolescent, we believe that there are many unique factors that exacerbate this time of imbalance and make it different.

One of the ways in which it appears to be different is because growth and processing seem to be especially rapid in the gifted and intense teen. In addition, asynchronous growth is often uneven across many aspects, intensifying feelings of discomfort and alienation. Many gifted teens operate in broader spheres of influence; they are more actively engaged in terms of both input and impact. This can intensify feelings of responsibility and remove focus from an individual's healthy development of ego.

Some destabilizing factors are common to all teens but appear intensified for those who are gifted due to intense desire and compelling drive to integrate experience. These include biological hormonal influences, the segregation of the age group from the rest of society and culture, a decided lack of cohesion between school subjects within secondary education, and where deep involvement does not arise in the academic environment and little to no integration of self with subject matter occurs. All students have a need to see the connection between subject matter and the world in which they live.

Most gifted teens possess an increased ability to learn quickly, a heightened facility of memory, and more rapid capacity to process, integrate, and connect ideas and information. These capacities are often obstructed in some way in formal learning environments. Gifted teens often have greater facility for discernment, differentiation, intuitive knowing, and penetration into meanings of events and experiences. These differences interact to create conditions in which it is difficult for them to be adequately mirrored by others. As a result, opportunities to engage deeply with true peers are rare.

To reiterate, all of these innate differences are more than likely influenced profoundly by arrested and/or precocious development and/or repressed functionality. In the absence of "good enough" environments, there will be no developmental cohesion, interfering with a healthy and naturally unfolding maturation.

What Is Needed to Support Intense Adolescents

We have identified some important aspects and areas for improving these conditions—to encourage healthier and more positive trends and to help counteract some of the more unhealthy and negative consequences of existing environments. We offer the following suggestions:

- Encourage multi-generational involvement and exposure.

- Truly honor the dignity and unique personhood of the child's essence—while at the same time addressing needs for guidance and appropriate boundaries.

- Pay attention to *wisdom and ethical regard*—as much as possible—in choosing courses of action and other decision making (Moyle, 2005).

- Attend to developmental tasks with conscious guidance and engagement of resources that are commensurate with a child's innate capacity (potential and ability).

- Realize that chance factors are uncontrollable and represent authentic interaction with a living environment—they create impetus for accelerated growth, robust maturation, and characteristics of flexibility and resilience in a child's character.

- Provide opportunities for the emergent adolescent to shoulder personal responsibility and decision making in a step-wise fashion. This acquired capacity needs to be buoyed by effective communication between parent and offspring and wholehearted belief in the inherent wisdom of the evolving teen.

- Provide opportunities to interact with mentors, with "true peers," and act, as well, in mentoring or supervisory positions to exercise all aspects of their interpersonal dimensions and foster important community building.

- Create curriculum that integrates subject matter which allows for—and, indeed, encourages—original thought, that develops intellectual risk-taking, and that requires full engagement of the intellect, world view, social/emotional aspects, and moral reasoning.

Chapter 5

The Emperor Has No Clothes: Exquisite Perception, Stress, and the Gifted Child

Annemarie Roeper, Ed.D.

Some gifted children seem much more resilient to stress than others. Some even seem to invite it. Others avoid it. We may not be able to fully understand gifted children's differences in response to stress, but we must provide them with the resources to deal with it, for the world is full of daily stress.

Let's Begin with a Story
We all know the story of "The Emperor's New Clothes"?

Once upon a time, there lived an Emperor who loved fine clothes more than he cared for ruling his kingdom, managing his armies, riding through town, or even going to the theater. All he really cared about was owning and wearing fine new clothes. One day, two tailors, who were actually swindlers and thieves, came to town, boasting that they made the finest cloth and that it was a special cloth, too. This cloth was so very special, they said, because in addition to being exquisitely beautiful, only those who were very bright and especially fit for their office in the court would be able to see it at all. It would be invisible to others.

While this pretend cloth was being woven, the Emperor would send members of his council down to check on its progress, and each would come back exclaiming and describing the exquisite beauty and intricate pattern of this wondrous cloth. Word spread throughout the kingdom of the beauty and magic of the fabulous cloth, as well as the great cost of it.

Finally, the Emperor could bear it no longer and headed to the looms to see the work of the pretend tailors himself. Not wanting to expose himself as stupid or unfit for his own office by admitting that he could not see the cloth, he, as his advisors before him had done, exclaimed that it was indeed the finest cloth he had ever seen. All of his followers strained their eyes in attempts to see the cloth, which they could not. Nevertheless, they all exclaimed, as the Emperor had done, about the beauty of this magnificent cloth.

With the Emperor's approval, the two tailors sewed a new suit of clothes for him from this cloth that did not exist. They played their roles well, staying up into the wee hours of the morning, working and sewing, maintaining their ruse.

In the morning, the tailors dressed the Emperor, and although he was just in his underwear, everyone in the court admired his new clothes and readied him for a procession through the town. Even his pages went along with the deception, pretending to carry his train behind him.

As he paraded through the town, all of the villagers cried out at the beauty of the Emperor's new finery. They all went along with the deception, and out of fear of being called stupid or a simpleton, they claimed it to be the most beautiful outfit ever. Never before had the townspeople taken such a keen interest in their Emperor's clothes. The excitement spread through the town until one very small child said, "But the Emperor has nothing on at all!!!" The father echoed these words and said, "The child tells the truth." And the crowd echoed, "BUT HE HAS NOTHING ON AT ALL!!!"

The Emperor thought to himself, "Well, the procession has started, and so it must go on!" So the court parade continued, heads held high, and the train that wasn't there at all held higher than ever.

This story serves as a metaphor for the lived perceptions of many gifted children. Gifted children see and feel more acutely than others. This is part and parcel of their giftedness, and yet at the same time, it can be a source of great stress. Unfortunately, their perceptions and realizations are not always received as positively by family or the larger community as they were for the child in the story of "The Emperor's New Clothes." As a result, gifted children experience stress.

Stress: Considering the Environment and the Gifted Child

Gifted children experience pressure and stress from two main sources: the environment and themselves. Some of the outside pressures are common to all gifted people. We live in a world geared to the average, where most thought processes and resulting actions are simple and accepted. They are often based on single classifications and single contrasts. This is the way it is done, whatever that might be, and this is how we shall continue. Gifted children, however, see and react to the nuances and complexity of the problems surrounding them and act accordingly. They see the gray areas, the overlaps, the exceptions, and the contradictions. Consequently, gifted children are out of step with the environment, and this ever-present difference is a stress-producing element for a number of reasons (Roeper, 2004b).

Before we can appreciate the ways in which gifted children are subject to stress, we need to explore further what this term means. What is stress? In the most elemental sense of the word, it means pressure, an impact. In order for stress to exist, there must be something that receives it, something on which something else makes an impact. Stress exists only if there is something to be stressed.

We say that an individual "receives" stress, or "experiences" stress. But *how* does this happen? And *what* in the person receives the stress? The heart? The brain? The body? In my opinion, how a person reacts to all experiences, including stress, depends on the state, the development, and the uniqueness of the person—the most inner Self of the person. It is the Self that experiences the stress. The Self is the beholder, and stress is in the eye of the beholder (Roeper, 2004b, 2007). What is quite stressful to one person may not be at all stressful to another; it depends on one's Self.

And so we must consider another question: What is the Self? The Self, I believe, is the interior of a person to which everything else is exterior. Stress usually develops out of the relationship between the inner Self (the core) and outer Selves (how we portray ourselves to others); sometimes it stems from only the inner Self. Are the inner and outer Selves in tune with one another? Are they partners, or are they antagonists? Education at its best can be defined as the positive nurturing of this relationship between the inner and outer Self.

Stress is neither negative nor positive. It depends, rather, on how the Self receives it and on the state of the Self. I believe that stress can be a positive force under the right conditions; it can prompt us to strive for new ideas and solutions that we otherwise would not have sought. I will elaborate on that notion further on in this chapter. First, I want to discuss the ways in which stress affects gifted children.

Because of their complex thought processes, gifted children are often misunderstood—or they are not understood at all. They get negative feedback and criticism, or they experience a certain perplexed reaction, or they get no feedback at all. If their perceptions and ideas are not understood and acknowledged, they surely are unlikely to receive appropriate feedback. Other children, less complex in their thoughts, get the exchange of ideas and reactions that they expect to receive. This is not always the case with gifted children. Instead, there is little or no exchange of ideas in the gifted child's everyday world that is on his or her level, and that creates unfulfilled needs and stress. These children are likely to work alone on their projects and in developing their thoughts. They lack intellectual or creative interchange. Because they get no resonance for their ideas, they become bored or frustrated, and this boredom and frustration is experienced as stress.

If, however, their giftedness is understood because they produce an identifiable product, such as learning how to read at an early age or achieving outstanding success in math, a different type of stress may occur—pressure from one's parent's or teachers to perform. In this case, the gift receives the attention, not the person. This, too, creates a certain kind of stress. For example, children who already know how to read in kindergarten will most likely be called upon to read when visitors are present. Even though they enjoy the attention that they receive, they realize that it is their gift, not themselves as unique persons, that is receiving the attention.

Other pressures that gifted children experience are a product of the giftedness itself. These pressures include:

○ Recognizing the state of the world and the dangers that surround us and not being able to do anything about them. Or perhaps feeling the need to do something but experiencing great anxiety at how these feelings and ideas will be perceived.

○ Realizing that adults are also unable, and often unwilling, to face the global situation. For example, many young gifted children reacted with enormously complex feelings in response to the events of 9/11, the war, and terrorism. They may feel deeply engaged in developing greater understanding of such complex problems yet also overwhelmed by their deep feelings and advanced awareness.

○ Recognizing injustices in personal life as well as society creates a number of related stresses and strong feelings, such as anger, frustration, and a compulsion to do something useful. But without environmental supports, gifted children may feel powerless to make an impact. They feel lonely in the depth of their caring about injustices. Average children, especially the very young, are generally not as aware, nor do they feel as deeply about the problems and injustices of the world, especially those in faraway places. Gifted children, by contrast, feel a kinship and often make these problems their own.

The personal pressures do not always relate to the here-and-now or to actual events, but to worries and concerns about the future. The future is real to gifted children, and they react to it at an early age. They also are concerned at an early age with death and other existential concepts, but they don't necessarily have the abilities to handle this expanded awareness either emotionally or intellectually.

One of the greatest pressures on gifted children is the pressure to be perfect. Because of this, they often have unrealistic expectations and standards for themselves and strive desperately to achieve them. They may want to dance the perfect ballet or play a piece of music perfectly. On the other hand, they also fear their own superiority in competitive situations because they do not want to receive reactions from others, especially when, as is often the case, these others include their own parents. Conversely, they may suffer from the opposite pressure, namely the urgent need to win in competitions. Their need for perfection shows clearly their lack of personal power because they are not able to be perfect. (For more information on perfectionism, see Silverman, Chapter 9.) They realize that they are small Selves surrounded by a large awareness. They deeply perceive their helplessness.

In addition, gifted children experience stress from the complexities that they realize. They cannot categorize things as easily as other children because they are aware of the various ways in which those things might be categorized. They, at times, cannot pursue goals as completely or directly as they might like because they always see the other side of the argument and the consequences of certain actions. This leads to great difficulty in making commitments and often leaves them outside of groups. More average children, who think in more typical ways, can accept goals more readily as their own, whereas to gifted children, everything may seem relative. On the one hand, they find it difficult to make an absolute commitment to a single position. On the other hand, they feel the pressure to be deeply involved and to reach for certain goals. Even if they select goals, however, they encounter impediments that prevent their attaining them in daily life. This creates stress and results in friction and irritation.

Additional tension is produced because the stress on the gifted may not be recognized by others, or may be misunderstood, or may not be viewed as legitimate by teachers and parents. These sensitive children, then, often do not receive recognition, relief, or help. But they need relief from stress. The stress that they experience is not ordinary stress. For example, a gifted child may not be heartbroken if she loses a spelling bee, but her inability to express her complicated, deep thoughts in an English composition may send her into a depression, even if the teacher is perfectly satisfied with the quality of her work.

Another example: A high school boy is in trouble because he does not do his homework, although he really would like to. In addition, he is experiencing feelings of desperation and despair because he never seems to have time to finish the symphony that he has on his mind all the time. He is under two types of stress: outer stress to do his homework and fulfill normal expectations, and internal stress prompted by his own inner creativity. Probably, neither of these is recognized by the significant adults in his life; they see no reason for him not to do his homework. They do not understand how it feels to be pressured to finish an incomplete symphony that one hears in one's head.

Gifted children need feedback even more than adults do. Often, their perceptions, special goals, and desires do not receive adequate recognition, while conventional goals are commonly recognized and applauded. This leaves gifted children alone with their goals and their dreams. Out of this grows another kind of stress. There seems to be a basic need in every human to measure one's achievements or abilities against a standard or a norm. Gifted children, however, often have goals and achievements for which there are no means of measurement, so these goals and dreams may never be recognized by others at all. How often, then, do gifted children know that they are achieving the goals that they have set for themselves? Albert Einstein and Albert Schweitzer, for instance, had types of giftedness that bore tangible results. They received positive feedback, although this happened only late in their lives. Many other gifted people never receive positive feedback for their goals and accomplishments precisely because the accomplishments are difficult or impossible to measure. How do we measure understanding that is more complex than that of others? And how can gifted children maintain their drive in the face of indifference or scorn?

Another source of stress for gifted children is the lack of role models and mentors. Because they often move in new directions, there are no models for them to follow. It is like the explorer who thinks that she will make a discovery, but since it has not been made before, she cannot be sure. Many gifted people have original thoughts and ideas and create original products that may not be accepted. History abounds with great creators whose work was not recognized for its extraordinary potential and worth until decades or centuries later. This can leave the gifted individual without true peers, feeling isolated and lonely.

There is another dimension of how stress affects gifted children. They not only receive stress, they also create it. Gifted children create a kind of discomfort in their surroundings, for by their mere existence, they uncover shortcomings. They question and challenge traditions and the status quo and are not comfortable doing things just because everyone else is doing them. Their experiences are unconventional; their needs are not typical, and society—many schools and other institutions—is unable to fulfill them. The gifted high school student who would rather write a symphony than do homework has been led to believe that his education will fulfill his personal needs. When he finds out, however, that this is not the case, his disappointment in the environment's failure to fulfill its promise creates a sense of dissatisfaction in his surroundings.

The gifted do not accept neat, simple categories; they expect society to think in complex ways, as they do. They expect society to look honestly at itself and to perceive things about itself that it cannot and does not want to see.

It is always a source of amazement to see how well gifted children know their teachers and parents. The children are aware of both the strengths and weaknesses of the significant adults in their lives. They expect adults' behavior to be consistent with their words. They do not understand when adults say, "Do as I say, not as I do."

At the same time, while gifted children feel that they are expected to look up to adults, they sense when adults feel threatened and insecure, even when they try to pretend otherwise. In that sense, gifted children feel betrayed in their sense of rightness and justice. And because they cannot reconcile this, they may challenge adults' authority and superiority. This tension, then, is another source of stress, both within the Self of the gifted child and in the environment.

Dabrowski's theory highlights this tension—the tension between "what is" and "what ought to be" (see Chapter 2). Often, gifted children are consumed by the pursuit of the greatest potential—in themselves, in others, and in their world.

This same sensitivity and drive toward improvement is a two-sided potential, bringing both joy and pain. Many gifted children recognize the problems in their environment, yet they simultaneously see the beauty of their world. Because these children are so sensitive to their parents and other close adults, another factor frequently enters into the situation that makes it difficult for them to cope. At a surprisingly young age, many gifted children take on responsibilities that are quite beyond their actual ability to influence others. Because many, if not most, gifted children experience the world with greater sensitivity and clarity than other children, they are also keenly aware of the difficulties and deficiencies in the world around them, as well as the difficulties and deficiencies in the adults to cope with these aspects of their realities. The gifted children feel an obligation to change the world, fix the problems of which they are keenly aware, and make the world a better place (Roeper, 2007).

This sense of responsibility, which grows directly out of their sensitivities and intensities, then repeats itself throughout their growth. They have a deep need to believe in their own strength and capacity for making a difference and to influence their world. In fact, often, this desire to do good and make a difference becomes an anchor for their sense of Self and a source of comfort for them.

I remember clearly many students with whom I worked closely over the years, sharing their concerns for the future. One 14-year-old girl went through periods of great desperation over issues including world hunger, war, and the environment. She was most insightful and well-informed about current events and poor choices that had been made around many difficult issues. Her response was clear and steady: "We have to believe in a better future. We have to keep this vision and make the change ourselves."

Positive Stress

Earlier in this chapter, I said that stress might be a positive force under the right conditions. How might that be? Stress is involved in creative effort, in trying to solve a difficult problem, and in stretching beyond one's current capacities. The first and most important way in which we can help gifted children in their paths toward personal development is to help them understand stress and how to use stress effectively. By helping them develop these understandings, they will be better poised to recognize their own capacities, understand personal coping strategies, and muster the strength to meet the challenges of their inner strivings and the challenges inherent in their environments.

One way that parents and teachers can best support gifted children in their development is by recognizing that emotional growth and personal growth are a necessary part of the educational process (Roeper, 2004b, 2007; Piechowski, 2006). Most educators and parents these days seem to believe that, for gifted children, emphasis must be placed first and foremost on their intellectual development. But intellectual development rests on the development of the child's Self, on his or her insights and deeper sensitivities. In fact, we cannot separate one from the other. It is this very separation that makes gifted children experience stress as a negative force.

The foundation for the development of one's sense of Self is laid very early in childhood. Young children internalize how their parents feel about them. In early childhood, they have no other source of discernment about who they are in the world. Their feelings mirror those of their parents. Do the parents view their children as extensions of themselves to fulfill their own needs? When this is so, children's Selves depend on their parents, and they cannot develop a healthy sense of autonomy. There is a lack, an unfulfilled need. We must, therefore, look at ourselves, our own needs, and see how we tend to relate them to children. This is true in a different way for teachers also. We need to see children as separate, autonomous beings.

One way in which we can help gifted children cope with stress is to have empathy for them. The goal is not to identify with them, but to empathize with who they are and try to meet their needs for self-exploration and self-development as best we can. Of course, this must also be balanced with the needs of the family and the needs of the classroom—a delicate balancing act, indeed. But we need as best we can to look at the child as the autonomous being and independent individual that he or she will ultimately be.

We need to look at gifted children on their own terms and not compare them to Tyrone or Amy down the street.

This is not the same as being permissive. It does not mean that we need to follow children's wishes and desires all of the time, because that may not be what they really need. It simply means thinking in terms of the developmental potential of our gifted children rather than the arbitrary expectations, relatively speaking, of the world.

It is important that young children feel support in terms of coping with both internal and external pressures. I have often thought that the supportive family or classroom provides a sort of cocoon in which the children find shelter and space as they develop their Selves in such a way as to protect themselves and to deal effectively with the pressures, desires, and excitement of growing up. Empathy, understanding, and emotional nurturing are essential supports for the development of young children.

As they grow older, the form that empathy takes may change. If they are well-understood and well-supported, they will have the skills they need to increasingly cope with internal pressures and the pressures that surround them. Then, our relationship will be to listen closely and keep our eyes open to their perceptions as they venture farther out into the world, looking where they are looking, and listening as they share their stories and explain their ideas and perceptions. Listening and respect are essential to mirror the development of children, to support them in developing a strong sense of Self. They are also essential to maintain healthy relationships into young adulthood and beyond.

The child who recognized that the emperor had no clothes on was surely a gifted child with insight and a strong sense of Self. While he experienced stress in the environment, seeing these events unfold so differently than the adults around him claimed, he also had a strong sense of Self. It certainly must have caused no small measure of anxiety in him to see how everyone else was fooled, yet because his sense of Self was strong, he had the strength to do something about it. One very lovely element at the end of the story is that others recognize and acknowledge the truth of the child.

This small child receives appropriate feedback and mirroring, validation, and affirmation for his truth and his experience. We can wish this for all of our gifted children, and as caring adults, we can provide this, too. With our willingness to step into their shoes, hear their truths, see with their eyes as best we might, and provide feedback and support, we will encourage them along the path toward the development of their highest potential.

Chapter 6

Dabrowski's Theory: Possibilities and Implications of Misdiagnosis, Missed Diagnosis, and Dual Diagnosis in Gifted Individuals

Edward R. Amend, Psy.D.

Nine-year-old Ford had severe temper outbursts in response to intense frustration—which resulted in a diagnosis of Bipolar Disorder (BPD). He was anxious and frustrated much of the time, and others viewed his intense and wildly-varying emotions as inappropriate reactions to situational stressors. Ford had also been identified as a profoundly gifted youngster, although no effort had been made at school or at home to understand this aspect of his personality or the role that giftedness and overexcitability might play in his difficulties. The educational environment was not meeting his academic or intellectual needs, but the report on file at the school did not in any way relate his very high intellectual abilities to his current problems. Instead, the school administrators and teachers who worked with Ford saw the boy's difficulties as pathological and biologically based. After all, he had a parent who had been previously diagnosed with BPD. His problems were clearly interfering with his development, and the consulting psychiatrist prescribed medications to attempt to manage his behavior, with limited success.

Ford's parents then contacted a psychologist who specialized in work with gifted children for a second opinion. This follow-up evaluation confirmed that Ford did indeed show mood-related difficulties and explosive tendencies. He also showed extreme intellectual and emotional overexcitability, with heightened—yet frustrated and unproductive—reactions in response to an inappropriate educational environment that moved at a slow pace and did not provide any accommodations for his advanced abilities. Unfortunately, he and his family had come to understand all of his problems as only pathological and not related to giftedness or overexcitability in any way. When treatment addresses the gifted traits and the corresponding needs, as well as the mood swings, there is a way to help Ford.

To date, medication has helped to stabilize some of the mood swings, but it has been largely ineffective in managing Ford's explosive tendencies. Addressing the boy's complex situation will take a strong clinician who is willing to embrace both the pathological and overexcitable aspects of Ford's personality. While it is possible that Ford will continue to need medication to address the biological aspects of his difficulties, helping him accept himself (both strengths and concerns) is necessary. Only if he understands and accepts himself can Ford learn to manage his emotions and behavior effectively to allow re-integration at a higher level. However, if Ford and those closest to him continue to perceive his behaviors as solely pathological, it is possible that he will remain disintegrated or re-integrate at a lower level, becoming entrenched in negative patterns. The course of intervention and the frame of reference taken by those involved with Ford will affect the path of his development—and both his and his family's future.

Ford's case of dual diagnosis (gifted and bipolar) and the difficulties that come with these two exceptionalities highlights the complex intersection of giftedness, overexcitability, environment, and pathology. Clearly a gifted individual, Ford was also experiencing mental health challenges.

Kazimierz Dabrowski and his colleagues, upon whose work much of this book is grounded, viewed mental health and developmental potential differently than other theorists and clinical practitioners. Dabrowski and colleagues would likely accept both the pathological and overexcitable aspects of Ford's life because, in Dabrowski's view, genuine mental health involves both disintegration of internal psychological structures *and* active developmental processes or dynamisms. According to Dabrowski, personality development and psychological growth do not follow a prescribed path from birth to adulthood to old age. Instead, development depends on various internal and environmental processes in interaction. The following example, presented by Dabrowski and his colleagues (Dabrowski, 1970), highlights the difference between Dabrowski's views and those of traditional mental health professionals:

> *The contrast between a developmental and a nondevelopmental psychiatric approach comes out very pointedly when we consider the problem of diagnosis of two individuals: one that has a strongly integrated primitive mentality, with intelligence totally subordinated to instinctive drives, unhesitating, shrewd and ruthless in the pursuit of his aims, and another, subtle, sensitive, full of doubts and scruples, consumed with disquietude, anxiety, feelings of shame and guilt. The first may be a very successful president of a big company, president of a labor union or a Caribbean state, as well as a boss of a criminal gang, while the latter is notorious among artists, thinkers, and writers. Which of them represents mental health, which of them needs psychiatric and educational advice, and possibly medical treatment?* (p. 118)

This question is central to the issue of misdiagnosis of gifted individuals. How does one conceptualize genuine mental health?[1] Dabrowski's answer is pertinent in relation to the misdiagnosis issues presented here.

> *The answer from the standpoint of the theory of positive disintegration is very clear. In the first instance, we have a typical case of primitive, even psychopathic structure, which creates daily injustice and puts in danger and fear everybody around. If an individual of this type would receive proper educational and psychiatric treatment in his childhood, many social calamities could be avoided. In the second case, we have an individual with a great human developmental potential, possibly a creative contributor to*

---

1 The scope of this chapter does not allow for a complete discussion of Dabrowski's views of mental health, and a brief overview will follow. The reader is referred to Elizabeth Mika's excellent chapter in *Dabrowski's Theory of Positive Disintegration* (Mendaglio, 2008a) for a more complete discussion.

> *the progress and growth of society. The fact that the first type of individuals is generally considered mentally healthy, and the second mentally sick, indicates that the society itself is primitive and confused.* (Dabrowski, 1970, p. 118)

In Dabrowski's view, the crux of mental health is not balance or a lack of problems, but rather imbalance and some measure of personal disintegration. Dabrowski's views contrast starkly with many traditional views of mental health, and the possibility of misdiagnosis stems from his conclusion that the problems traditionally associated with mental illness are actually signs of a developing personality.

Misdiagnosis and Missed Diagnosis of Gifted Individuals

Both misdiagnosis and missed diagnosis are problematic errors for various reasons. Many clinicians who specialize in working with gifted individuals recognize these issues, though formal research on misdiagnosis is limited (Webb, Amend, Webb, Goerss, Beljan, & Olenchak, 2005; Hartnett, Nelson, & Rinn, 2004). Nevertheless, misdiagnosis of gifted children and adults has received some attention in the professional literature (e.g., see Webb, et al., 2005) and occasionally in the popular press. There has been even less focus on missed—or overlooked—diagnosis, though this problem has been reported informally among colleagues.

What roles do Dabrowski's theory of positive disintegration (TPD) and the concept of overexcitability (OE) play in the misdiagnosis of gifted individuals? Both relate to the possibility of misdiagnosis or missed diagnosis in gifted children and adults, and this chapter will discuss how they relate to the diagnostic process and to misdiagnosis, as well as discussing some potential misdiagnoses that seem associated with OE.

To understand how misdiagnosis and missed diagnosis may be related to TPD, one must first understand Dabrowski's view of mental health and psychopathology. In a sense, Dabrowski viewed certain psychopathological symptoms (particularly neurosis and even some psychoses) as an essential step toward personality development. One must, he posited, experience symptoms related to disorders in order to develop fully (Mendaglio, 2008b). Thus, one could argue that misdiagnosis is frequent in individuals who are high functioning and fully developed in personality terms; the behaviors (or symptoms) they experience (e.g., excessive anxiety or compulsive behavior) along the path of development do not indicate pathology, but rather reflect a mentally healthy process of development.

Diagnostic errors arise when professionals misinterpret behaviors, or when they simply interpret behaviors in the context of artificial diagnostic schemas. Whether misdiagnosis or missed diagnosis, there are associated costs, and accurate diagnosis is important to avoid the two equally problematic situations. Both misdiagnosis and missed diagnosis occur when giftedness and its characteristics (such as OE) are confused with a pathological condition such as Attention Deficit Hyperactivity Disorder (ADHD), Obsessive-Compulsive Disorder (OCD), Oppositional Defiant Disorder (ODD), or Asperger's Disorder. First, missed diagnosis occurs when a clinician fails to make a diagnosis of a true disorder because the behaviors are either thought to be related to giftedness alone or are perhaps obscured by giftedness, which may help an individual compensate for symptoms of true pathological conditions like ADHD. In other cases, a gifted individual may purposefully camouflage or hide pathological behaviors, causing the correct diagnosis to be missed. Or a professional may overlook a disorder in the belief that the behaviors simply represent a "quirky" gifted individual. In cases of missed diagnosis, the misattribution of behavior results in a failure to accurately identify giftedness or the disorder when one is (or both are) actually present.

Second, and particularly germane to Dabrowski's theory of positive disintegration, is misdiagnosis, which occurs when a disorder is inaccurately diagnosed in a gifted individual, though the disorder is not actually present. In such cases of misdiagnosis, the behaviors of concern are often better explained by giftedness, OE, or the process of development that Dabrowski called TPD than by the diagnosed disorder. In these cases, if treatment can address the giftedness and foster growth and development, the problematic behaviors will decrease or, in some cases, disappear or extinguish. However, with a misdiagnosis, professionals are more likely to eschew such interventions in favor of treating the "disorder" by medication or therapy to relieve the symptoms, which may be counterproductive to re-integration.

Either situation—missed diagnosis or misdiagnosis—decreases the chances that proper interventions will be implemented. A missed diagnosis could result in no treatment and thus no opportunity for growth, while an inaccurate diagnosis may lead to a view of the behaviors as something to eliminate rather than something to embrace and help one grow. Without accurate diagnosis and appropriate interventions, positive results will be minimal.

The Diagnostic Process

The diagnostic process for psychologically-based disorders used by psychologists, physicians, and other healthcare and counseling professionals (collectively referred to as clinicians throughout this chapter) is based on specific behavioral criteria set forth in the *Diagnostic and Statistical Manual of Mental Disorders—Fourth Edition, Text Revision* (DSM-IV TR) (American Psychiatric Association, 2000). This manual, considered the standard for clinicians, contains behavioral descriptors that are criteria for all of the recognized mental disorders, ranging from well-known childhood disorders such as ADHD and Asperger's Disorder to disorders such as Schizophrenia, Bipolar Disorder, and Major Depression. It is important to note that giftedness is rarely considered in the diagnostic process, even though the authors of the DSM-IV TR acknowledge in several instances that mental capacity or intellectual functioning, if limited or retarded, can affect behavior and has diagnostic implications.

Partially as a result of the omission of giftedness from the DSM-IV TR, most clinicians receive no training about the characteristic behaviors and needs of gifted individuals and/or how the behavioral presentation of gifted individuals may differ from others. This lack of basic information about giftedness is problematic and increases the likelihood of misdiagnosis of gifted individuals. If such information is included in future editions of the DSM, gifted individuals will have a much better chance of being diagnosed and treated appropriately.

Clinicians are trained to assess and categorize human behavior, looking for clusters and patterns to determine the best explanation for them. The diagnosis is meant to be the beginning and to direct the intervention process. Correct interventions can only be carried out with correct diagnosis. For example, if a physician mistakenly identifies an infection instead of allergies, the prescribed antibiotics will likely not help or lead to a positive outcome. Likewise, if a clinician views a gifted individual's OE or disintegration as pathological rather than a developmental process, proper intervention is unlikely. Misdiagnosis and inappropriate treatment lead to two specific negative consequences: potential side effects from improper treatment, and lack of proper treatment that can help.

Clusters of behaviors are important diagnostic signs, though the presence of behavioral indicators alone does not constitute enough for any particular diagnosis. There must also be impairment. An "impairment" criterion is required for all diagnoses in the DSM-IV TR; the behaviors of concern must negatively affect functioning in at least one area, and sometimes in at least two areas (e.g., social settings, work, or school). Thus, hyperactive behavior, by itself, does not indicate a diagnosable condition of ADHD. However, if that hyperactivity is significant and interferes with an individual's ability to learn, demonstrate knowledge, interact with others, or otherwise function effectively in the school or work setting, then a diagnosis of ADHD may indeed be appropriate. In gifted individuals, the behaviors being considered must be distinguished from OE and/or disintegration. Dabrowski would take this a step further and argue that even behaviors that are interfering may be a sign of positive growth.

Thus, without specific knowledge of TPD and OE, for example, clinicians are unable to "frame" behavior in light of this information, just as the physician who is unaware of a particular disorder or its medical presentation would be unable to appropriately categorize that medical condition. In the same way, a clinician would be unable to use giftedness, disintegration, or OE to explain a gifted individual's behavior, leading to misattribution and possibly to misdiagnosis and inappropriate intervention.

Giftedness as a Part of the Diagnostic Process

The gifted individual, by definition, is different from the norm. In today's world, there is a tendency to see anything different as abnormal. For clinicians and some school personnel, differences that are outside of the norm are often considered to be pathology that needs to be cured. On the one hand, today's culture has become more accepting of certain mental illnesses; there is less stigma associated with disorders such as depression and anxiety. One need only watch an evening of television or read a popular magazine to recognize this. Topics rarely discussed in past years are now frequent subjects of public discourse. On the other hand, increased awareness and acceptance of mental health issues has also led to increased use of medication to treat the symptoms of these disorders as people look for a relief. These days, alleviating symptoms of depression and anxiety with medication is seen as natural and positive by both physicians and patients. Who wouldn't want to rid himself of such negative and unproductive behaviors?

But what if these symptoms were productive and actually a necessary step toward development? What if standard treatments that alleviated symptoms actually decreased the likelihood of true positive development and genuine mental health? This is what Dabrowski proposed in his theory of positive disintegration. His death in 1980 meant that he did not witness the surge in medication management. He steadfastly believed that disintegration and personal disharmony were harbingers of advanced development. TPD posits that disintegration, signified by behaviors that may include anxiety, is *necessary* for personality development.

Dabrowski particularly noted that the conflict between the real self and the ideal self, or the frustration resulting from the way things are and the way that one would like them to be, certainly will result in discomfort and anxiety. One could argue that gifted individuals, with their advanced cognitive processes, are more likely to be keenly aware of these differences. However, intelligence, in Dabrowski's view, is not sufficient for development, while the experience of higher-level emotions is essential for advanced development.

How one views this discomfort and, ultimately, the steps that one takes to address it help determine one's course. Viewing emotions as neurotic anxiety that must be eliminated immediately through the use of medication is less likely to yield the positive disintegration and subsequent personality development than the view that the conflicts must be embraced through struggle in order to resolve them and re-integrate at a higher level. Dabrowski saw anxieties not as something to remediate, but rather as something to celebrate. Writer Frank A. Clark once remarked, "We find comfort among those who agree with us—growth among those who don't." The disintegration described in Dabrowski's TPD often represents that disagreement, either within oneself or between oneself and the world, that eventually leads to growth. He believed that comfort with self and society often indicated basic or initial integration, as he conceptualized it, and that growth would only arise when discomfort and subsequent disintegration occur, hopefully resulting in secondary integration. People who disagree make us uncomfortable; if we have insight and self-reflective tendencies, we are more likely to explore the differences and grow as a result.

The term *disintegration* usually evokes negative images in one's mind, and the process of disintegration relates to many processes, ranging from emotional disharmony to the complete fragmentation of personality. Yet this concept, described by Dabrowski, is not only a potentially positive force, but also is a component *necessary* for development (Dabrowski, 1964). Positive disintegration enriches life and spawns growth. This basic tenet of TPD reveals the possibility of misdiagnosis, as seen in the following vignette:

> *Five-year-old Harrison is about to enter kindergarten. At the end of the previous school year, the preschool teacher expressed substantial*

concerns about Harrison's ability to remain still and on task. "Harrison doesn't complete tasks expected of a child his age," she offered as proof of a pathological difficulty. Then, school officials danced around the topic of medication, because they were convinced that Harrison had Attention Deficit Hyperactivity Disorder (ADHD), though they were careful never to directly state that conclusion.

Harrison's parents suggested to the school that the work might not be challenging enough and that lack of academic "fit" might be a factor. The parents suspected that Harrison was gifted because he had a huge vocabulary at a young age and read early. "He loves making jokes and is intensely interested in airplanes, space, and birds," they said. They reported that at home, Harrison was active and involved in many activities, and focus was not an issue there. However, his elaborate projects never quite turned out in reality as he saw them in his head.

In school, Harrison avoided challenging tasks and politely refused challenging work when it was offered to him. When, at parent request, teachers provided advanced work, Harrison seemed distracted from it and often failed to complete it. This confirmed the school's opinion that Harrison had ADHD and simply could not maintain his focus without one-on-one attention. In their opinion, giftedness had nothing to do with the problems. They told Harrison's parents to seek evaluation to determine the cause of Harrison's inability to follow through with work, and they said that his admission to school the following year would be contingent upon the results of the evaluation and the parents' response. The parents understood this to mean that Harrison would be admitted back to the school only if he was on medication to help him comply and complete work like the other students. After all, the teacher simply couldn't continue to provide excessive one-on-one attention to get Harrison to complete the day-to-day tasks expected of him.

The parents took Harrison for a thorough evaluation, which revealed elevated—but not clinically significant—levels of hyperactivity and inattention. Further evaluation revealed a profoundly gifted youngster with intellectual abilities and academic skills far above his age and grade expectations, but also a frustrated youngster with significant asynchrony in his development.

While his cognitive ability was precocious, his motor and social developmental levels, for example, were generally age-appropriate.

Harrison was significantly concerned about his competence; he saw a huge discrepancy between the quality of his work and the quality of his thoughts. He did not like what he was producing any more than the teachers did, and at merely five years old, he began vividly seeing the difference between his real self and his ideal self. When project after project failed to turn out as he so clearly saw in his head, he became discouraged. Not surprisingly, he lacked confidence in his ability to complete tasks to a specified level. These feelings created reluctance to engage in school, and his negative behaviors emerged as a result.

The importance of incorporating giftedness into the diagnostic process is clear in this example. Harrison showed many symptoms that could easily have been mistaken for ADHD, and an uninformed clinician may have placed this five-year-old on medication to help him comply and complete tasks as the other students did. Instead, reframing his behaviors in light of his giftedness and OE allowed for positive management and growth. Harrison and his parents began to understand and accept his OE, his asynchronous development, and his lack of confidence, as well as their relation to his giftedness. The school grudgingly allowed Harrison to show mastery and accelerate to appropriate curriculum, while accepting the limitations associated with his age. They allowed frequent opportunities for movement and accommodated his thirst for knowledge by directing him to appropriate resources. Without this positive frame and appropriate interventions, the outcome may have been quite different.

Of course, some gifted individuals do experience clinical difficulties, as the gifted are not immune to problems. When these difficulties are seen as related to giftedness and OE, they can be addressed in a way that promotes re-integration at a higher level, as seen in the following vignette:

Serena, a seven-year-old girl finishing the second grade, was referred for a consultation after she began lying about her behavior and her teacher reactions at school. She was beginning to refuse to go to school, often commenting about how much she hated it. She began having stomachaches each morning and occasional crying spells, during which she expressed her intense negative feelings. She retreated from social interactions and seemed to enjoy her favorite activities less than she had at the beginning of the year. Her sensitivity was clearly evident, and she began compulsively pacing the house and sneaking food into her room.

In school, Serena began to perceptively recognize the difference between herself and other students. Her interests were different and more intense. She could not talk with anyone—not other students or even teachers—about her interests in the stock market crash and the Great Depression. None of the other second graders knew what those were, let alone had an interest in discussing the finer points of those difficult times. Teachers had no interest in talking with this second grader because those topics were not covered at that grade level. Serena hid her interests as best she could, sometimes denying them to try to fit in. In class, teachers reprimanded her for being off-task and urged her to stay on topic when she answered questions in more depth than the teacher was seeking. "She needs to stay on track and stop blurting out information about the topic that doesn't answer the questions," the teachers said.

The school did not see Serena as bright, and certainly not gifted, but rather as an average student who was frustrating to teachers, somewhat impulsive yet disengaged, and beginning to show some negative behaviors that were common among other disengaged students at the school, such as lying and failing to complete assignments. The school's response was to enforce stricter discipline, including extra assignments and staying in for recess, but this simply fed Serena's dishonesty, as she was able to tell tales to her parents that seemed plausible. Despite communication between home and school, the problems escalated in both settings. New behavior problems arose at school, and more sadness and anxiety showed in Serena's behavior at home.

Serena, at only seven years of age, was experiencing a depressive episode with associated anxiety resulting partially from a mismatch in curriculum—she was disintegrating. Her treatment focused on management strategies for her anxiety and depression, combined with supportive interventions and curriculum modifications. She and her parents were educated about the needs of gifted children, OE, and the social/emotional aspects of growing up gifted. With new tools and a new frame, Serena's mood and behavior quickly improved. Her parents began to foster her interests and accept her differences. Giftedness became a part of Serena that she and those around her accepted—it did not define who she was but was incorporated into her developing persona. The school eventually accepted her abilities, modified the curriculum through subject acceleration, and incorporated Serena's interests whenever possible. Her parents explored ways to make Serena's "dream" of visiting the New York Stock Exchange come true. With OE and giftedness as a backdrop, Serena's development returned to a positive track—she had re-integrated at a higher level.

Gifted Behaviors, OE, and Disintegration: Excuse or Explanation?

Vignettes like these are typical scenarios for the few clinicians specializing in work with gifted children. When clinicians explain to educators or other professionals how a gifted child's behaviors (or "symptoms," as others may see them) are related to her giftedness, the clinicians are often met with disbelief. When clinicians discuss OE and its relation to an active child's difficulty sitting still long enough to take an examination, they often hear responses from others ranging from slight annoyance to outright hostility. Some say things like, "How can you *excuse* a child's behavior just because she is gifted?"

Excusing behavior is not the goal; the goal is understanding it, explaining it, and ultimately embracing it. In most cases, the behavior must still be changed—after all, it is impairing functioning. The non-productive behaviors must be adapted into productive ones in a way that *promotes* development rather than *stunts* it. In Dabrowski's view, behavior expressing developmental potential is a necessary step toward development—rather than a pathological impediment to it—and will foster the processes of behavior change, personality development, and personal growth. Thus, Serena's anxiety and depression are acknowledged, processed, and resolved. Her giftedness and OE are accepted as healthy parts of herself to be shaped and nurtured rather than extinguished. Likewise, Harrison's and Ford's maladaptive behaviors are partially explained by giftedness and OE, allowing individual understanding and growth.

OE and TPD can provide not only clinicians, but also gifted individuals and their families, an explanation other than pathology—an explanation to use as a tool for further development. The behavior is not excused but rather reframed, embraced, and addressed in a positive way that allows for further development. Essentially, treating behaviors as pathology and possibly medicating a child for the immediate comfort of others (i.e., to get a child to comply) may stop the process of further personality development. However, when behaviors like Serena's and Harrison's are explained in the context of positive disintegration and OE, management strategies addressing the frustration can be used to help them through the process of re-integration at a higher level.

Dabrowski's Theory and Misdiagnosis

Unfortunately, a clinician who is unfamiliar with TPD and who is trained to describe and categorize behavior may see a negative process at work and identify the pathological condition to which it is associated, while neglecting the potentially positive aspects of the behavior and process. Each level of the TPD brings forth some difficulties that, if not clearly understood as part of the process of development, could easily be viewed as pathological or negative. For example, clinicians may see egocentrism and lack of empathy, which are common behaviors associated with Level I, Primary Integration. At Level I, these behaviors predominate, and one must begin to disintegrate or experience anxiety and discomfort if one is to progress.

At Level II, Unilevel Disintegration, social aspects begin to influence the individual, and the person begins to experience inner conflict. Because anxiety arises due to this inner struggle, the behavior, on its face, may at first appear pathological. However, in reality, it is a part of a developmental process. The key for clinicians, although difficult, is to determine which behaviors are productive and part of a positive re-integration process and which are indeed pathological or adevelopmental. Mika (2008) clearly states the potential concern with misdiagnosing the behavior: "By pathologizing disintegrative experiences associated with creativity and self-transformation, we stigmatize individuals undergoing accelerated growth and add to their burdens rather than help relieve them" (p. 153).

Without knowledge that the disintegration can, indeed, be positive, it may be interpreted by the individual and clinician alike as pathology. Those who do not understand TPD often regard any evidence of disintegration and OE as negative. When adults label the high activity level of a child like Harrison as "hyperactive" or the behavior and sensitivity of Serena as "inappropriate," how do those children begin to understand their behavior? Do they see it as a positive developmental step? No. They are more likely to view it as something to rid themselves of, or at least try to manage differently. They may see the behaviors as parts of themselves that they do not want to maintain.

Thus, when Harrison is "hyperactive," he frowns upon himself or his behavior—significant guilt may arise when he is unable to control the behavior to others' satisfaction. When Serena is told that her behavior is simply unacceptable and that she must conform to the normative behavior and interests of the class, she begins to doubt herself and further deny her real self. Alternatively, reframing the behavior in light of OE and disintegration may allow them and others to seize the positive aspects. They will then be able to use this perspective to grow and develop and to avoid the non-productive guilt arising from the misattributions of the behaviors as negative.

The perspective of the child and others, including the clinicians involved, will largely determine whether this child will disintegrate in a healthy, positive way that allows him growth or whether he will disintegrate negatively in a way that stunts and precludes development. Others' reactions will affect his future behaviors, and a label of "pathology" will undoubtedly influence the outcome. A clinician who is aware of the concept of OE can help the individual embrace the behavior and grow.

OE and Misdiagnosis

OE in an individual is particularly likely to trigger misdiagnosis, or at least mislabeling or misattribution. OE is a heightened response to stimuli—an action or reaction that exceeds what would typically be expected. The heightened response may last longer or occur more frequently than expected (Dabrowski, 1996). Numerous sources (e.g., Mendaglio, 2008b; Piechowski, 2006; Webb, Gore, Amend, & DeVries, 2007) describe heightened sensitivities in gifted individuals, and research (e.g., Bouchet & Falk, 2001; Tucker & Hafenstein, 1997) has shown their widespread prevalence in the gifted population. The difference between OE and what would be considered a typical action or reaction is found in the frequency, intensity, or duration of the action or reaction.

When OEs manifest themselves in a gifted individual, the potential for misdiagnosis increases, since someone unfamiliar with Dabrowski and TPD can easily misconstrue any of the five OEs. OE and its characteristic behaviors are often mistaken for mood disorders, attention disorders, impulse control disorders, anxiety disorders, and many other diagnostic disorders. The term itself, *overexcitability*—particularly the prefix "over"—

implies *too much* of something. Too much emotion, too much activity, too much sensitivity—any of these can be easily misinterpreted or misattributed. Just think of how many times we have remarked to our own children, "Calm down! It is not that big of a deal," or "You don't have to cry about that! You're overreacting." Too much reaction makes some people uncomfortable, and negative responses to the reaction are common. The child or adult who is the recipient of those responses may see her own behavior as problematic indeed, rather than something that can lead to further development. She may see herself as "unacceptable" or "unwanted."

Dabrowski's description of psychomotor OE is an example here. His conceptualization of psychomotor OE includes an excess of energy, rapid talk, and restlessness. Yet these descriptors are also among the primary behaviors listed for Attention Deficit Hyperactivity Disorder. Some argue that psychomotor OE, as described by Dabrowski, is similar to modern-day conceptions of ADHD (Mika, 2006). Others argue that, though the outward behaviors are similar, the "cause and the cure are completely different" (Goerss, Amend, Webb, Webb, & Beljan, 2006).

Psychomotor OE may also present as impulsive behavior (e.g., acting out), compulsive behavior (e.g., excessive talking or organizing), nervous habits, or extreme competitiveness (Dabrowski, 1996). If the behaviors are taken only at face value, it is easy to see how misdiagnosis could occur—a clinician simply reviewing the behaviors and marking them off a list (e.g., the diagnostic criteria for ADHD or an anxiety disorder such as Obsessive-Compulsive Disorder from the DSM-IV TR) could easily come to the conclusion that the behavior fits a particular DSM-IV diagnosis.

The problem here is that typical interventions for treatment of ADHD or OCD often include medication as a part of the treatment plan. Conversely, if the behaviors are seen as part of a developmental process, one can see how the clinician would take an entirely different approach toward treatment—an approach to foster development and re-integration at a higher level rather an attempt to stop the very behaviors that may cause growth, which ultimately may cease the behaviors of concern. The impulsive or compulsive behaviors may actually be a pure form of anxiety necessary for growth.

Sensual OE, which is often present in artists and creative persons, involves heightened experience of or response to stimuli in any of the five senses: seeing, smelling, tasting, touching, or hearing. Artists experience the world differently than the typical individual, and creativity abounds. While many people enjoy art, some *experience* it, and these latter ones are likely those with sensual OE. With any heightened experience, sensory overload may arise, bringing with it excess anxiety or nervousness. Indeed, many studies show a higher prevalence of mental heath issues (as traditionally defined) among artists (e.g., see Piirto, 2004), and Dabrowski would likely describe those eccentricities and "symptoms" not as problems, but rather as signs of disintegration—a step toward growth.

It is easy to understand how someone who hears, sees, or smells things that others do not could be labeled with a pathological condition. Some individuals with sensual OE react strongly to odors or sounds. The young boy who reacts loudly due to strong smells coming from the school cafeteria or the girl who hears the lights buzzing and cannot focus on her work might be labeled with a behavior disorder for simply failing to comply with the demands of the school setting. Certainly, a child who "sees" things that others do not (i.e., experiences visual information in a different way) would, at minimum, be viewed as odd or strange by peers and possibly teachers. The tendency to label anything outside of the norm as unacceptable or pathological also impacts this situation, often heightening others' reactions. Misdiagnosis is certainly possible in these situations.

Intellectual OE, often associated with highly gifted individuals, is characterized by an almost insatiable desire for knowledge and understanding. Curiosity abounds, often with a search for precise answers. Probing questions and persistence in the pursuit of interests and passions are common, sometimes to the exclusion of people and things that others may see as important. When these passions are obscure and/or narrowly focused, they may easily be viewed as a symptom of Asperger's Disorder.

Asperger's Disorder, a disorder on the Autism Spectrum, is characterized by difficulties with social reciprocity and interactions. Another major component of the disorder is the intense interest in and fascination with a particular topic. Intense interest or passion for a topic is also a common characteristic of gifted children and adults. As anyone who has excelled in a field of study can attest, an intense interest is necessary, and it may also cause some temporary neglect of and disconnection with other important people and things. Some anxiety may arise when the individual notices this disconnection, but a person without Asperger's Disorder also recognizes the temporary inability to address it due to the demands of the current situation.

If such an individual described his anxiety, fascination, and exclusion of others to a clinician, a plethora of diagnostic possibilities would be evident. Asperger's Disorder is a possibility that can be quickly ruled out in an adult if there is a typical developmental history and no previous social difficulties. Yet for a child with a checkered social history and some school problems, this disorder may be seen as a reasonable diagnostic option. Anxiety disorders like Social Phobia (also called Social Anxiety Disorder) or personality disorders like Avoidant Personality (a pattern of social inhibition and hypersensitivity to negative evaluation) or Schizoid Personality (a pattern of social detachment and limited emotional expression) might be pinpointed in an adult. But viewing this experience with a TPD and gifted frame, however, can allow for these *temporary* disruptions to be seen as necessary toward growth, rather than pathology that requires constant management throughout life. Allowing the individual to embrace these anxieties and move toward higher-level integration is necessary.

Imaginational OE involves a richness of imagery, a love of fantasy, and a unique perspective. Individuals with imaginational OE may lose themselves in daydreams or create worlds with stuffed animals or other toys, complete with sports teams, villains, businesses, and a town newspaper. This type of creative imagination can lead to possibilities heretofore unseen—exciting discoveries, astonishing inventions, or even breathtaking fears. These fantastic fabrications can take a child away from things that others see as more important at the time, like cleaning her room or doing homework. When observed in school, these behaviors could be plausibly seen as the inattentive type of ADHD, characterized by distractibility and lack of task focus. Some might view an adult lost in a dream world of his own creation as out of touch with reality, but that same adult could develop intriguing new approaches to solving problems, or he might invent a new product. If the person is seen as so out of touch as to be unable to participate in the world as others do, the "daydreaming" could be labeled delusional, schizophrenic, or even dissociative. The syndicated cartoonist Mike Peters was told that he was wasting time with his constant doodling when he was in school. Many of his teachers thought that he would amount to nothing; he did not fit the norm. Mr. Peters is still drawing, his cartoons appear in many newspapers around the country, and he won a Pulitzer Prize for them.

Caring and empathy are qualities that we hope our children and other loved ones embody. Emotional OE, characterized by just these traits, can be easily misunderstood in its extreme form. Individuals possessing this OE are highly sensitive to their own and others' feelings. With its complex emotions and intense affective expressions, emotional OE is often the first noticed by others (Lind, 2001). The vast range of feelings, intense highs and lows of mood, and the sensitivities to self and others that come with emotional OE can appear to be a clinical mood disorder such as Bipolar Disorder (Probst, 2007), a chronic disorder characterized by mood swings and emotional instability. Healthcare professionals might also identify mood disorders, such as Major Depression and the milder-but-longer-standing Dysthymic Disorder, if the predominant mood is negative. In addition, they could diagnose (or misdiagnose) anxiety disorders like Generalized Anxiety Disorder (worry over many things) and Panic Disorder (intense anxiety reactions in certain situations) in the emotionally OE person.

Of course, overexcitability need not be negative; OE can manifest as a positive force, particularly when more than one OE is present in an individual. Consider, for example, the combination of intellectual and emotional OE, which might describe a creative scientist like Jonas Salk, whose intense search for understanding and extreme compassion for the human condition led him to the polio vaccine. A combination of intellectual and imaginational OE could, perhaps, describe Albert Einstein, a man who saw possibilities where others saw nothing at all. Imagine what the world might have been like if these two men's unquenchable thirst for knowledge or creative thought processes had been labeled pathological due to their extreme nature. Salk and Einstein embraced their passions—though others did not always support them—and provided the world with innovations that changed the course of history. Similarly, Eleanor Roosevelt and Maya Angelou, two women who experienced great emotional upheavals in their lives, moved beyond their personal turmoil to contribute to politics, history, literature, and humanitarianism. The contributions of both have made the world a better, more compassionate place.

Needs, Recommendations, and Considerations

Clearly, some behaviors indicate pathology and require clinical intervention through typical means, including medication management. Dabrowski certainly did not believe that all forms of neurosis or psychosis help one on the path toward personality development. After all, gifted individuals are not immune to true psychological disorders, particularly those with a biological basis or ones that involve a chemical imbalance. Dabrowski also described the low-level integration of psychopaths, as well as the process of unhealthy (i.e., negative) disintegration that results in mental illness or lower-level re-integration in other persons. Thus, not all disintegration seen as outward behaviors such as anxiety and conflict will lead to positive outcomes.

How, then, is a clinician to determine whether a gifted person is experiencing disintegration that is unhealthy or disintegration that aids positive development? Only a clinician with sound clinical judgment and a solid footing in TPD will even be able to begin to sort out the nature of these conflicts. Without the understanding of positive disintegration, OE, and the many other aspects of TPD, a clinician will most likely apply the behavioral criteria of traditional mental health diagnoses and risk misdiagnosing an individual who is experiencing positive disintegration.

In the present mental health climate, quick diagnosis is a necessity due to insurance and managed care requirements. Other barriers to competent mental health services for gifted individuals, such as limited availability and insufficient training, may lead to treatment with medication to alleviate the very "symptoms" that could lead to further disintegration, further personality development, positive change, and true mental health as Dabrowski conceptualized it.

Finding an appropriate clinician—one who is trained in giftedness and Dabrowski's concepts—is difficult. A national organization called SENG, Supporting Emotional Needs of the Gifted (www.sengifted.org), is attempting to address some of this void by offering continuing education courses for mental health professionals who wish to get training about the psychological and behavioral traits of giftedness and their implications. SENG has also developed a brochure to help parents and others ask the necessary questions, such as those in Tables 6.1 and 6.2, in order to determine the suitability of potential mental health professionals.

Table 6.1. How Do I Know if My Child Needs to See a Psychologist or Therapist?

It isn't always easy to determine if a child could benefit from professional help. To help decide, consider the following:

○ Are the intensity, duration, or frequency of the behaviors in question (e.g., tantrums, crying spells, aggressiveness, withdrawal) interfering significantly in school, at home, or elsewhere?

○ Are the behaviors causing family difficulties? Is there an increase in sibling rivalry, excessive bickering, or other distress? Have these behaviors resulted in increased tension between you and your spouse?

○ Have there been marked changes in the child's eating or sleeping patterns? Or a marked increase in mood changes?

○ Do you suspect possible drug or alcohol use?

Adapted from Webb, Gore, Amend, & DeVries, 2007.

Table 6.2. How Do I Find an Appropriate Practitioner?

It is vitally important to find a therapist who understands giftedness. To determine whether a therapist understands giftedness and related issues, consider asking some of the following questions:

○ Do gifted children have special needs? How do they differ from non-gifted children?

○ Are there any particular problems or behaviors that you see in gifted children?

○ What are some of the particular social and emotional needs that you have noticed in the children you serve?

○ How do you distinguish among behaviors associated with ADHD and characteristics of the gifted?

○ What percentage of the clients you see is gifted?

Adapted from Webb, Gore, Amend, & DeVries, 2007.

Finding a clinician with whom an individual can feel comfortable and develop a sound therapeutic relationship is necessary, and questions such as those in Tables 6.1 and 6.2 or in the SENG brochure can increase the likelihood of this. Finding someone who accepts and understands OE in a way that allows an individual to embrace her OE as an integral part of herself and her developing personality is priceless. Increased awareness of giftedness and its characteristics will allow researchers and clinicians alike to further explore these issues to decrease the likelihood of misdiagnosis.

For those who work directly with gifted individuals, it is clear that misdiagnosis occurs, and all too frequently. Research on the misdiagnosis of the gifted is limited, and case study analyses are often a first step to promoting additional research. Hopefully, clinicians who have seen misdiagnosis occur will begin to develop a literature base of case examples and publish them in professional journals. Then, researchers may begin to formally study the possible overlap among disintegration, OE, diagnosis, pathology, and positive adjustment.

Many questions remain. For example, what role does one's environment play in misdiagnosis or misattribution? How does an individual's personal perception of his behavior influence self-management? How does reinforcement from others lead to positive disintegration and development? Are traditional mental health labels helpful or harmful to the process of emotional development of gifted individuals? Are situational manifestations of anxiety more likely than global displays to lead to personality development? How can one distinguish more consistently between healthy and unhealthy disintegration? Where is the line between positive maladjustment and general maladjustment? Although Dabrowski's original writings shed light on these questions, continued formal exploration through systematic research of TPD and the concept of overexcitability is needed. In the end, enhanced understanding of these relations will allow more accurate identification and more appropriate interventions.

Chapter 7

Integrating the Intense Experience: Counseling and Clinical Applications

P. Susan Jackson, M.A., R.C.C., and
Vicky Frankfourth Moyle, M.A., L.P.C., L.M.H.C.

Why Intensity Is an Important Factor in Counseling

Individuals make the decision to seek counseling for a variety of reasons. The overarching motivation for many is to relieve mental suffering and get help to actualize a desire for change in their lives. Many suffer from difficulty or inability to overcome untenable inner feelings of tension or distress. This may take forms that vary widely in depth and span, such as response to crises events, depression, anxiety, and feeling unsuccessful in the world, to name a few. However, many "intense" individuals may seek help because of feelings that don't seem, on the surface, to be "that big of a deal." They seek therapy because of feeling pent-up, immobilized, indecisive, or incomplete; feeling diffused, a felt sense of the emerging meaning of the experience that they aren't living fully (Gendlin, 1997); feelings of discomfort, incompatibility, or lack of fit in some context; feelings of shame or guilt, self-repudiation, or self-silencing; the feeling of being misunderstood, misinterpreted, or that relationships are unreciprocated by others at similar levels of complexity or commitment.

Counseling as we advocate it begins with the *experience* of the client and the importance of a multilevel awareness by all members involved in an interconnected system of care. We emphasize the particular role of the counselor in a dynamic, co-created counseling relationship—essential for work with intense individuals. This co-creation between client and counselor, in which healing and change occur in the creative space between committed individuals (Clarkson, 2003), is a conceptual model used in integrative, transpersonal, and contemplative therapeutic approaches. We offer two vivid case examples to emphasize aspects of the almost unbearable tension of being (and becoming) that is experienced by persons with intense natures. For further reference, we refer the interested reader to other case examples (Jackson & Moyle, 2009; Jackson, Moyle, & Piechowski, 2009) in which client intensity plays a significant role in guiding therapeutic intervention.

A sufficiently complex and integrated conceptualization by the counselor of the client's experience and difficulty is crucial. The ability to assess a client's development and potential across a full spectrum of capacities, as well as the skill and sensitivity to address the client on multiple levels of communication, awareness, and understanding, is key to establishing rapport and effecting change.

A Note to Adults on "Problem" Conceptualization

The counselor or therapist must keep in mind that underneath a desire for change may lurk many confounding variables, such as significant psychological wounding that may stem from abuse, attachment issues, narcissism, etc. The counselor must be well-grounded in an integrative understanding of ethical and clinical sound practices—aware of the possibility of opening up potentially volatile issues—and he or she must have knowledge of, if not experience with, issues of mental illness. An in-depth conceptualization of clinical mental health practice is essential for nuanced and knowledgeable diagnosis/assessment/treatment befitting the special population mentioned here.

This does not imply that persons with intense natures coming for counseling are necessarily mentally ill. Some will have diagnosable problems; our contention is that many will not. The ability to make a differential diagnosis that is entirely mindful of the uncommon intensities and idiosyncratic nature of the highly creative person is of critical importance. In particular, we draw the reader's attention to the excellent work in this area by Alice Miller (1982, 1983, 1991a, 1991b, 1998), who wrote *The Drama of the Gifted Child*.

Adults come to counseling usually of their own free will—they are self-motivated and refer themselves to a counselor. Children, more often than not, are referred by some adult in their lives—usually because their external behaviors cause friction in the environment. Children rarely (and legally cannot) come to counseling of their own accord; it is an adult who is the final arbiter—and the one who often defines the problem. A child may, in fact, be baffled by a referral to a counselor. He or she may have an awareness of being the source of someone else's distress but confused about the reasons why this might be so.

Human behavior can broadly be described as an attempt to equilibrate the experiences of inner and outer realities as we express ourselves in the world. All individual actions have—for good or ill—essential purposes, and behaviors are undertaken in response to internal or external stimuli. Because of this, behaviors represent coping mechanisms that cannot simply be forbidden, erased, or removed without scaffolding to replace them. Children, even gifted children, rarely have the experience, awareness, objectivity, or the language to describe or completely comprehend how they are feeling or to explain why they are acting as they are. They often do not have a metacognitive understanding of their own processes, and they may be embedded in a family structure that is dysfunctional in some way (not obvious to the family) in which they have little power or direct effect. Often, they are stymied by adult narcissistic patterns within their families of origin. Also, many adults who bring children to counseling lack conscious awareness and are constrained by their own strong defenses. These dysfunctional patterns and defenses might, in fact, be a confounding source of difficulty for the child, and they may be exacerbating a problem. Additionally, many adults profess to be willing to accept responsibility for their role in a difficulty but are unable to do so.

Carl Gustav Jung claimed that the greatest gift we can give our children is a clear field of consciousness. What did he mean by this? In addition to the concepts of archetypes and the collective unconscious, one of his great contributions to the field of psychology was the idea of the Shadow (Jung, 1969). Just like a lurking physical shadow, this psychic Shadow is subtle, difficult to see, hard to capture, and disappears in the right kind of light. It represents unmediated impulse—all of which is hidden, and often difficult for us to face, in our own personalities. It includes the parts that we don't want to admit and the aspects of ourselves that seem to get in the way of our best efforts (but it sometimes drives them as well), for automatic unconscious behaviors come from the same source as that which fuels our feelings of energy.

But raw and unexamined aspects of our consciousness can be passed on to our progeny. Becoming conscious of, facing, and transforming the Shadow—which is partly our "own" concoction, partly inherited from our ancestors, and partly a species transpersonal "birthday present"—could be considered one of our most important tasks in this lifetime. Socrates claimed that the unexamined life is not worth living. We would emphasize that the *examined* life is certainly *more* worth living, and certainly more worth passing on to those who follow us. It is a responsibility that we owe to our children and all of the children in our care.

Children are embedded in family and social/cultural systems, and they are dependent upon parents and other adults to model the ways in which one should develop and be human. Children learn by mimicry, and this is as true for the task of learning to become the best unique and unrepeatable self that each of them can possibly be as it is for the job of learning how to tie their shoes.

One of the first steps, then, in counseling for children is for the adults in their lives to embark upon the journey of doing their own psychological work—endeavoring to really be honest about putting effort into resolving their own "unfinished business" and inherited "garbage"—unconscious resentments, fears, angers, and unlived life. Any adult bringing a child to counseling should be willing to participate in investigating his or her own contribution to the "problem," and be open to the possibility of change as well.

It should be noted here, however, that encouraging and facilitating this adult commitment to self-exploration and change may be tricky. The psychological defenses of highly intelligent, intense, and sensitive individuals are most often complicated and entangled. Aspects of the Shadow function—deep-seated fears, and feelings of shame and incapacity—often lie beneath the surface and, in addition to being unrecognized, in adults may be codified and rigid.

The wise therapist is patient and purposeful. The goal is to bring new insights, new behaviors, and mutually beneficial patterns of interaction into the family system, while at the same time protecting the well-being of the child. A hasty or incautious approach is counterproductive. The gifted child's seemingly maladaptive behavior may in fact be serving the maladjusted positions and modus operandi of other family members. A focus on the "problem" behaviors of the child may be a smokescreen for a deep-seated and unconscious defense of the adults' or siblings' deeper issues. The child may be unwittingly carrying those painful, buried issues—expressing this burden in his or her conduct and interactions. This is especially true of intense and sensitive children who, often entirely unconsciously, seek to meet the multi-layered needs of those around them, *even if it does them harm.*

In the early phases of counseling, it is essential that the clinician stabilize the child while working toward building an authentic and entirely trustworthy liaison. Increasing resiliency and self-awareness through the development of a safe and responsive relationship—independent of all family/community ties— is vital. Affording the child a variety of many-faceted experiences to encourage expression of all aspects of his or her growing self is important. This revealing of self emerges naturally when the psychotherapeutic experience is sufficiently attentive, flexible, and inclusive of complexity.

A therapeutic plan might include reducing a child's systemic tensions through play therapy and relaxation exercises. It might include experiences in expressive modalities such as art therapy and psychodrama. The "wisdom of healing environments" (Podvoll, 1990) could be employed by exposing the child to nature and the natural world. Interactions with animals can reduce tensions while building relationship and self-knowing.

Opportunities to express wide-ranging, penetrating, and multilevel feelings are vital components of effective counseling with gifted children. Many sensitive and intense bright children have limited vocabulary to express complex feelings. Most have little practice in doing so with another person who can reflect the complexity, power, and subtle nuances of the spectrum of their feelings while keeping an objective view on the overarching themes in the child's development. Allowing the very inhibited and introverted child to control, to a large degree, the cadence and kinds of interaction occurring in those initial meetings can be profoundly validating. For others with more dominant personalities, it is essential to establish the therapeutic environment as one requiring mutual engagement and reciprocity in interactions, full commitment, and respect for boundaries. Without any particularly conscious effort, many highly intelligent children endeavor to be entirely self-referencing and self-sustaining—because they are dubious that others can reflect their thoughts and emotions. Such children *appear* to be entirely narcissistic and unwilling to participate, so it is important to be sensitive to these outer defenses that may be masking grave doubt and past disappointment.

Cyrus: A Case Study of Anxiety and Academic Failure

The following case study offers insight into this dynamic of apparent narcissistic presentation, while providing first-hand exposure to the subtle interplay of psychotherapy with this special population.

Cyrus, an eight-year-old boy, was referred to therapy for violent mood swings and acute noncompliance at home and school. His psycho-educational evaluation revealed superior intellectual ability, with significant discrepancy between his potential and his level of performance in both reading and writing. Cyrus had very poorly developed fine-motor skills and disabling weaknesses in the cognitive functions required to process language.

As might be expected, Cyrus exhibited particularly unenthusiastic responses to school. Persistent academic failure and lack of recognition for his extraordinary comprehension, exceptional visual memory, and sophisticated humor resulted in acute anxiety that alternated between withdrawal and aggression, both at home and at school. The lack of a meaningful conceptualization for his uncommon intellectual, emotional, and imaginational sensitivities had resulted in ineffectual and sometimes inappropriate responses from both his family and the educational system. For instance, he was given the chance to participate in a musical recorder class as part of his differentiation plan. The intention was to provide another avenue for personal expression and an opportunity to interact with older students more in keeping with his intellectual ability. However, this decision, while extremely well-intentioned, paid no heed to his fine-motor difficulties and the frustrations bound to result from a confrontation with discrepancies between the imagined harmonies of the music in his head and his utter incapacities in the mechanics of playing an instrument. His speed of processing, in which he envisioned his overt incapacity in detail (practically before the class had even begun), caused him to not be able to even pick up the instrument. His refusal was interpreted as defiant behavior, rejection of an invitation to social community and higher-level opportunities, and a lack of engagement with true peers. In addition, this incident was prefaced with a public appeal to the class by the principal, encouraging them to participate wholly in the new experience, in which all students would be beginners together. Cyrus' simple behavioral response belied the complexity within. He was bereft—filled with shame, aware that he had broken the social contract, and unable to communicate his shame.

Cyrus defined himself as a failure and grasped at any opportunity to control the environment around him. Extreme frustration, low self-esteem, and almost total psychic shutdown had confounded two psychiatrists and his learning support team.

Most times, Cyrus refused to engage at all. When he did engage other people, he preferred to control all aspects of the engagement on self-appointed terms. He appeared to be power-hungry and highly insensitive to the needs of others. At times, for instance, he became bossy with his younger brother. The younger sibling was also an exceptionally bright boy, possessed of a tender heart and a huge imagination. In an attempt to optimize their often complex and wide-ranging play activities, Cyrus tended to dictate the terms of engagement. Because of his exceptional nonverbal abilities, he could easily and rapidly imagine the outcome of circumstances and interactions—they played like movies in his mind. He greatly valued the playtime with his younger brother and wanted to share the deep synergy of relationship with him. When his younger brother offered an alternative point of view, however, Cyrus often had a hard time letting go of his imagined scenario. He could become intractable and incommunicative, and his incapacity with verbal expression compared with his brother's facility exacerbated his frustrations. At the time of admission to therapy, his very caring parents—highly successful university professors—were battle-fatigued, confused, and at their wits' end.

At his first meeting, Cyrus had difficulty even entering the clinic building. Although the trees enveloping the entrance and the dog asleep on the walkway drew his attention, he was extremely reluctant to cross the threshold. Careful observation through the clinic window revealed how effortlessly he responded to the natural world and how gentle he was with the sleeping dog. Eventually, he entered and was ushered into the consulting room.

Given the hesitant nature of Cyrus' approach to the building, the therapist was exceptionally careful in her opening dealings with him. She kept her voice tone low and was especially attentive to his guarded body space, his direct eye contact, and his gentle nature. Overall, she sustained a genuine and congruent pattern of interaction, while expressing a welcoming and confident attitude. The therapy room was spacious, with more than enough room for Cyrus to express himself through movement and play, and it provided varying proximity to the therapist. Through subtle mirroring, humor, and steady verbal encouragement, she made every effort to convey empathetic response to even the most discreet verbal or nonverbal behaviors. At times, a quiet appreciation of his exploration of the therapy room provided affirmation of Cyrus's evidently evolving frame of reference.

An initial verbal exchange revealed his interest in mythological themes, science and nature, and imaginative play of all kinds. His extreme sensitivity was acutely apparent in the immediate reactions showing on his face, in his body movements, and in his speech. He exhibited heightened responses to all aspects of the environment and to the therapist's behavior and comments (although their expression was very subtle). After a time, his ardent insight and probing humor revealed itself more openly.

To provide the most non-threatening medium, congruent with his temperament and interests, the therapist gave Cyrus a 10-foot length of brown butcher paper and access to dozens of play-therapy objects. With very little direction, he began creating an imaginary kingdom with many complex characters and fitting challenges to illustrate the archetypal hero's journey. Using objects of his choice, he profiled various states of chaos, struggle, and resolution. At the end of the hour, he was relaxed and interactive. It was the very first time in three years that he had completed an hour of therapy without entering a state of rage and leaving amidst chaos. He was happy to carefully place all of the therapy objects back in their appropriate places, as he recognized the need for order and appreciated the effect on the next patient of an orderly and predictable environment in which to work.

What is critical to note here is the response of the therapist to this complex, sensitive, and clearly wounded child. In the open space of the consulting room, she sat on the floor, quietly observing, making almost no comment. Occasionally, Cyrus asked for advice: "Should this object be included?" "Where should that one be placed?" She was careful to remind him that he was the ultimate arbiter of the process, while encouraging him to occasionally attend to other perspectives. In particular, she invited him to stand behind her so that he could consider how the scene was evolving from her perspective—from another person's vantage point. At those times, he became very still and focused and made comments that sometimes acknowledged her point of view and sometimes held firm with his own initial impressions and thrust. He seemed fascinated and delighted by the experience of entering the mind's eye of another person in an obviously synergistic process.

Eventually he began to interact more freely with the therapist and to encourage her to participate in the building of his many-faceted empire. He seemed greatly relieved to be exchanging his ideas. She was careful, in this initial meeting, to let him take the lead, while gently making it very clear that respect for property and the welfare of others was an inviolable rule.

In this way, Cyrus was ushered into a communion and deep synergy— a dynamic and rich exchange of thoughts, feeling, impressions, and ideas. Reduction of his overall psychic tension and appreciation of his complex inner world were important starting points for effective psychotherapy. Most importantly, Cyrus had made initial steps in forging an alliance with another person in a reciprocal and beneficial manner. Trust in the process and in his psychotherapist were critical components for the success of this initial meeting. Over time, this experience in therapy, combined with extensive educational adaptations, reframed Cyrus' ways of interacting in the world.

The Intensity that Cannot Be Seen

We have a tendency to think of intensity as an external attribute— something that can be seen. Psychologist Kaye Redfield Jamison (2004) emphasized this idea when she all but claimed the characteristic of the intense energy which she called "exuberance" to be the exclusive domain of individuals with extraverted personalities. Even if one accepts her premise (which we do not), one must allow for another kind of intensity that is internal—e.g., passion that an outside observer cannot witness directly. It *might* be that introverts would be most likely to experience such inner intensity, but that is speculation. In any case, we have found in our experiences with clients that extraordinary energy, strength, concentration, depth of feeling, intellectual interest, and emotional excitement—of an inner nature—is often present in individuals with extraordinary capacities for action, but that it is often hidden or masked and goes unnoticed by others.

Intensity *may* arise from being moved by an external source, and it *may* be visible as passionate, effusive exuberance and energetic activity by an observer. However, we would like to focus particularly on intensity that *feels*, to an individual, like a deep responsiveness within and that arises from an essentially creative encounter in the inner psychic milieu between a unique client and his or her apprehensions in the world. Our focus will be on the personal experience and meaning for the client, bringing with it deep respect for the phenomenology of a unique and unrepeatable human being.

Intensity of an inner nature is the driving force behind advanced human development in Dabrowski's paradigm. He emphasized the particular over-excitabilities (OEs) of intellect, imagination, and emotion in his theory, believing that the presence and integration of these three OEs were most predictive of advanced development. He defined an internal mental environment, the inner psychic milieu, where basic automatic and unreflective instinct is brought into tension and conflict with new awareness and realization of alternative ways to be and become. He theorized that a disintegration of stable but more primitive personality structures is essential to develop to the level of a truly authentic and ethical, unselfish individual. Thus, Dabrowski (1964, 1966, 1967, 1970, 1972) provided an invaluable map of the inner experience of remarkable persons for professionals in education and the counseling and health professions. So, too, he provided profound validation where none existed for those individuals experiencing such conflicts and positive disintegration from the inside.

Most importantly, Dabrowski normalized the idea of disintegration as an *essential* process in human growth and development. Thus, the uncommon (and frequently shattering) experience of multilevel disintegration—psychic turmoil manifested, in part, by multifaceted depressive phenomena and extreme anxiety—has meaning and, ultimately, purpose. While this knowledge does not ameliorate the direct experience, an individual can find solace in framing such an intense and overpowering experience in a paradigm of growth. Knowing that others have survived such intense periods of discontinuity and have emerged as more integrated, fuller, more authentic, and more complete human beings can provide great comfort.

Keys to Effective Therapy: Grounding and Stamina

This phenomenological experience of inner intensity had never been conceptualized or described in quite such a psychological way before Dabrowski. Although Dabrowski paved the way for a new recognition of the importance of imagination and emotion, along with the intellect, in the development and evolution of individuals, he gave less emphasis to the two other excitabilities: the psychomotor and the sensual.

We believe that these two somewhat neglected OEs have significant potential for utilization in counseling and clinical applications dealing with intensity. Invigorating and developing the sensual and the psychomotor capacities can be key to helping a client integrate him- or herself. The capacity for sensual connection and aesthetic arousal utilizes the client's own physical body to provide grounding in the actual world, and the invigoration of psychomotor capacities provides energy to create, pursue, persist, and persevere in the communication, manifestation, and transformation of one's ideas.

Dabrowski was clear about the role of creative expression as a crucial medium for the integration of an individual's most authentic emergent capacities. In fact, Dabrowski correlated increased potential for creativity with a capacity for higher-level development. In his work with clients, he observed greater creative drive in those individuals experiencing what he termed *multilevel disintegration*. Such drive can manifest in many ways as bursts of creative impulses in varied mediums. Ultimately, they are attempts to transform not only physical materials, but also one's own self.

The Loneliness of Inner Intensity

Inner intensity provides fuel for a rich and complex interplay between imagination, intellect, and emotion in the inner psychic milieu, giving rise to a higher-level plasticity in the brain. And while it may lead to self-motivated and authentic action, it can also create an isolated world, setting those individuals apart from others in significant ways. This kind of development and experience can be very lonely for those so endowed.

This inner intensity has an inevitability about it that may feel overwhelming to anyone—child, adolescent, or adult—but locked inside, intensity can be frighteningly alienating and potentially volatile. This inner intensity can generate insights and imaginative leaps, but unless the internal responses have outward expression, there is a tendency for shutdown, implosion, and deep distress. A human being must be able to balance intrapersonal facility with interpersonal relationships and agency in the world, and the give-and-take exchange between the environment and the individual is crucial to the human experience of meaning and connection. The ability to take into oneself aspects of existence from the outside, then to change and be changed by this meeting and ultimately recombine the inner experience with outer expression, is essential to an integrated personality and to a feeling of overall well-being. This exchange should be a satisfying, fluid, invigorating, and effective experience. We are embedded in the world, and we cannot exist without it.

If there is inadequate responsiveness or lack of proximity with a sufficiently reciprocal and synergistic environment, this profound transmutation between the inner and outer world can feel hopeless and devastating. However, a therapeutic encounter with an understanding clinician of sufficient capacity can help enliven and heal an individual and can help a client to discover his or her own resources to create connectivity with the external world. When this therapeutic alliance is framed in informed empathy and truly unconditional regard, an unprecedented foundation for growth is created. It may be the first time that the intense individual with the proclivity for advanced development has encountered circumstances in which his or her perceptions and inner reality can materialize—unfettered—in a meaningful and auspicious way.

This need for reciprocal exchange is surely the most essential of human needs, without which a human life lacks significance. To be able to probe the essence of oneself and the world—*as perceptions and understanding emerge*—in a responsive and affirming context breathes life into an otherwise stalemated existence. Individuals endowed with the most sensitive and acute discernment are in particular need of scaffolding, reflection, and encouragement for their unique and unrepeatable pathway in life. The anxiety that underlies many intense individuals' lived experiences is often the result of a lack of understanding from others and a scarcity of meaningful encounter, thereby creating insufficient resources for growth.

Fynn: A Case Study of Intensity

Fynn (a 19-year-old male, exceptionally gifted) came to counseling after a weeklong stay in a psychiatric ward for major depression and disturbing suicidal ideation. As a condition of release from hospital, he was required to engage in intensive psychotherapy for what was clearly a long-standing mood disorder. The provisional psychiatric diagnoses suggested bipolar tendencies and the possibility of Asperger's Disorder. Fynn had been identified as a gifted learner early in his schooling experience, although he received inconsistent support for his high cognitive ability and no recognition of his exceptional emotional sensitivity, rich imaginational acuity, and deep need for inquiry. He wrote in his journal, which he shared with the therapist, the following:

> *Tonight I've been thinking a lot about life, and I've been watching some of a documentary on American-Iraq historical relations. I am really disgusted by a lot of the things I see, but they only confirm my suspicions and sense of many international relations in general. I am in great need of exceptional experiences—some consistent feeling that I need to find a calm place at last, and peace. My feelings remain that I have been educationally neglected and pacified, and this pisses me off! I am very pissed off by this feeling of neglect by the system, and to an extent by my ignorant yet loving parents.*

In his first counseling session, Fynn appeared to be an unusually sensitive young man with a probing, complex conversational style. He exhibited a razor-sharp faculty for analysis, a penchant for introspection, and an ability for remarkably rapid mental processing. He demonstrated noteworthy idealism and a need to evaluate all aspects of human functioning. He seemed to be very harsh in his self-evaluations and was especially critical of others, though in an idealistic way.

At the onset, his overt facial expressions were difficult to read; over time, he relaxed and unveiled (verbally and nonverbally) aspects of his inner world. An overriding sense of acute and deep-seated fatigue radiated from him. He seemed to be struggling with a need to keep himself together while urgently seeking guidance and support. He hinted at weighty feelings of despair and bleakness. At the same time, there was an untouched sense of wonder and trust that was palpable in his gestures and comments.

Fynn's depressive profile included suicidal ideation; a depressed mood (evident for more than two months); blunted motivation; a flat affect alternating, at times, with excessive feelings of euphoria; excessive irritability; difficulties concentrating; disturbed sleep patterns; and insufficient appetite for food. As is common with major depression, Fynn's capacity for analysis outstripped his capacity for synthesis. Fynn could probe and pull things apart, but he was increasingly inadequate at putting them back together. This functional incapacity was extremely disturbing for someone normally adept at mental synthesis of any kind. The inability to synthesize his impressions and thoughts contributed to Fynn's feeling of estrangement and personality disunity, which then intensified significantly a state of hyper-vigilance and anxiety.

Fynn's self-destructive fantasies were rooted in a need to gain mastery over a self-system in chaos, and suicide represented ultimate control. Lacking familiar internal psychic moorings and external psychosocial supports, this disarray and disunity were extremely terrifying.

> *Since our meeting yesterday, especially, I have noticed rapid polarizations of emotions and mental states. The first of these two opposite mindsets is the old depression mindset: I feel tired, frustrated, self-defeating, suspicious, nervous, awkward.... I suffer some tension, have difficulty "seeing" my surroundings and focusing on passages in books, and I don't feel whole or present. The second state is more enjoyable, but less familiar: I feel more energized, hopeful, (a very unfamiliar emotion, Hope)...self-encouraging, trusting (or at least capable of defending myself), calm, charming, fluid, I am more-or-less free of tension, see my surroundings with*

impressive detail, am more engaged in reading, and I feel more whole and present. That is, I feel "I am here, all of me; here is a fine place to be; also, I am a fine person to be, and the future will take care of itself." This is all very confusing, but I expect from what you've told me that it's just part of the healing process. I prefer the more hopeful state of mind, but it is unfamiliar and scary! The sudden mood switching makes me tired!!

It was helpful for Fynn to reconsider the cycling of mood state from the vantage point of the theory of positive disintegration (TDP). Dabrowski specifically conceptualized major depression as having a profound developmental purpose and, with appropriate support, a positive outcome. From the perspective of TPD, the bi-phasal aspect of what we might erroneously label Bipolar Disorder—alternating phases of low mood and extreme excitation—invites new ways of perceiving and increased self-awareness. In the depressed state, the patient finds himself drawn toward self-criticism, self-analysis, and possible inferiority. In the phase of excitation, wherein the mood is elevated, the patient finds himself inspired with enhanced inspiration, facility of synthesis, and vividness of associations. By becoming aware of the nature of these states and using the perceptions gleaned to develop an objective view of the developing self, the internal psychic milieu is strengthened, and higher-level development is supported.

It became obvious that Fynn was intensely lonely, deeply desirous of meaningful interaction, and yearning for reflection of a teeming, dynamic, and multifaceted inner world. In his own words, Fynn talked about a "suffocating loneliness through my struggles." He was a writer and an artist and was exceptionally wide-read in philosophy, politics, technology, literature, and science. He was an individual brought to silence by the wonders of nature, a musician of certain talent, and a poet. Clearly, his presenting mental status was of grave concern and required a focused and strategic therapeutic plan. Notes from the counselor's log at this point in the therapy included:

Fynn has very high developmental potential. He demonstrates an overexcitability profile uncommonly rich in the emotional, imaginational, and intellectual dimensions. Trouble-free expression of his heightened sensual and psychomotor capacities appears to be muted by the overriding depressive condition. Still, Fynn expresses a remarkably wide range of consciousness and a desire for extreme variety of experience.

His intellectual overexcitability is extraordinarily fluid, full-bodied, and penetrating, his need to know and explore voracious. Facility with emotional expression is extremely limited and a source of great dissatisfaction to him. It is clear that he is hypersensitive to the mood states of others and his environments. With gentle encouragement, Fynn manifests complex and many-layered feelings yet is easily overwhelmed by emotional interactions of any kind.

Marked anxiety is evident—his face is taut and upper body especially unyielding. Exceptionally shallow breathing patterns are in evidence, and he reports the occurrence of panic attacks that are particularly unsettling for him. Fynn intellectualizes most of his feelings. He seems unsure and disoriented when gently encouraged to pay attention to and describe his overall mind-set without his habitual hyper-intellectual spin.

The Asperger's Disorder diagnosis suggested by the psychiatrist appears to be erroneous. Fynn is entirely capable of reading social cues and of interacting with others. Rather than a reduced ability to respond to the reactions of others, Fynn expresses a hyper-capacity for attending to others' communicative cues that often overwhelms him in an excess of stimuli. When overwhelmed, he shuts down, and his patterns of communication become difficult to read. Fynn will need many opportunities to exercise latent interpenetrating perceptions and feelings, and he will need coaching in establishing reciprocal interactions with others. Encouragement and support throughout the process will need to continue due to long-standing anxiety and social rejection.

In Dabrowski's words:

The variety and cooperation between different ways of receiving these stimuli adds to this process. This sensitivity acting in the "unknown fields" of the inner and outer worlds brings about a need for new experiences, for uncertainty of experiencing, for hesitation, and disquietude, which in general terms means a process coupling excitation with inhibition. (Dabrowski, 1972, p. 66)

This back and forth process of intense experiencing alternating with hesitancy creates a loosening of familiar processes, a new edge of creativity in one's own being, and an opportunity to forge true psychic change. The counselor encouraged Fynn to appreciate the inherent rhythms of his psychic regeneration. Attention to grounding mechanisms of daily exercise, breath-work, meditation, a healthy and varied diet suited to his needs, and an orderly environment for working and sleeping were put into place.

Over several counseling sessions, it became obvious that Fynn was struggling to maintain interior equilibrium, and he experienced strong feelings of unreality, disconnection, and lack of personality cohesion. In this state, Fynn was exceptionally self-critical and evaluative about himself and others, the nature of human relations, and the state of the world.

> *I feel like a man at the world's end, when the greatest chaos of chaos resolves itself in the utter destruction of everything familiar. There is no more suffering, only a neutral calm of total resignation. I sometimes long for the abyss. My life is futility, vanity, dark comedy. I am the mason without bricks; I am the sailor without a boat; I am the thinker without knowledge. My past is a lie fed on lies, my future is a grey stretch of interminable road, and I'm merely a hitchhiker on that road. My mental life is poverty and pretension. The dogmas and dictums have worn my soul thin. What can I scrape from this empty bowl? I am the chasm that falls down myself. What can I find in empty rooms, when I cannot find myself?*

Fynn would need encouragement to temper his evaluative approach to all things with gentleness and humor as a mediating device. In a communication with his therapist, Fynn said:

> *I would LOVE it if you could somehow convey the importance I give to a sense of humor in dealing with my struggles and therapy. I recognize fully that full Laughter and Depression cannot co-exist, and so finding laughter means finding your way out of depression, however hard that is....*

After a few weeks in therapy, Fynn declared that:

> *The most impressive mood change in the past week(s) is the ability to feel things like hunger, tiredness, gladness, and sadness. To me, that represents a softening of my emotional shell and willingness toward vulnerability to circumstances, in light of the new advantages they may present (like therapy).*

Within this overall complex framework, Fynn's ability to probe his inner world and to see multiple dimensions in the environment around him were noteworthy. He began to be more consistently aware of others, of physical aspects of his environment, and of the social agenda that previously had overwhelmed him. In telling the story of his life, Fynn revealed that he had been at odds with a good number of the milieus he grew up in: home, school, church, and aspects of the community. This "positive maladjustment"—conflict with and rejection of the prevailing social standards and attitudes in keeping with a felt sense of a higher moral imperative—had operated in Fynn's outlook for some time and was a driving force in much of his behavior and thoughts. His challenge of the status quo in his family life and in academic settings was often excessive. Fynn acknowledged the impetus behind his behavior in these statements, written at the beginning of his therapeutic program:

> *My tenacity and ferocity seemed somewhat unrelated to the incidents, in a righteous obsessiveness and fighting spirit. It was like I chose these times to use all the energy of my emotional baggage to fight against situational representations of injustice against me. I love this sentence, too, and it reminds me of my dad, and a bit of my mom: "extraverted consciousness is unable to believe in invisible forces...."*

Fynn's profoundly introverted nature infused with rich imaginational, emotional, and intellectual characteristics was radically unlike his parents. His father, a brilliant and successful businessman, prided himself on the suppression of emotion, most often displaying dispassionate and so-called "objective" behavior. Success in the world, using intelligence to maintain efficient systems and pleasant relationships, was his mandate. His own father had been a scholar and a recluse and, in his judgment, was "unsuccessful in providing for his family." The legacy for Fynn's father was deep mistrust of intellectual pursuits and firm adherence to a philosophy of pragmatism. His mother, on the other hand, was an extreme extravert, also very successful in the business world, but prone to unbalanced displays of emotion and unreasonable rants. Like Fynn, she was very complex and emotionally labile. Both parents cared a great deal about Fynn and were often at a loss about how to support their son with his idealistic, passionate, tenacious, and complex style of operating in the world. Fynn had just two close friends and had felt socially isolated for some time.

121

Despite his obvious brilliance and capacity to engage in the world, Fynn revealed his need for withdrawing from external stimuli in ways that might have been (to others) signs of morbidity and perhaps disturbing conduct. He described his newly widened emotional stance and capacity for deeper emotional engagement and the seemingly necessary withdrawal: "It's definitely representative of a greater, overarching mood shift. Music has more significance again. However, that said, I have noticed that after such lucid 'emotional episodes,' I have a strong tendency to retreat again...."

Fynn's overall therapeutic program involved attention to diet and exercise, meditative practice, creative and musical pursuits, and studies of various areas of interest. Reduction of extreme tension coincided with increasing self-expression. It was essential that Fynn harness his deepest creative intentions while clarifying and exploring his most authentic sense of self in several contexts. He had been shut down a very long time. His hypersensitivity and vulnerability to the often-erratic emotional tone in his home environment precluded him from developing a healthy autonomy that was critical for his personal evolution.

Fynn was encouraged and provided with opportunities to engage with others of all capacities and, of critical importance to him, with members of the exceptionally gifted population. Thus, in addition to benefiting significantly from the professional clinical relationship, Fynn engaged latent relationship capacities to connect with others who infused his system with new energy and affirmed his deepest sense of self.

> *In my free time, I am reading about bee keeping and starting to read about fishing, and thinking about relaxation principles. I have SOME continuing issues with stress, but I am breathing deep when I feel pains, and at times I feel the most relaxed I have been in a loooooong time. One day I would like to have property to have large gardens and bee-keep. I think that in my spare time now I will also read about planting, and the different regions of the country.*
>
> *Running, being as I described a fundamentally non-logical activity (except of course in limited circumstance inapplicable to me), taps into some of the "animal" part of the human psyche, I think. This could tie in with the catharsis in some way, but the point is, I feel that exercising healthful body activity that taps into that animal instinct in a controlled way is a way of harnessing the*

energy of that deep psychic element, and becoming comfortable with it. I'm sure this is in the literature somewhere....

> *My head feels tired and grumpy, and I actually lose visual focus (I notice this about when I get down) because I hate doing these registrations and having to face how far behind I see myself to be, relative to where I "should" have been at this point. I fought so long, was so misunderstood, and now it's humiliating to me. Just the same, it is bittersweet, and that means I have some sweet. I feel much better personally, thanks to our work at the clinic, even though it's frustrating to go back to catch up courses from a few years ago in my struggles.*

Fynn wrote the following poem to mark the vast improvements in his well-being and the resurgence of hope and purpose. The final stanza underscored his recognition of the role that his disintegrative process played in developing a more authentic and realized sense of self.

A haggard man was I
When I staggered through your door,
And for weeks and months I waffled
With an overload of garbled stories

Flailing for an explanation,
Desperate with new postulations,
Tired on the floor

But now I'm writing poetry,
And bad cartoons,
And more than that, I feel again—!—
And feel that maybe life has something more—

With therapy and work and beer
I see that poetry's a job for living people,
Not for grammatical corpses.

Living's a very ungrammatical business, too
(And oh, how I was a grammatical corpse—
Frozen in a jam of ill contemplations)

Now, I don't need beginnings
And I almost don't need endings—skip 'em!
Periods are out of fashion, sometimes()

I've learnt:
If I can take my insanity, and
swallow it like a pill a thousand times
I'll be the sanest man on earth.

Integral Intensity Counseling: A Summary

These two case studies show that a therapeutic encounter of deep meaning and sufficient complexity can help to facilitate the transformation of cognitive functioning, emotional fatigue, and stymied processes of living in the world. In each instance, exceptional sensitivity and almost immeasurable intensity were fundamental features in the challenges experienced by both young men. Their rich inner worlds and their capacities for deep intellectual, emotional, and imaginational penetration into the world around them resulted in a surplus of feelings and impressions that were exacerbated by an insufficient reciprocity in the environment.

Psychotherapy with clients of such intense and sensitive natures demands a great deal of the therapist in terms of conceptual sophistication and sensitivity to the presenting issues. Nevertheless, the rewards are immeasurable. For the client, the feeling of being truly met, in the context of a deeply meaningful exchange, provides hopefulness and new energy for creativity. This co-creation of human sensitivity and connection may take place in a professional arena, but its effect is derived from real relationship in space and time, which the client deeply feels. The nature and consequence of such intense, mutually contemplative, and integrated encounters can catalyze the intense client into profound levels of reconstruction, filled with renewed acceptance of self and of purpose and meaning.

Dabrowski's theory of positive disintegration remains one of the best guides for describing the experienced inner turbulence, deeper meaning of conflict, and idiosyncratic behavior of individuals endowed with extraordinarily intense capacities. Dabrowski helped us to see the transformational potential in what had previously been seen as merely dysfunctional behavior, emotion, and cognitions—describing the multilevel growth process to the world. For the helping professional, he emphasized acceptance of the client and, where possible, guiding development toward authentic personality expression on the highest levels of realization. We have found reason to reconsider the two "neglected" psychomotor and sensual OEs, suggesting that they can be employed as important potential agents of stamina and grounding for the client.

We have made the case for recognizing inner intensity—deep responsiveness that is often overlooked and may be intentionally hidden from others—as a variable that cannot be ignored and cannot be separated from the client's essence. And finally, we want to emphasize the danger of misdiagnosis when insufficient attention is devoted to understanding this intensity, its meaning to the client, and its essential role in the development of his or her emotional and personality growth.

Authors' note: All names used in the above case studies are fictitious in order to preserve client confidentiality.

Chapter 8

Overexcitability, Giftedness, and Family Dynamics

Susan Daniels, Ph.D.

Parents of gifted children often must devise their own means of understanding problems and issues that arise from their children's giftedness. There are few guidelines to follow for children who differ from average children not only in intellectual development, but also in social and emotional development. (Lovecky, 1992, p. 18)

Overexcitabilities affect more than the individual; they influence everyone around, including family members. Parents with strong OEs are likely to have children with strong OEs (Lewis, Kitano, & Lynch, 1992; Tieso, 2007b), and the resulting intensity within the family can be quite dramatic. As an outgrowth of a research study, described below, I was able to identify some common themes within families with OEs, and some interesting family dynamics as well.

In 2002, Michael Piechowski, Frank Falk, and I received a research grant from the SENG (Supporting Emotional Needs of the Gifted) organization to develop and validate an instrument to identify and assess OEs in young children. By using as a model the existing OEQ-II (Overexcitability Questionnaire – II)—a 50-item Likert scale questionnaire with an eighth-grade reading level—we created an instrument for assessing OEs in children in grades three through eight. As a second phase of that research study, I interviewed parents regarding their experiences of their children's OEs, patterns of OEs in their families, and the impact of OEs on parenting and family dynamics.

The interview transcripts—stories from these parents of gifted children—are lengthy and complex, a first indication that gifted parents share cognitive and personality traits with their children. Parents of gifted children generally have a wealth of ideas and questions about their child's development, as well as fabulous vocabularies and verbal skills. Reading and analyzing these transcripts and the stories they told was both exciting and daunting, and it revealed many insights. Prior to conducting these interviews, and to provide a context, I read earlier research and literature. Here is a summary of that information.

Giftedness in Families

Giftedness can be considered to be a quality of a family, rather than a quality that sets the child apart from the rest of the family. Silverman (1993a) states, "When one parent's IQ is known, the child's IQ can often be predicted within 10 points" (p. 171). Therefore, when a child is identified as gifted, it is likely that the parents are gifted as well (Kline & Meckstroth, 1985; Meckstroth, 1991; Tolan, 1992).

It is also commonly noted that parents of gifted children find it difficult to acknowledge giftedness in themselves. Although they recognize gifted traits, behaviors, and issues in their children, and may even realize that they have some of the same traits, they often still have difficulty raising their hand in an audience of other parents of gifted children when a speaker asks how many of the adults in the audience are gifted. Yet as Stephanie Tolan (1992) remarked, "it is hard to help one's child resolve issues one has not yet resolved for oneself" (p. 8).

Knowing this—that parents seldom feel comfortable describing themselves as gifted—prompted me to consider a central question: Are parents of the gifted and highly gifted aware of overexcitabilities in themselves and in their children, and what impact does their recognition of the overexcitabilities have upon the family?

Several research studies of giftedness in families have investigated what factors contribute to gifted development (Ross, 1979). A few considered the social/emotional components of gifted family life (Cornell & Grossberg, 1987; Sebring, 1983; Solow, 1995). At least one study (Gaunt, 1989) found that parents of moderately gifted children differ from parents of highly gifted children in how they perceive their children's learning characteristics, social and emotional adjustment, school experiences, and social and emotional experiences. However, few studies specifically addressed the impact of the child on the family (Bloom, 1985; Cornell, 1984), and none investigated how gifted characteristics of the parents interact with gifted characteristics of the children.

Cornell (1984) was one who asked, "How does giftedness influence the family?" (p. 3). Using rating scales and a structured interview, he examined how parent perceptions of giftedness affected the gifted child and the family. Solow (1995) investigated the ways in which parents think about and explain the social and emotional development of their gifted children, and then she examined how this influenced their interpretation of the child's behavior.

Impact of Overexcitabilities on Development and Family Dynamics

While the OEs confer certain developmental advantages, they also present stress and create challenges for the gifted individual (Lovecky, 1992) and the family (Schetky, 1981; Silverman & Kearney, 1989). In addition, it seems likely that the existence of—as well as particular constellations of—OEs in gifted and highly gifted families create certain social/emotional challenges for the entire family (M. Piechowski, personal communication, July 7, 2002). Piechowski (1991) observed:

The stronger these overexcitabilities are, the less welcome they are among [others] unless they, too, are gifted. Children characterized by strong overexcitabilities are often made to feel different, apart from others, embarrassed, and guilty for being different. (p. 287)

Some challenges associated with overexcitability impact the family directly. Schetky (1981), for example, noted that gifted children have "high energy drive, both physical and psychological," and that they can be "physically and mentally exhausting to live with" (p. 2.). Even in infancy, parents must cope with and respond to early behaviors associated with overexcitability. For example, one parent of a highly gifted child commented, "When other babies were getting 12 hours of sleep, I was lucky if he slept six hours. I figured he was smarter than other children because he had been awake twice as long" (Silverman & Kearney, 1989, p. 52).

More than one study demonstrated that gifted children and adolescents exert a great deal of pressure on the family (Bloom, 1985; Buescher, 1991). Parents, brothers and sisters, and even grandparents have indicated being affected by the fervent needs and intense behaviors of gifted and talented children and adolescents (Bloom, 1985; Buescher, 1991; Silverman & Kearney, 1989).

However, few researchers or clinicians have investigated patterns of OEs in gifted and highly gifted families, and there is a clear need for more research in this area (Tieso, 2007b). As a result, the nature and scope of the influence of OEs upon family dynamics and parent-child interactions for the moderately gifted and highly gifted is largely unknown.

The SENG Research Study

During development of the Overexcitability Questionnaire for Children, I met with groups of parents, explained the OEs, and gave them some background on Dabrowski's theory. Later, I met individually with parents who volunteered for the study and administered a semi-structured interview. I asked all participants the same set of questions, and I also asked them to expand and clarify whatever points they made. Additionally, I encouraged the parents to add questions and experiences that they felt were relevant to the investigation of overexcitabilities in young gifted children and in family dynamics.

Each parent had a copy of the list and a description of overexcitabilities (see Chapter 1) for reference during the interviews. The interview questions were as follows:

1. Please share with me any examples or experiences of overexcitabilities that you have encountered with your children in each of the five areas: psychomotor, sensual, imaginational, intellectual, and emotional.

   a. What are specific examples in each of these OEs?

   b. Are any of them especially evident in your child?

   c. Could you describe or tell how this OE is most apparent in your child?

2. Do you feel that these qualities are more evident in your child (or children) than in other children? If so, how so?

3. Can you think of a time when a friend, family member, teacher, extracurricular activity leader, or coach pointed out that your child displays some of these characteristics?

4. In what ways have these traits impacted you, your family interactions, or your parenting?

5. Are there any other prominent characteristics of your child that you would like to discuss?

6. Is there anything else that you would like to add or any questions that you might have for me?

Essentially, questions 4, 5, and 6, combined, ask: "How do these characteristics and traits emerge within your family, and how has this affected your parenting and/or your family dynamics?" The parent interviews yielded dozens of hours of tapes, which we then transcribed. All names were changed to protect privacy. In the sections that follow, the story of one family, whom I will call the Miller family, represents the narratives of many other families. I will then discuss the typical themes that emerged through the interviews of all of the families, and I will include sample statements from a few of the parent participants.

The Miller Family

Sherie and Patrick Miller are the parents of one girl and two boys. Patrick is a professor of sociology, Sherie is a social worker, and there is approximately a 15-year age difference between the two. Patrick has three grown children from a former marriage, two of whom were formally identified as gifted. Sherie and Patrick have three young children: Nate (nine), Gwyn (eight), and Marlan (four). Nate reads far beyond grade level and has been identified as intellectually gifted; he particularly enjoys writing and illustrating stories about dragons. The school district has nominated Gwyn for participation in their visual and performing arts (VAPA) enrichment program due to her advanced drawing and painting abilities. And Marlan has been reading chapter books since he was just three years old. Sherie and Patrick are candid that the intensities and sensitivities of their highly excitable children have created both great joy and great frustration for them as parents.

Psychomotor OE

Sherie says, "Nate is not always in a real intense psychomotor OE place, but when he is, Oh!!! It's almost as though he's in his own little world. He'll talk really fast, and he laughs loud and hard. He just sort of 'takes off' and swirls in his own energy. And he brings Gwyn into it!"

Gwyn, they say, is certainly energetic, but given the descriptions of each OE, they would not describe her behavior, generally, as overexcitable in terms of physical expressions and qualities. Yet she is susceptible to influence from her two brothers. Marlan, at four, is quite physically intense as well. Patrick says, "He moves…well, a lot…except when he doesn't! No, really, this is a kid that's almost always on the go. However, sometimes, if we are lucky, he'll take the ever-so-infrequent nap. Whew!" Often, they say, Nate is the catalyst. When his energy and activity levels are high, this seems to trigger Marlan's energetic responses, and Gwyn can get caught up in the bustle of energy as well.

Sensual OE

Gwyn is highly sensually overexcitable and has complex reactions and responses to sensual stimuli. As Sherie said, "She gets sooooo delighted with color, texture, fabric.… When we gave Gwyn and her best friend matching princess dresses, Tianeme, Gwyn's friend, simply smiled, but Gwyn beamed and noted all of the details, stroking the fabric and running it over her cheek. Of course, every irritation—an itch or some other physical discomfort—has to be described in every detail, too! Gwyn also has a beautiful voice and loves to sing, accurately replicating songs she hears on videos or recordings, but she sings mostly for herself. She won't do this in front of just anyone! She does really love to be center stage and the center of attention, but only with people she knows. She is almost morbidly shy with new acquaintances. Yet she also says she already knows that she wants to be a dancer and a choreographer and a costume designer when she grows up. She's a pretty complex kid when you think about it."

Gwyn is prone to both self-stimulation and self-soothing. She went through an intense period of crossing and uncrossing her legs, and finally her mother said that she had to tell her, "You must do this in private." Sherie noted, "Her sensitivity to taste and dislike of many food tastes and textures means there's much she won't eat." Patrick's sister said of her, "She's wired, and she's wiry." Gwyn just turned eight, and they said she's just beginning to wear a size six. However, there are some things that she consistently likes to eat, her parents noted, including both sugar and bread. Sherie commented, "It seems that carbs soothe her. We work hard to make sure that the carbs going in are healthy; carrot cake—made with whole-wheat flour and agave nectar rather than sugar—is a big favorite. Don't get me wrong, she would love to down fudgy cupcakes with thick butter-cream frosting, but lots of white sugar and processed food seem to really make her wired, and then she crashes. So we work the fruits and vegetables into foods in ways she enjoys. Anyhow, between her finicky eating and high activity level, she's a thin girl."

Patrick noted that at first, he didn't think that Marlan showed many traits of sensual OE. Then it occurred to him that "Marlan pays close attention to visual qualities and the way things look and the way he wants them to look. If drawings don't turn out to please him, he cries." Also, he said, "The other day, we got a new cushion for the porch swing, and it's flowered on one side and dark brown on the other side. It was showing the floral pattern, and he turned it over because the brown matched the trim of the house. I mean, I don't think many four- or five-year-old kids notice stuff like that." As the discussion progressed, Marlan's personal aesthetic sensitivity became more and more apparent.

Imaginational OE

Sherie at one time was an avid still-life and portrait painter, and she still paints miniatures as her busy schedule—professional and personal—allows. Patrick writes short stories, some of which have been published in collections. Assuredly, creativity and imagination are valued in their household. Both parents read to the children daily, and art and design materials are readily available in their home. The family seems to have an innate proclivity toward honoring imagination and cultivating creative ideas.

During her interview, Sherie elaborated on Nate's imaginational OE in detail: "I hate to say that Nate is overexcitable in every area. I mean, he's not overexcitable in the sensual area. But 'imaginational' so speaks of Nate. He craves stories. We read to him constantly—things like Harry Potter and Narnia—advanced books. And he likes nonfiction, too, as well as lots of fantasy."

She said that Nate's imagination keeps him from being bored and that he is, for the most part, very self-entertaining. "I've noticed on the chart of OEs 'low tolerance of boredom,' and you know, Nate doesn't like boredom, but he doesn't get bored—or let himself be bored for very long. Nate can be happy playing with a stick."

Further, Nate's imagination interacts with his emotional sensitivity to provide an unusually alert awareness of possibilities around him. Patrick elaborated: "Nate engages in animistic thinking, too. When he was a little younger, maybe four or so, he insisted that plants have feelings, and he expressed concern that it might not be a good idea to cut the grass. We assured him that cutting the grass was similar to cutting his hair—which he doesn't particularly mind—and that it was just part of taking good care of the lawn, along with watering it and the like."

Sherie and Patrick both also discussed dreaming as another significant aspect of Nate's imaginational OE. He has had a range of vivid dreams, describing them and discussing them in great detail with his parents since his early childhood. His dreams have ranged from the everyday—events that happened at school, for instance—to fantastic dreams of flying carpet rides and living in early colonial times. His dreams for one stretch of time involved episodes of extreme nightmares, and just when his parents were becoming concerned, they stopped as suddenly as they began. Patrick described the range and vividness of Nate's dreams: "For a while, we weren't getting any sleep due to his bad dreams of monsters and the like. But he's also had dreams that led to beautiful drawings and stories, too. There was a period where he had, oh, maybe three or four 'magic carpet' dreams in about a two-week period. He described his dream so very vividly. He was flying low over several lands and observed people and animals and the goings on of a town. So we got his art supplies out so that he could illustrate his dreams. Then he expanded them with a longer story that he made up and created a small book of them."

Gwyn is inclined to play make-believe games and invent stories at every opportunity. She, they say, is very fond of traditional fairy tales and likes to play them out and stage plays with her friends in the neighborhood on a regular basis, with an audience of younger and older children, as well as any parents who might be supervising. Sometimes she'll recruit her older brother's participation, although while he is highly imaginative, he doesn't like acting or performing very much. Marlan, on the other hand, does improvise little stories, but since he is younger, he's more inclined to play alone or with one or two of his age mates than with his older sister's friends. Gwyn enjoys social time and group play with a small group of close friends, and she is quite happy to play alone and amuse herself as well.

Gwyn is also quite artistically inclined. She was identified to participate in her school's art enrichment program because after her classwork was finished, she always chose to work in an art center or draw at her desk. At home, she has an art box that she can take outside on a picnic table, where, Sherie says, "messy work is always allowed." Gwyn can get quite absorbed and paint for long stretches at a time. She creates realistic art in a large watercolor tablet and also paints vivid and elaborate abstract paintings on sheets torn from a roll of large white craft paper that is available to her and her two brothers at all times in the family's mudroom at the back of the house. Patrick said, "We have a portable CD player that Gwyn can take outside, too. She loves children's music and classical music. Sometimes she will, as she says, 'paint the music.' Last week, she painted a sheet of bright swirls and then took marking pens and drew in these tiny shapes and elaborate designs. We asked her what her painting was about, and she said, 'Butterflies and wind.' We really should keep a journal about these things, huh? But then, where would we find the time?"

"With three children who are all imaginative and artistically inclined, the art spreads out from the refrigerator and down a long hallway," Sherie said. "Some favorite paintings and drawings have stayed up for a long time, and others come and go." She went on to describe Marlan's musings and inventive play around the house: "Marlan always has his own view of the world. Right now, he thinks he's a wizard; he introduces himself as a wizard and refers to himself as a wizard. We're just going with it for now. We got him a magic wand, and he 'manages' things around the house with it—like, he'll wave his wand and say things that please him, like, 'Now would be a good time for dinner,' and 'The wand says Marlan can stay up for another half hour.' The wand doesn't always work for him, of course, but it seems to be a very good outlet for his imagination right now."

"The wand doesn't always work for him" is somewhat telling about the Millers' parenting approach. Both parents elaborated that they will engage with Marlan in his story and his fantasy play, but if his wand suggests activities that are outside of family rules, then they will set limits for Marlan and his magic wand. One night, they insisted that the wand be put away for a while; Marlan's cherished wand was not going to interrupt his bedtime or the process of getting ready for bed.

Intellectual OE

Intellectual overexcitability was evident in the interview process with the Millers from our first exchange. Both Sherie and Patrick interjected with questions, insights, personal revelations, and relevant anecdotes throughout the interview process. In addition to providing accounts of intellectual OEs in each of their three children, they conveyed that their house is "virtually decorated in books—classic and modern." While the Miller children consistently smuggle flashlights into bed, Sherie and Patrick similarly have gone through more mini-reading lights than they say they can count in the 10+ years of their marriage.

Nate tends to find one topic that drives him for some period of time, until he connects with the next. Sherie said, "Yes, Nate's hyper-focused. He's an avid reader. He'll go to bed and turn on the light. When we come in three hours later, he'll still be going through books. And he's only nine. I mean, I expect that out of 12-year-olds, 15-year-olds, I suppose, but he's only nine."

In contrast, Sherie said that Gwyn's interests are often captured by each moment. "Gwyn's intellectual interests emerge through whatever captures her imagination at that time. She's very fanciful. She gets captivated by things that delight her, in the environment or in her mind. One day in the spring, she watched a Monarch butterfly in our garden for the longest time. Then she did a 'butterfly dance' around the yard, and after dinner, she asked if we had any books about butterflies or if we could spend some time looking up butterflies online. The next day, she took out art supplies and drew a bunch of butterflies, and finally, she wrote a butterfly story. She stays with things a long time."

Marlan, on the other hand, while very curious, has yet to pursue a particular topic in depth. He still reads picture books and seems to be very visually oriented, taking in much information from observing the physical environment and then responding with related questions. Patrick elaborated that this carries over to a very active and hands-on approach to satiating his curiosity. He said, "Marlan is sort of all over the place. Although he's very bright, there are some ways that he almost seems younger than other kids his age. He still asks questions like when he was a toddler. He's curious, and he's relentless. 'How come? Why? And what if?' are probably the most frequent words he uses. Endless questions. And he wants to look inside everything to see how things work."

Emotional OE

Nate and Gwyn are both deeply emotional. Nate is especially aware of and responsive to others' emotional states. Sherie elaborated with her own observations and by recounting a discussion with one of his teachers:

"Nate's also, well…I would say overly empathic. He can experience other peoples' feelings as if they were his own. And sometimes he is just overly concerned about other people's feelings and circumstance. He wants to help everybody and fix everything. We've had long talks about boundaries.

"His teacher has talked about his emotional fluency. This comes up in response to stories. The other kids give, you know, simple, concrete responses, and Nate gave this well-developed, complex, emotionally sensitive response to what he thought the character might be feeling. The teacher showed it to me in utter amazement."

Gwyn, on the other hand, is highly attuned to her own emotional ebb and flow, and her emotions span a broad range. Both parents spoke at once about Gwyn's feeling states, interjecting back and forth, in this interview excerpt: "Gwyn is definitely highly emotional. Her emotions are almost euphoric when she's really happy. She'll jump up and down and clap her hands and squeal. I mean, when she's happy, her face will light up the room. She's radiant!! She's generally a pretty positive kid, though she'll cry really hard if she's disappointed. She is extremely sensitive to the people she cares about—very attentive. But when she first meets somebody, she'll be really shy and withdraw. Her responses are extreme here—almost flat affect. Once she's comfortable, though, she'll warm up, and the inner glow returns."

Themes and Threads throughout the Parent Interviews

Complete analysis of the interviews, conducted over a two-year period with more than 20 parents, will be an ongoing project. In the meantime, a few themes have emerged: accepting and accommodating differences; adult recognition of giftedness; big ideas and healthy grandiosity; emotional flooding; grief for a lost vision of a "normal" child; moral and ethical awareness; relationship of parenting style, communication, and discipline approaches; resources and resiliency; and adult well-being and self-care. I will discuss each theme in detail, using excerpts from parent interviews as illustrations of the connections and parallel experiences across the families.

Accepting and Accommodating Differences

Many parents became aware quite early of the depth and intensity of their children's knowledge and insight into the world around them, as well as to their own feelings and internal states and rhythms. They were able to give numerous examples of ways in which the perceptions and experiences of these children differed from most of their age peers. Many parents realized that they had to accept that their child was different, and they began the journey of gathering information and sorting out what that might mean for their family's daily living, as well as for their long-term plans.

> We found ourselves asking over and over again, "Is this normal"? And after a while, we realized that any attempts to figure out what was normal for Haley were futile. She's just not a typical kid. You know, it's not like I can chat with the parent down the street very easily. Really. One of our neighbors was talking about how much fun it has been now that their son, who just turned two, is talking in full sentences. Haley is almost three, and she is reading picture books. And it's not just her ability to read that's so different; it's her need to know about everything, too. This child has a billion questions every day. We're lucky that, after doing some reading, one thing led to another and we found…a private school for gifted children that also has a preschool program.

In the case of multiple children—with different and varying patterns and degrees of overexcitabilities—the process of discerning and developing an understanding of the range of these differences becomes even more complex. Many families had to make significant changes to accommodate the intellectual and social/emotional needs of their gifted children. Sometimes this meant relocating for a better school fit or driving long distances for a private school option. Birth order may be a factor, and less excitable siblings may have resentment toward the more excitable one(s).

Adult Recognition of Giftedness

Developing an understanding of their children's unique intellectual and emotional capacities brought their own development into consideration anew for many of these parents. More than just a few of them questioned their own abilities, their own potential, and the implications for their parenting as well.

> We wondered, "What does this mean about us as parents and as people?" Discovering that gifted children are children with above-average abilities and potential, we asked ourselves if we have, or may have had, high potential as well. Were we ever identified as gifted? If not, why not? Both of our sets of parents have passed away, so these are questions that will likely remain open. Yet they

bring on other questions. Are we living up to our own potential? And…what do we need to know or be able do to in order to raise these children of high potential?

These considerations brought with them the desire for more information regarding giftedness in families and adults.

Big Ideas and Healthy Grandiosity

Many accounts of advanced interests coupled with detailed plans emerged from these interviews. Some of the children had complex projects that they conjured and described in great detail to seemingly anyone who would listen. Some had persistence and drive around these ideas that just wouldn't stop, even from a very young age. One of the more elaborate projects that came to fruition and a positive resolution, due in large part to the efforts and persistence of a dedicated gifted program coordinator, was the building of a robotic arm by an ingenious five-year-old with a very capable fifth-grade assistant. Jacob's mother recounted the story as follows:

One incident that turned out well for Jacob's big ideas comes from when he was just four and went to kindergarten for part of the day. To make a long story short, Jacob has advanced reading and thinking abilities; he reads in areas that interest him all the way up to the high school level, but he's actually a bit delayed in the development of his physical skills. So after Jacob was relentless in talking about his plans and diagrams for building a robotic arm for weeks on end, the gifted coordinator organized two one-hour times each week when he could get together with a gifted fifth-grade boy who really liked robots, too. Jacob told the boy all of his ideas for the design of a robotic arm, and the two boys built one together.

One highly gifted 10-year-old girl had written a novella that she called "futuristic historical fiction." She wrote her life story, autobiographically from birth, and projected forward through college and into her early career, including descriptions of where she was living, what her apartment looked like, and what work she was doing to preserve the marine environment. These endeavors appear to integrate intellectual abilities along with intellectual, imaginational, and emotional overexcitabilities. Their passions, and perhaps a dose of what Grobman (2006) has called "healthy grandiosity," seem to propel these children with the persistence needed for effective development and pursuit of their inventions and plans.

Emotional Flooding

Every parent had an account of deep or dramatic emotions to relate. Not only did their children show heightened sensitivity and awareness of their own and others' feelings, but also, there were times when these children were overcome and overwhelmed by their own emotions. For Gwyn, from the Miller family, adverse reactions to sensual and physical experiences could result in emotional flooding.

> *Sometimes she's very dramatic about negative emotions. For example, just a few days ago, we were over at a family friend's house, and Gwyn was playing on the lawn, and the sprinklers came on suddenly. Well, she threw her head back, and her hands were helpless at her sides, and she just wailed. She did nothing to help herself. Now mind you, only two days before, she was playing in those sprinklers and got herself completely wet by choice.*

One young man, usually very gentle and caring, had strong outbursts of anger when overly frustrated, overtired, or overwhelmed.

> *He has a deep anger place, but you know, we've used a lot of emotional vocabulary with him to help him speak of and better understand his strong emotions. Typically, when he's in the angry place, the only thing that works is time and space. He needs a time-out and, if possible, a distraction. I'll give him a book, and if he can go to another place in his imagination, that helps.*

Another young boy beamed and jumped for joy with pleasure, but he reacted just as strongly if plans were changed or if he was unable to finish an activity that he'd started, especially if this occurred just before bedtime. His mother told me:

> *Oh, he has very intense emotions—great jubilation when things are going well, and great drama when he experiences disappointment. You cannot change plans on him. He just loses it. I mean, he's not awful. He, at five years old, just realizes that he doesn't have control over the situation, and he'll just cry. I think that early on, he experienced greater frustration and anger [than normal], and he would have pretty spectacular temper tantrums.*

Grief for a Lost Vision of a "Normal" Child

Several parents talked of their experiences of coming to the understanding that gifted children are different, yet most also wondered what having a more typically developing child would be like. More than a few acknowledged that they at times wished for a more average child. For example, one parent likened her child's personality to the dramatic qualities of a popular cartoon character and shared that she both wondered what it would be like and at times wished she had a more average child. She said:

> *Okay. This is really hard to admit, but, well, you know, Carlos has been compared to Calvin from "Calvin and Hobbes" more times than I can tell you. He's smart, and he has a great imagination, and he's stubborn as can be. He's a handful and then some. I love him; I love him so much. But there have been so many times, too, and I'm not proud of this, but I just wish I had a normal child, you know? I wonder what that would be like. Sometimes I just wish he were a normal kid.*

Other parents explicitly addressed that there was a period of sadness when they realized that there were some typical aspects of development that they would never experience with their child.

Moral and Ethical Awareness

Several moral and ethical themes recurred across the interviews—early awareness and concerns with issues of justice; concern for the well-being of others; questions of right, wrong, and the relativism of these concepts; questioning death and the possibility of life beyond; and interest in philosophy and social issues.

> *Nate is very curious. He is always reading, and he pays close attention to the world around him. It's almost as though he's hyper-vigilant, he so closely attends to the world around him. He really pays attention to what other people are doing, and he's conscious of what other people's actions mean. For instance, he'll talk about when a child violates another person in some way, and he'll discuss the implications of the person's actions and ask lots of deep "why" questions. Not in a "shame-shame" way, but trying to understand the background and rationale behind their actions. He processes moral and ethical issues at almost an adult level, and this seems tied to his reading as well. He just keeps reading and reading and*

reading. He asks deep questions about the world—for instance, about global warming, responsibility for the environment, for children less fortunate in far away places, and so on. These concerns have brought him to tears on more than one occasion.

Parents typically were touched by their child's sense of caring and concern, yet at the same time frequently felt some concern themselves for how and to what extent to delve into these areas that are advanced concepts—and for some, burdens—to manage at their child's young age. More than a few children acted on this early awareness and sense of responsibility by contributing in a positive way by volunteering at school or in their communities to make a positive contribution toward issues that concerned or inspired them. Some of the families volunteered at their religious institutions, local libraries, humane societies, and other service organizations. They then discussed the volunteer activity in depth, and the related areas of social and ethical concern went far deeper beyond the time of the actual service activity.

Parenting Style, Communication, and Discipline Approaches

An issue for many parents was developing an appropriate parenting style. They realized that their parenting experiences were different from those of most parents, and they were concerned with issues such as how much to share authority in setting limits and how open communication should be concerning "adult" topics. Most, however, recognized that even though their children were quite bright intellectually, their life experience and judgment lagged behind, and these parents were authoritative, though seldom authoritarian, in their parenting style. As one parent said:

Remember that WE are in the parental driver's seat—that even if they can produce a better argument than I can, I still get paid the big bucks to make the final call. Because I am the parent, I can say, "It just doesn't feel right to me," or "I don't have the energy for that right now," and things like that can be a good enough reason for setting a limit. It is important not to give up parental authority just because they can out-argue me. Also, family sharing of choices for read-alouds, field trips, etc., make a big difference in cooperation.

Resources and Resiliency

Some parents experienced concern and even dismay over whether or not they had the resources to adequately parent and provide for the needs of their gifted child. Yet most recounted impressive resourcefulness in accessing materials online and connecting with other parents and community members. One couple spoke appreciatively of the resources available through their school district:

> *We feel so fortunate that we live where we do. I mean, this district is really trying to provide appropriate programs for gifted kids and, well, for their parents, too. First, the district GATE coordinator started by giving a series of parent talks. Then, about a year later, they held a parent discussion group. That was a life-saver for us. It's hard to put into words what it feels like to be with other adults, other parents, who have kids with similar or comparable abilities and interests [when you've never really had that before]. It's such a relief. As a parent of a gifted child, it can feel very isolating; it's great to find others who can relate.*

Another parent described the resourcefulness that emerged within a group of parents at her child's school:

> *We started a G/T parent co-op. We have a resource library at one of the schools where parents can check out books on gifted kids. And we also have a babysitting co-op, too. It's almost impossible to find babysitters anymore in general, at least where we live. So if we swap babysitting time, then it's a double bonus. We get to go out for a while, and our kids get a play date. I mean, they don't all get along really, really well, but we find combinations that work.*

For most of the parents, information about gifted children was certainly essential, but connection with other gifted children and their parents provided a true sense of community that supported the families' growth and greater well-being.

Adult Well-Being and Self-Care

In discussing the impact of overexcitabilities on the family and the experience of parenting gifted children, the needs of the children are usually at the fore of discussion. Yet the intensified needs of the parents must not be marginalized or forgotten. Parenting highly sensitive and intense gifted children brings with it a bevy of unique joys and exhilarations, and also additional stressors for the individual parents and the parents as a couple.

> *Our son is in the highly gifted range. He's been accelerated in school, and that's been good. But we have had more meetings at his*

school—from first grade to fourth grade—than I would imagine most parents have in their child's entire school career. It's very time-consuming, and there are times when we've both been just exhausted. We need to make sure that we find time for ourselves, which can easily evaporate if we don't pay attention.

As has been discussed throughout this book, it is essential for the optimal development of gifted children that they learn strategies for self-nurturing and for modulating their overexcitabilities. It is also important that their parents have as much support as possible and the opportunity to refuel their own energy stores. One mother stated:

As a single mother—especially, I think, with a gifted child—I really feel that I need some extra support. My family doesn't live nearby, but when my mom comes to visit, it gives me some time for myself. Sometimes, I just need more sleep. Sometimes, I need a good cry. Sometimes, I need a quiet cup of tea. Sometimes, what I really need is to nap for a good long time—like maybe a day or two.

One particularly expressive quote from *Helping Gifted Children Soar* (Strip & Hirsch, 2000) reflects the experiences recounted in this chapter especially well: "Parenting a gifted child is like living in a theme park full of thrill rides. Sometimes you smile. Sometimes you gasp. Sometimes you scream. Sometimes you laugh. Sometimes you gaze in wonder and astonishment. Sometimes you're frozen in your seat. Sometimes you're proud. And sometimes, the ride is so nerve-wracking, you can't do anything but cry" (p. 3).

Chapter 9
Petunias, Perfectionism, and Level of Development

Linda Kreger Silverman, Ph.D.

The Saga of the Petunias and the Chipmunks

We live in the mountains where it is not uncommon to have snowstorms as late as June and as early as September. The Almighty has been our Gardener during our short growing season, enchanting us with a lovely array of wildflowers. Recently, I was moved to plant large pots of petunias and pansies all around our deck to lend their glory to the view. I had a flower box built on the edge of the patio. I became deeply attached to my flowers. I diligently tended them every morning and evening, watering them with *Miracle Gro* and pruning the dead blossoms. The pots were a perfumed profusion of deep purple, lilac, pink, yellow, and white.

And then the adorable little chipmunks came. Well, they used to be adorable…. They devoured *all* of the blossoms in the flower box and then began to munch on the ones in the pots. Dismayed, I tried to distract them. Their cousins, the squirrels, love bird food, so I put out a dish of bird food for the chipmunks. They ate the bird food and had my petunias for dessert. To deter them, I tried moth balls in stockings, cayenne pepper, rags dipped in vinegar, hole-punched bottles of ammonia stuck in the dirt; two kind of animal repellent, and raw eggs mixed with cayenne pepper. No luck.

All of my joy vanished. Twice a day, I would come out on the deck and fret about the eaten and half-eaten blooms. Then a friend came to visit. She said, "Linda, 99% of your flowers are absolutely gorgeous. Why don't you just enjoy them?" Of course, she was right. Aside from the sad stems in the flower box that captured my entire attention, the rest of the pots were heavy with blossoms—enough for the chipmunks and me to enjoy.

Nevertheless, I was still on a mission to save *all* of my petunias from the scourge of the chipmunks. I continued to fret. The very next day, it hailed—a true Rocky Mountain hailstorm. Pea-sized hailstones carpeted the deck. My blossoms were devastated, and so was I. I nearly cried as I examined each pot around the patio and the deck. Not a single bloom was intact. Then I went to the front deck and saw that two of the pots protected by the overhang were spared. I was ecstatic to find survivors.

That was when it dawned on me that I had lost out on a great deal of joy before the hailstorm because I was so preoccupied with the flowers that I had sacrificed to the chipmunks. From that day on, I became extremely grateful for every new blossom. The plants weren't destroyed, just the blooms. Soon the pots were overflowing again with beauty. When the frost descended in early autumn, I took some of the pots of petunias indoors, and lo and behold, they lasted all winter long.

Obviously, there is a moral to this story. Suppose that instead of fussing about the petunias that became chipmunk fare, I had delighted in the perfect way the other flowers grew, with sunshine, water, and appreciation? It was my perfectionism that led me to plant the flowers in the first place—to add to the beauty. It led to the construction of the flower box and my lining the patio with flower pots. The flowers were the perfect touch. Perfection and beauty are intertwined. It is the perfectionists in this world who create beauty. The chipmunks taught me the price of focusing on what is "wrong." My lesson was to see the situation differently—to concentrate on what was perfect instead of what I perceived to be imperfections.

Is Perfectionism Bad or Good?

Perfectionism is a potent force that can immobilize or energize, depending on where we focus our attention. If we feel incapable of attaining internal standards or meeting the expectations of others, it can cause paralysis and underachievement. It also can be the passionate drive that leads to extraordinary creative achievement—an ecstatic struggle to move beyond the previous limits of our capabilities (Silverman, 1999).

Perfectionists set high standards for themselves, and they experience great pain if they fail to meet those standards. They are besieged with guilt and shame that few seem to understand. Their unrelenting self-criticism appears maladjusted. Even when others applaud them, they often feel miserable, aware of how much higher they aimed. They may feel that they have cheated themselves and others by not fully utilizing their abilities. Those who perpetually remain in this self-castigating state live unhappily ever after and give perfectionism its bad name.

But this is only part of the story, albeit the one that receives the most attention. The extent of joy that it is possible to experience is directly related to the intensity of the struggle in which we engage to reach our goals. Perfectionists are capable of being totally in Csikszentmihalyi's (1990) flow, unfettered by time constraints or the judgments of others, when the activity itself becomes the reward rather than a means to an end.

Giftedness and Perfectionism

The gifted often set unrealistic standards for themselves, fight windmills and City Hall, persist when others have given up, and envision the possibilities even in the face of disaster. They push themselves beyond all reasonable limits to achieve goals that they feel are important. While this idealism may seem unjustified to an outside observer, it has the potential to change the world.

Giftedness and perfectionism are soul mates. Perfection is an abstract concept. It takes an abstract mind to grasp its meaning and to cherish a vision that does not exist in the concrete world—to yearn for "what ought to be" (Silverman, 1983). Facility with abstraction is the *sine qua non* of giftedness; this quality differentiates the gifted from others throughout the lifespan.

Asynchronous (uneven) development of the gifted also gives rise to perfectionism (Silverman, 1993c). Gifted children set standards according to their mental age, not their chronological age. A nine-year-old mind makes promises that six-year-old hands cannot keep. In addition, many gifted children have older playmates, so they tend to set standards appropriate for their more mature friends.

At a very young age, gifted children have the cognitive capacity to predict consequences of their actions; therefore, they are more likely than average children to be successful in their first attempts at mastery. From their earliest years, they have been able to avoid failure. Each success creates the expectation that they will succeed in the next task, no matter how difficult the challenge. Since they are accustomed to success and relatively unfamiliar with failure, gifted children can become failure-avoidant.

School exacerbates perfectionistic tendencies in the gifted. Giving all children the same level of work regardless of ability makes it too easy for

147

gifted children to get the highest grades. They come to see themselves as "A students" and can get addicted to A's. In her study of gifted college students, Speirs Neumeister (2004a) found that early academic success was a factor in perfectionism.

> *Though all were identified as gifted in elementary school, none of the participants found their early school experiences to be chal-lenging. In fact, some of them said they never experienced challenges in school until they reached their AP courses nearing the end of high school. John believed his ability to master the cur-riculum with ease had a strong influence on the development of his perfectionism. He said, "My perfectionism now might have come from the fact that I never really did fail at anything when I was younger. The expectations [for perfection] just grew." John explained that, had he encountered any academic difficulty at a young age, "then it would be acceptable once in a while, and my perfectionism wouldn't be that high." (pp. 266-267)*

Lack of challenge and stimulation can also feed perfectionism in another way. If schoolwork is too easy, some gifted children will do any-thing to complicate the task just to make it worth doing, such as trying to accomplish it perfectly. This was revealed in Schuler's (1997) study. The majority of the students found the work that they were expected to do unchallenging—requiring a minimal amount of intellectual effort—yet they poured their enormous energies into achieving the highest grades pos-sible. There is no joy in demonstrating mastery of a skill or concept that one learned long ago; therefore, artificial rewards, such as grades, become the only satisfaction possible. In fact, the participants in the study conducted by Speirs Neumeister, Williams, and Cross (2007) indicated that homo-genous grouping and appropriately challenging coursework helped to decrease their perfectionism. Unchallenging schoolwork, combined with the high premium placed on competitive grades, fosters "dysfunctional" perfectionism in gifted youth.

Within the context of Dabrowski's theory (Dabrowski, 1964), per-fectionism takes on new meaning. At the lower levels of development, it is a distortion of the desire for self-perfection. In the service of development, it becomes a driving force within the individual to live a life imbued with higher-level values. Perfectionism manifests as dissatisfaction with "what is," and a yearning to become what one "ought to be" (Dabrowski &

Piechowski, 1977, p. 42). There is an inner knowing that there is more to life than the mundane, as well as a desire to create meaning of one's life by doing the best that one is capable of doing.

Measuring Perfectionism

Perfectionism is a controversial area of inquiry. There are researchers who see this trait in a positive light and others who see it negatively. Those who recognize positive aspects of perfectionism are more likely to find a connection between it and giftedness. When it is conceptualized as pathological, little evidence emerges of perfectionism in the gifted. The problem often stems from the instrumentation. Biases on the part of researchers inevitably seep into the instruments that they construct and interpret. Only miserable gifted people would admit to perfectionism on a negatively-tinged survey.

I remember how excited I was the day I encountered the 10-item perfectionism scale that appeared in *Psychology Today* (Burns, 1980). I fully expected to get 100%. To my chagrin, I only achieved a middling score. So I analyzed the items to see where I went wrong. I aced all of the items related to high standards (e.g., "An average performance is bound to be unsatisfying to me"; "If I try hard enough, I should be able to excel at anything I attempt."), but I failed all of the items measuring fear of failure (e.g., "People will probably think less of me if I make a mistake."). This item didn't make much sense to me, as I had seen so many perfectionistic, gifted children purposely make mistakes to gain the acceptance of their classmates. But I knew that introverts were afraid of failure and I am an extravert, so I wondered if that was the reason I did so poorly.

The more I examined what was being written about perfectionism, the more convinced I became that the writers were indiscriminately mingling idealism, introversion, preoccupation with one's flaws, fear of not being able to live up to others' expectations, striving to attain excellence, and making unfair demands of others. This strange amalgam was held responsible for an alphabetical inventory of ills: alcoholism, anorexia, anxiety, bulimia, chemical abuse, decreased productivity, depression, excessive cosmetic surgeries, fearfulness, gastrointestinal distress, hypomania, insomnia, low self-concept, migraines, narcissism, obsessive-compulsive personality disorder, panic disorder, passive-aggression, performance anxiety, poor self-control, procrastination, psychosomatic disorders, respiratory ailments, sexual compulsions and dysfunctions, shame, social phobias, suicide, troubled personal relationships, Type A coronary-prone behavior, workaholism, and writer's block (see Chan, 2007, for illustrative citations). I clearly saw perfectionism in all of the gifted children and adults I worked with, but without the pathological symptoms.

Gifted people tend to work hard to achieve difficult goals. They can immerse themselves for years in a quest (e.g., understanding the relationship between energy and matter). Idealistic, they are often disappointed when they discover that others do not share their values. Many are not satisfied unless they feel they have done *their personal best*. These are all positive aspects of perfectionism that have been noted repeatedly as characteristics of the gifted (e.g., Buescher, 1985; Chamrad & Robinson, 1986; Clark, 1988; Davis & Rimm, 2004; Freehill, 1961; Gallagher, 1990; Hollingworth, 1926; Karnes & Oehler-Stinnett, 1986; Kerr, 1991; Kramer, 1988; Lovecky, 1992; Manaster & Powell, 1983; Robinson & Noble, 1991; Roedell, 1984; Roeper, 1991; Webb, Gore, Amend, & DeVries, 2007; Webb, Meckstroth, & Tolan, 1982; Whitmore, 1980).

Ten years after Burns' (1980) "unidimensional scale" of perfectionism came out, "multidimensional" scales of perfectionism appeared (e.g., Frost, Marten, Lahart, & Rosenblate, 1990; Hewitt & Flett, 1991a; Slaney, Rice, Mobley, Trippi, & Ashby, 2001). The two used most extensively in studies of gifted students both bear the same name: *The Multidimensional Perfectionism Scale* (MPS) (Frost, et al., 1990; Hewitt & Flett, 1991a). These tools were considered more sophisticated than Burns' test because they measured different aspects of perfectionism, were longer (35 items and 45 items, respectively), and had more validation studies. Both were based on a negative view of perfectionism (Chan, 2007).

Here are some sample items from the *Multidimensional Perfectionism Scales*:

FMPS (Frost et al., 1990)

○ Concern over Mistakes: "I should be upset if I make a mistake."

○ High Personal Standards: "I set higher goals than other people."

○ Parental Expectations: "My parents wanted me to be the best in everything."

○ Parental Criticism: "As a child, I was punished for doing things less than perfectly."

○ Doubts about Actions: "Even when I do something very carefully, I often feel that it is not quite right."

    ○ Organization: "I am very good at focusing my efforts on attaining a goal."

HMPS (Hewitt & Flett, 1991a)

    ○ Self-Oriented: "It makes me uneasy to see an error in my work."

    ○ Other-Oriented: "If I ask someone to do something, I expect it to be done flawlessly."

    ○ Socially Prescribed: "The better I do, the better I am expected to do."

A decade later, Slaney, et al. (2001), recognizing the negative impression of perfectionism permeating the two prior multidimensional scales, constructed the *Almost Perfect Scale – Revised* (APS-R), which attempts to provide a more balanced perspective. The APS-R is composed of questions that probe whether a person's perfectionism is adaptive or maladaptive.

The most recent instrument on the block, the *Positive and Negative Perfectionism Scale* (PNPS-12), was developed by David Chan (2007) in Hong Kong. In his conceptualization, perfectionism can be positive and healthy when it focuses on "high personal standards" and "a realistic striving for excellence," or it can be negative and unhealthy when it "focuses on a rigid adherence to personal high demands, as well as a preoccupation with the avoidance of mistakes" (p. 79). This child-friendly, 12-item self-report scale is in Chinese; it contains six healthy manifestations (e.g., striving to be perfect in what one does well) and six unhealthy manifestations of perfectionism (e.g., missing opportunities because of not tolerating imperfections).

A series of questions probing perfectionism in academically talented students was developed as part of an ongoing longitudinal study (Perrone, Jackson, Wright, Ksiazak, & Perrone, 2007). The four questions were: "I need to achieve perfection"; "I need to do better than most others"; "I need to do as well as most others"; and a reverse scored item, "I don't feel a need to excel in this area." Even though there is a competitive tone to these questions, with no item related to doing one's personal best, the authors found that perfectionism led to positive outcomes.

Research on Perfectionism and Giftedness

Once valid instruments became available, academically talented college students and children in gifted programs were sought as subjects in a number of studies—sometimes just to validate the instruments (e.g., Vandiver & Worrell, 2002). These studies attempted to determine empirically if the gifted are more perfectionistic than the general population, and if this trait is adaptive or maladaptive. The results proved equivocal (Baker, 1996; Chan, 2007; Kline & Short, 1991; Kramer, 1988; LoCicero & Ashby, 2000; Parker & Mills, 1996; Parker & Stumpf, 1995; Perrone, et al., 2007; Roberts & Lovett, 1994; Schuler, 1997; Siegel & Schuler, 2000; Sondergeld, Schultz, & Glover, 2007; Speirs Neumeister, 2004a, 2004b, 2004c; Speirs Neumeister, et al., 2007).

Roberts and Lovett (1994) reported much higher levels of perfectionism among gifted junior high school students than among non-gifted students. Kramer (1988) found greater degrees of perfectionism in gifted than in non-gifted teens, as well as more perfectionistic tendencies in females than males. Baker (1996) found higher levels of perfectionism in exceptionally gifted ninth-grade girls than in girls of average ability. Kline and Short (1991) reported increasing perfectionism in gifted girls as they went from elementary to high school. In LoCicero and Ashby's (2000) study, males of high ability were more perfectionistic than males of average ability. Schuler's (1997) study of 112 gifted adolescents in a rural setting indicated that 87.5% had perfectionistic tendencies; no gender differences were found. In their analysis of gifted sixth, seventh, and eighth graders, Siegle and Schuler (2000) found perfectionistic tendencies across all socioeconomic, racial, and ethnic groups.

However, in a study of 600 gifted sixth graders and a comparison group of 418 sixth graders from the same schools, Parker and Mills (1996) found few differences between the academically talented and the control group. In a second study, Parker (1997) found that 32.8% of his gifted sample were nonperfectionists, and in a third study (Parker, 2000), 38% of the gifted sixth graders were nonperfectionistic. Frost, et al.'s *Multidimensional Perfectionism Scale* (1990) was the measure employed.

How one defines perfectionism plays a critical role in one's findings. In "The Perfectionist's Script for Self-Defeat," Burns (1980) distinguished between "the healthy pursuit of excellence by men and women who take genuine pleasure in striving to meet high standards" and "those whose standards are high beyond reach or reason, people who strain compulsively and unremittingly toward impossible goals and who measure their own worth entirely in terms of productivity and accomplishment" (p. 34). Burns' distinction between perfectionism and striving for excellence has been echoed by other writers (e.g., Adderholdt-Elliott, 1987; Greenspon, 2000; Hendlin, 1992). The definition of perfectionism proposed by Frost, et al. is "the setting of high standards of performance which are accompanied by tendencies for overly critical self-evaluations" (1990, p. 450).

Hamachek (1978) may have been the first to suggest that that there are two varieties of perfectionists: healthy and neurotic. He said that "normal" perfectionists derive pleasure from accomplishing difficult tasks, whereas "neurotic" perfectionists never feel that what they have done is good enough. Building on Hamachek's perspective, several researchers have found healthy aspects of perfectionism in the gifted.

Parker (1997) conducted an investigation of 400 gifted sixth graders with Frost, et al.'s (1990) scale, along with several other measures. Three groups emerged from his study: 32.8% were nonperfectionistic, 41.7% were healthy perfectionists, and 25.5% were "dysfunctional" perfectionists. Parents' and children's perceptions closely matched. His research supported the existence of both normal and neurotic perfectionism. He concluded that "the overriding characteristic of perfectionism in these talented children is conscientiousness, not neurosis" (Parker, 1997, p. 556). Employing a larger sample of 820 gifted sixth graders, and several other instruments for cross-validation of the constructs, Parker (2000) reported that 42% were healthy perfectionists and 27.8% were "dysfunctional."

> *The ACL [Adjective Checklist] descriptors suggested individuals who were organized, dependable, and socially skilled. Their ACL scaled scores indicated students who were conscientious, achievement-oriented, well-adjusted, and socially at ease. It appears that these students could be characterized as healthy perfectionists, whose perfectionistic strivings motivate them to successfully achieve.*
> (pp. 176-177)

Schuler (1997, 2000) studied gifted adolescents in a rural setting. Both "healthy" and "dysfunctional" perfectionists were revealed. The healthy perfectionists had a strong need for order and organization, accepted mistakes, enjoyed the fact that their parents held high expectations for them, had positive ways of coping with their perfectionism, had adults who modeled doing their best, and viewed effort as an important part of their perfectionism. The dysfunctional perfectionists were continuously anxious about making mistakes, held extremely high standards for themselves, perceived that others held excessive expectations for them, internalized negative remarks from others, questioned their own judgments, lacked effective coping strategies, and exhibited a constant need for approval.

Chan (2007), studying 317 Chinese gifted children in Hong Kong from seven to 18 years of age, found that the students tended to endorse positive perfectionism more than negative perfectionism. Positive and negative perfectionism could be differentiated, but Chan did not find support for the validity of self-oriented and other-oriented factors. Positive perfectionism affected life satisfaction and positive affect.

These studies suggest that there is a high correlation between certain aspects of perfectionism and giftedness, and that perfectionism is multifaceted, with both healthy and unhealthy forms (Chan, 2007; Parker, 1997, 2000; Sondergeld, et al., 2007; Speirs Neumeister, 2004a, 2004b, 2004c; Speirs Neumeister, et al., 2007). In interpreting this research base, it must be kept in mind that negatively-tinged instruments color the results.

Dabrowski's Levels as a Template

Dabrowski's theory presents another lens for examining perfectionism in the gifted population. According to Dabrowski (1964, 1972), there are various levels of development, from narcissistic self-absorption to a life of pure service. This is not an age-related theory of development—we don't start out as sociopaths and end up as saints. Individuals tend to be predominantly at one or two levels throughout the lifespan. Perfectionism looks completely different at each level of development.

Level I

At Level I, the individual is only concerned with the self. In the service of egocentrism, perfectionists become tyrannical. They don't see their own imperfections; instead, they focus on the flaws of others. A person at Level I uses other people for self-gratification and self-aggrandizement. For example, a man at this lower level is attracted to a beauty queen so that he can show her off—"Look what I've got!" If anything mars her beauty, he is likely to humiliate her. A mother at this level of development expects her children to achieve in school, behave well in public, get accepted at an Ivy League university, and become a doctor or lawyer—to reflect well on her. The needs of the other person are never taken into account. The motto at Level I might be, "I'm perfect, but you're not."

In Hewitt and Flett's (1991a) *Multidimensional Perfectionism Scale*, this has been labeled, "other-oriented perfectionism." Other-oriented perfectionists set up unrealistic standards for others and focus on their flaws; this is accompanied by blame, lack of trust, and feelings of hostility toward others (Hewitt & Flett, 1991b). Parents with other-oriented perfectionism are likely to cause debilitating perfectionism in gifted children (Schuler, 2000; Speirs Neumeister, 2004a). These parents expect nothing less than A grades. When their children do not meet their expectations, the parents punish their children emotionally through disapproval or guilt, remove privileges, or even punish them physically. This type of parenting is a recipe for dysfunctional perfectionism in children.

Level II

The field of psychology generally views perfectionism as a "pervasive neurotic style" (Hewitt & Flett, 1991b, p. 456). Most of the neurotic forms of perfectionism are born in Level II. At Level II, individuals are at the mercy of the social group. They continuously ask themselves, "What will people think of me if I…?" They experience insecurity and feelings of inferiority toward others; they judge themselves as lacking in comparison with others. Polarized—"all or none"—thinking comes into play at this level: "Either I am perfect or I am worthless."

Writers who perceive perfectionism as a negative trait (e.g., Greenspon, 2000; Hendlin, 1992; Hewitt & Flett, 1991b; Pacht, 1984) focus primarily on the expressions of perfectionism at Level II. Greenspon (2000) describes perfectionism as a psychic wound, which is never healthy. The person needs to excel in order to bolster flagging self-esteem. For Hendlin (1992), perfectionism is a trap whose chief sign is obsession. Adderholdt-Elliott (1987) wrote *Perfectionism: What's Bad about Being too Good*, a book for students. Here is the description of the perfectionist from her revised, updated edition:

> *Perfectionists…live in a constant state of anxiety about making errors. They have extremely high standards and perceive excessive expectations and negative criticisms from others, including their parents. Sometimes those external pressures are real, sometimes they come from within. Perfectionists question their own judgments, lack effective coping strategies, and feel a constant need for approval. They fear being exposed as frauds or imposters. Many avoid the healthy risks that will help them grow, procrastinating, or refusing outright to try new experiences for fear of failure.* (Adderholdt-Elliot & Goldberg, 1999, p. 4)

155

Hewitt and Flett's (1991a; 1991b) "self-oriented" and "socially pre-scribed" types of perfectionism fit those at Level II.

Self-oriented perfectionism is an intrapersonal dimension charac-terized by a strong motivation to be perfect, setting and striving for unrealistic self-standards, focusing on flaws, and generaliza-tion of self-standards.... [S]ocially prescribed perfectionism entails the belief that others have perfectionistic expectations and motives for oneself. (Hewitt & Flett, 1991a, p. 98)

These two constructs overlap (intercorrelations range between .25 and .40) (Hewitt & Flett, 1991b). The socially prescribed perfectionist tries to live up to others' expectations or beliefs about others' expectations. The self-oriented perfectionist has internalized those values and imposes them on the self. The standards toward which self-oriented perfectionists strive are often introjected from family, friends, media, religious groups, etc. These individuals fight an inner demon who derides all of their attempts. The demon can never be satisfied. The focus of their attention is their own imperfections—they magnify their flaws and overlook their strengths, thereby providing a distorted mirror of their own existence. Self-deprecation is a debilitating form of perfectionism. At Level II, the motto is, "I'm not good enough. I'll never be good enough."

Newer research with gifted students suggests that not all self-oriented perfectionists are self-defeating (Speirs Neumeister, 2004a, 2004b, 2004c). While the construct originated with the study of individuals in psychiatric hospitals, it has taken a new twist. Speirs Neumeister (2004a, 2004b, 2004c) conducted in-depth interviews with 12 college honors students who had previously been in gifted programs. Six scored high on self-ori-ented perfectionism but low on socially prescribed perfectionism, and six had the reverse pattern. The self-oriented perfectionists had much healthier attitudes than the socially oriented perfectionists. They had high intrinsic motivation, set high standards for themselves, had a strong work ethic, and tried to do their best, but they were not overly concerned about grades or fears of failure (Speirs Neumeister, 2004c).

Level III

Healthier forms of perfectionism emerge at higher levels of develop-ment. At Level III, "multilevel development," the individual becomes a seeker of self-perfection. Instead of feeling inferior to others or feeling inad-equate to meet the expectations of others, the person becomes aware of his or her potential to be fully human and feels inferior to that potentiality. Gaining a glimpse of the possibilities in oneself for integrity, empathy, wisdom, and harmony is a powerful incentive for growth. The longing to become one's best self propels the individual to search out the blind spots, see the naked truth about oneself, and transform one's pettiness and lower-level instincts. The road to becoming one's highest self is an arduous journey that requires support and encouragement for undertaking this challenge.

Imagine, if you will, two layers of reality. Within the layer that most of us understand, there are persecutors, victims, and rescuers. There are winners and losers. Life is high drama. At a more evolved layer of reality, there are no polarities; there is only oneness. Within the human psyche, there are pulls from both of these realities. At Levels I and II, the pull from the lower reality is very strong, and there is little, if any, awareness that a higher reality is possible. At Levels IV and V, the pull from the higher reality is very powerful and actively directs the personality. At Level III, the individual becomes aware of the higher, but in the beginning is still caught in the lower. A struggle begins to climb out of habitual ways of being in the world. It is quite painful to know that there is a higher reality, while at the same time feeling incapable of reaching it. As a result, the individual at Level III lives with a vertical tension between "what is" and "what ought to be" in oneself. The motto of Level III could be initially, "I see who I want to be, but I see no way of getting there from here."

The dynamisms at Level III make clear that this is not a comfortable experience:

- Hierarchization (critical perception and evaluation of one's values)
- Dissatisfaction with oneself (frustration and anger with what is)
- Inferiority toward oneself (frustration at one's inadequacies)
- Disquietude with oneself (agitation and anxiety with what is)
- Astonishment with oneself (surprise and shock in regard to what is)
- Shame (embarrassment over one's deficiencies)
- Guilt (anguish over moral failure)
- Positive maladjustment (antagonism against social opinion and protest against violation of intrinsic ethical principles) (Dabrowski, 1977, p. 44)

Though uncomfortable for the person, these inner forces express different ways of evaluating one's personality and reflecting on one's character. They catalyze the work of inner transformation. Despite significant ups and downs at Level III, there is an upward trend, as higher-level reality exercises a stronger influence on the personality than lower-level reality.

A person who is experiencing these intense feelings can be easily misunderstood by a therapist whose concept of perfectionism is limited to the manifestations at Level II. It would take a therapist who has traveled the path of multilevel development to appreciate the importance of this internal journey of personal transformation.

Level IV

At Level IV, the individual has transformed much of the inner polarity and is able to commit to living a life permeated by high ideals. One gains greater capacity for self-reflection, for acceptance of others and of self. There is more self-regulation. Instead of being controlled by baser desires, such as possessiveness or trying to control others, one is able to easily access compassion and understanding of the plight of others. One's perspective is informed by a clearer vision of the meaning of life experiences. Perfectionism at this level is wholeness and the appreciation of the inherent perfection in all of life. The motto at Level IV is, "What ought to be will be, and I will make it so."

Level V

Level V is the perfection of the personality. It is life without inner conflict. It is a life directed by the highest guiding principles. At this amazing level of human development, the individual becomes a wise teacher, guide, and exemplar for others. Here, one achieves autonomy from the lower layer of reality fraught with confusion and violence. Life is lived in service to all of humanity, not in service of the ego. The motto for this highest level could be, "All is love." This is the transcendent potential for humanity—the greatest gift of Dabrowski's theory.

Healthy Perfectionism

While some continue to believe that healthy perfectionism is an oxymoron because of their definition of the term (e.g., Greenspon, 2000), it is important to recognize that for the gifted, "impossible dreams" may be within reach. Idealism should not be squelched. Setting high standards is a positive aspect of perfectionism, especially when it is coupled with the belief that one is capable of attaining those standards. Without the perfectionistic drive, there would be no Nobel prizes, no Olympic champions, no great art, no ballets, no opera singers, no scientists obsessed with finding a cure to cancer.

I believe that we hold a double standard when it comes to perfectionism. Few of us would buy a musical recording in which a few notes were missed. We expect perfection. The opening ceremony of the Summer Olympics in Beijing in 2008 was a celebration of the breathtaking perfectionism of the culture. Frankly, I want my surgeon to be a perfectionist who will put everything back exactly where it belongs—with no parts left over. If perfection is of such value in these arenas, perhaps we need to rethink our devaluing of it in children.

We have mixed emotions about how hard one should work to strive for excellence, and we give gifted children mixed messages. On the one hand, we exhort them to "do your best," and when they take us seriously, we tell them that they're too perfectionistic. To become good enough to be on the concert stage, one has to eschew all other distractions and focus all of one's free time on practice, practice, practice. If that is a young person's goal, what right do we have to impose our values of "well-roundedness" on him or her? We admire the fruits of the labors of those who are driven by their desire to achieve perfection, but we cannot cope with the personality trait that leads to those achievements. Since perfectionism shows up so often in the gifted, isn't it possible that it is a necessary and appropriate part of the gifted personality? You can neither create nor cure perfectionism. It appears to be natural.

> *When asked to describe how their perfectionism developed, the group of participants scoring high on self-oriented perfectionism found the question difficult to answer, for they could never remember a time in their lives when they were not perfectionistic. For that reason, they were quick to note that it seemed to be a tendency they had had since birth, an inborn characteristic.* (Speirs Neumeister, 2004a)

If the trait is not curable, then it is important to learn to channel this energy effectively so that it does not paralyze.

Channeling Perfectionism

For Counselors

Maslow (1971) equated the full realization of one's potential with the struggle for perfection of one's talents and capabilities. Maslow's description of the process of self-actualization sounds remarkably like Csikszentmihalyi's (1990) flow:

Self-actualization means experiencing fully, vividly, selflessly, with full concentration and total absorption. It means experiencing without the self-consciousness of the adolescent. At this moment of experiencing, the person is wholly and fully human. This is a self-actualizing moment. This is a moment when the self is actu- alizing itself. As individuals, we all experience such moments occasionally. As counselors, we can help clients to experience them more often. We can encourage them to become totally absorbed in something and to forget their poses and their defenses and their shyness—to go at it "whole-hog." (Maslow, 1971, p. 45)

Maslow invites counselors to encourage what others might discour- age: perfectionistic zeal. Robinson (1996) also regards perfectionism in the gifted as a potentially healthy trait, and she exhorts counselors to support what she calls "positive perfectionism":

Some therapists would label as neurotic those characteristics that are quite typical of bright youngsters. Indeed, therapists are trained to look for psychopathy rather than health in people who are "dif- ferent." ...Counselors, in particular, tend to see perfectionism as a neurotic trait. Although, in general, high degrees of perfectionism may be associated with lower degrees of self-confidence...support- ive adults can enable students to practice "positive perfectionism" (i.e., setting high standards for oneself, working to meet those standards, and taking joy in their attainment). (pp. 133-134)

Based on their study of perfectionism, Perrone, et al. (2007) came to a similar conclusion:

The findings of this study lend support to the idea that perfection- ism can lead to positive outcomes, such as achievement of one's potential in education and other life roles. Thus, counselors may not want to completely discourage clients from displaying per- fectionistic tendencies. Rather, counselors should assist clients in channeling these tendencies toward specific goals.... (p. 120)

For Teachers

It is important to give gifted children challenging enough work so that they have the opportunity to struggle to learn. It is a disservice to a gifted student to get an A without applying any effort. Schoolwork has to be sufficiently differentiated so that advanced students earn their grades. When they sail through school getting A's without trying, they are unprepared to deal with the challenges that they will face later. If classwork is too easy, some students will complicate it to create their own challenge. This feeds perfectionism.

Adelson (2007) created an excellent table of actions to encourage healthy perfectionism in the classroom. Like Dweck (2006), she recommends praising students for effort rather than achievement. A safe environment is essential for risk-taking; students are applauded for trying something new. Projects are turned in at various stages, starting with "sloppy copies," in which no erasures are allowed, and working on multiple revisions to help students take pride in the process rather than the product. Adelson has them critique their work and write "WIMIs,"—"Why I Missed It"—to assist her students in focusing on what they are learning from their mistakes instead of on grades.

For Parents

Traditionally, perfectionism has been blamed on the child's parents. Burns (1980) felt that perfectionism is learned from perfectionistic parents whose self-esteem is contingent upon their children's success. However, counselors and researchers generally have not found the parents of gifted children to be at fault.

> *Although the commonsense notion of the causes of perfectionism tends to lay the blame for the perfectionistic child squarely on "pushy," exacting parents, clinical experience shows this conclusion to be unwarranted. Many perfectionistic gifted children are the products of relaxed, easy-going parents with realistic expectations.... It seems possible that certain children are simply born with the combination of temperaments that create a need for an orderly environment, or conversely, an aversion to chaos.* (Kerr, 1991, p. 141)

Parker and Stumpf (1995) found no evidence that parents play a major role in the development of their gifted children's perfectionism. Employing Frost, et al.'s *Multidimensional Perfectionism Scale* (MPS) (1990), parental expectations accounted for less than 4% of the variance of their children's scores. In Schuler's (2000) study, healthy perfectionists perceived themselves as more perfectionistic than their parents, and dysfunctional perfectionists perceived their parents as more perfectionistic. This finding was replicated by Speirs Neumeister (2004a), using Hewitt and Flett's MPS (1991a). Gifted college students with socially prescribed perfectionism whose self-worth was tied to their achievement usually had perfectionistic parents with authoritarian parenting styles. However, healthy, self-oriented perfectionists had parents who did not expect perfection in their children. They gave their children unconditional love and support.

For You

○ *Appreciate the trait.* Understand that it serves a useful purpose. Ideals and high standards are good, even if it hurts when you can't always reach them.

○ *Reframe "mistakes" as learning experiences.* Perceive each outcome that was different from anticipated as a stepping stone to future accomplishments. Successful individuals do not expect instant successes. They see each "failure" as valuable information—a narrowing of possibilities leading them closer to success. One father said to his children, "Anything worth doing is worth doing wrong, because it is only by doing it wrong that you can learn to do it right."

○ *Set priorities for yourself.* Allow yourself to be perfectionistic in activities that really matter to you, rather than in everything all at once. No one can be perfect in everything; we all have to make difficult choices about what to strive for and where to settle for less than our best.

○ *Start a project instead of procrastinating.* Starting a task is usually harder than completing it. Perfectionism can work for you once you begin something that needs to be done. After you start a project, you attract ideas and resources as the concept percolates—even in your sleep. Putting it off delays the activation of your creative juices. While you might be relying on the adrenaline rush that occurs when you are racing to meet a deadline, the same adrenaline can also cause panic and paralysis. Furthermore, too much reliance on adrenaline can damage your adrenals. Move your start time further from your deadline, and you will be surprised at how much better you feel about the outcome of your efforts.

○ *Maintain high standards for yourself, but don't impose them on others, lest you become a tyrant.* It is fine to hold high standards for yourself but unfair to expect others to conform to them.

○ *Keep striving, even when your first attempts are unsuccessful.* Don't give up! With practice, you will come closer and closer to your goals. Read biographies of famous people who felt intensely frustrated in their efforts and overcame their obstacles through persistence.

○ *Don't punish yourself for failing.* Focus your energies on future successes. Try to be a model of self-acceptance, of willingness to look foolish and to admit to being wrong. Perfectionism facing backward leads to self-deprecation: "I should have known better." Perfectionism facing forward leads to improvement: "Next time, I'll do it differently."

○ *Hold on to your ideals, and believe in your ability to reach them.* Believe in your dreams. Support children in following their dreams.

○ *Recognize that there are good aspects and bad aspects to perfectionism.* You have choices about how you use your perfectionism. You can let it paralyze you with fear of failure, or you can use it to mobilize yourself toward unparalleled excellence. This drive can help you create a better world.

○ *There is pain in perfectionism.* Fear of that pain can inhibit you from trying anything, or you can deal with it courageously. Nothing is ever as bad as it appears. Teach children through your example that they can cope with this pain. It is a *good* pain. Help them realize that they are good problem solvers, hard workers, and emotionally strong. They may not be able to avoid the pain, but they can surmount it.

Conclusion

Just like the saga of the petunias and the chipmunks, the focus of one's perfectionism needs to be on appreciation of what is perfect instead of on imperfection. Perfectionism applied to oneself may lead to higher accomplishment, whereas perfectionism applied to others leads to unfair expectations, disappointment, and resentfulness. Perfectionism that translates into trying again and again leads to success, whereas perfectionism that results in paralysis, avoidance, anxiety attacks, and withdrawal guarantees failure.

Perfectionism facing forward leads to striving to create a better life, while perfectionism facing backward leads to self-flagellation, overconcern with one's mistakes, and wallowing in self-pity. The key is learning how to set priorities. Instead of obliterating perfectionistic tendencies, I encourage gifted students to channel their perfectionism into what they care about the most.

It takes great personal courage to live in that gap between "what is" and "what ought to be" and try to close it. The desire for self-perfection is painful, and not everyone is willing to experience that pain. This is what separates the person of high moral commitment in adult life from the apathetic person who is adapted to the limitations that currently exist in oneself and the world. As educators, parents, and counselors, our role is not to protect the gifted from their pain, but to reassure them that they have enough inner strength to use that pain in the service of their development.

Part Three

Still Gifted After All These Years—
Lifespan Intensity and Gifted Adults

Chapter 10

Advantages and Challenges of Lifespan Intensity

Ellen D. Fiedler, Ph.D.

"You have so much energy!" "I can't believe how much you do!"
"Don't you ever slow down?"

"Why are you always asking 'why'?" "Why do you always read
so much into everything everyone says?" "Can't you just sit back and
accept things as they are?" "You're analyzing this to death!"

"What's the story with your going on and on about flavors
and textures and sights and sounds and smells?" "I don't see what
the big deal is." "I can't understand why you have to have the tags
cut out of all of your clothes."

"You're always looking for other solutions to every problem
and other ways of doing things." "Why can't you just settle on one
good answer and get on with it?" "Why can't you accept that the
first one you think of may well be 'good enough'?"

"You're too sensitive!" "Why do you let all those things bother
you?" "Why do you always take everything to heart?" "I thought you
were going to outgrow this business of being so sensitive."

These and dozens of other comments and questions plague the lives of gifted adults, who have been criticized for their intensity and sensitivity throughout their lives, never quite understanding why others don't understand who they are, how they think, and how they feel. And yet those whose intensity permeates their very being actually do live life to a degree that regularly rewards them with peak experiences, great satisfaction, and joy. The up side of feeling all feelings to the "nth degree" is that the natural highs are higher, are more blissful, and are felt far more fully than those that others experience. The down side is that the lows are also more intense. Of course, there are both advantages and challenges to a lifetime filled with intensity.

Here is the paradox of lifespan intensity—"experiencing in a higher key" because of one's overexcitabilities, as Dabrowski called them (Piechowski, 2002). From childhood on, many gifted adults have spent all of their years living life to the hilt. One gifted adult described it as "living three lives in one." Many of these individuals immerse themselves fully in whatever they are doing— whether it be their work, their hobbies/avocations, or their relationships with friends, family, or even acquaintances. They tend to be fully present in the moment (sometimes oblivious to time and its constraints) and to imbue each encounter with relevance and meaning. Superficiality is unfamiliar territory for them, and they tend to go into far further depth in whatever they do or feel than others, thereby seeking and frequently finding great fulfillment even in everyday events—a sunrise, a chance encounter on a bus, a message from a friend, the laughter of children.

Others, however, "live lives of quiet desperation" (Thoreau, 1854/2004, p. 7). They find themselves concealing who they are—knowing how different they are from others—marking time, and waiting for a time when they can be themselves in surroundings where they can feel psychologically safe.

The Chameleon
by Ellen Dove Fiedler

> *Sometimes you see me; then you don't.*
> *I know the tricks for blending in.*
> *My color's bright,*
> *A glowing hue,*
> *Changing with your point of view.*
>
> *My awareness, truly keen,*
> *Makes me be sure*
> *I'm seldom seen*
> *Unless, unless it's safe for me—*
> *Safe to be all I can be.*

In surroundings where no threat
Causes me to fade and hide,
Filled with doubts
And deep despair,
Not quite belonging, anywhere.

If you will see me as I am
Then I can let you come inside,
Into a place
Where you can find
The treasures of my hidden mind.

I'll share my secret world with you,
Tell you my dreams,
My thoughts, my plans.
And then, at last,
Perhaps I can
Know who it is I really am.

Most gifted adults have repeatedly felt misunderstood by others. Furthermore, they have often found themselves on a lifelong quest to understand themselves, while longing to find kindred spirits with whom they might share life's journey in meaningful ways. Some gifted individuals seem to sail through life on untroubled waters, fully enjoying the opportunities available to them, while others battle inner storms and strong seas that seem to batter them from all sides (Fiedler, 1999).

The multifaceted aspects of intensity (psychomotor, intellectual, sensual, imaginational, and emotional), as described by Dabrowski's theory of positive disintegration (Piechowski, 1997), manifest themselves throughout an individual's lifespan. But the advantages and challenges of intensity have a paradoxical nature that can be viewed through several additional lenses, such as Erikson's theory of psychosocial development (Harder, 2002), Streznewski's (1999) exploration of the lives of gifted grownups, Sheehy's (1995, 2006) views regarding the cycles (and crises) of adult life, and Jacobsen's (1999) concept of everyday geniuses.

Erikson, Streznewski, Sheehy, and Jacobsen

Erikson's theory provides many insights for understanding childhood and adolescence (Harder, 2002). Streznewski (1999) learned from her interviews with gifted grownups about the mixed blessings of extraordinary potential at each of these life stages. Sheehy's (1995, 2006) work helps us understand some of the predictable cycles of adult life. Jacobsen (1999) provides descriptions of gifted adults who may be totally oblivious to their core identity—"lost within the fabric of a society that seems to have issued an edict against knowing oneself, being oneself, and expressing oneself in full" (p. 38). By considering the confluence of these perspectives, we can gain a clearer picture of the advantages and challenges of intensity across the lifespan of gifted adults.

Young Adulthood: Approximately Ages 18 to 35

The hallmark of this stage is characterized by Erikson as the psychosocial crisis of "intimacy versus isolation." At this point in life, most young adults are seeking companions and life partners, trying to find mutually satisfying relationships through friends and love relationships. This is when they are typically making their first decisions about meaningful friendships, living together, and/or marriage (Harder, 2002).

For many gifted adults, the search for kindred spirits often begins in earnest in young adulthood, and their friendships and love relationships may have an almost explosive quality. Successfully finding others with whom they can truly connect allows gifted adults to savor the joys of true intimacy—joys that they will experience with their characteristic intensity.

However, therein lies the challenge. Jacobsen (1999) indicated that "The chief complaint directed toward the gifted is that they think, do, say, imagine, or emote 'too much.' They are simply 'too-too' in comparison to the norm" (p. 126). Since only about 5% of the population is thought to include gifted individuals, kindred spirits may be few and hard to find. Furthermore, when the myriad differences within the gifted population are taken into consideration, the probability of gifted individuals finding each other diminishes even further. For example, someone who is passionate about history and spends every spare moment learning all he can about it may have little in common with others who don't share his passion, and they quickly lose interest in hearing every detail and nuance of whatever historical information this person is currently devouring, contemplating, and yearning to share. Gifted adults may have to search far and wide to find others who share their sometimes esoteric interests or even to find someone who laughs at their sometimes quirky jokes. This challenge follows young gifted adults into the workplace, where the entry-level positions that they find themselves in can result in their being lost in the crowd, unable to find others with whom they otherwise might feel a genuine sense of connectedness.

If connections that lead to intimacy are not successful, or when attempts to form close relationships explode in their faces, isolation is typically the result, with some gifted young adults distancing themselves from others, more convinced than ever that they are aliens from another planet and that there is no one here on earth with whom they can relate. They may meet this challenge by simply deciding to be "happy loners," basking in their solitude, or they may become cynical and scornful of others, defensive and bristling with every encounter that seems to validate the ways in which they see themselves as far too different from everyone else to bother relating to them.

> *Both the speed and complexity of a gifted person's thought process can make for barriers to communication and connection. Those barriers can be created by other people who don't understand, or they can be created by the gifted person, deliberately. Some people screen out the pain of rejection; some simply prefer their own company. Some people find it very difficult to explain their difference to anyone, and...they settle for isolation.* (Streznewski, 1999, p. 191)

The issue of identity formation is also related to intensity at this stage of life. As Sheehy (2006) noted, "Most theorists agree that more than anything else, it is successful work experience that helps a young person resolve the conflicts of dependency and establish an independent identity" (p. 91). However, if this is true for the general population, what might this mean for gifted young adults, whose intensity raises questions for them regarding their identity and creates unique issues for them regarding their career paths? Their intensity may be simultaneously a catalyst for either intimacy or isolation. For instance, if a gifted individual feels that she is a "minority of one" in the workplace, her feelings of frustration are likely to be intensified; she may experience an identity crisis, with isolation as a logical consequence. However, if she finds at least one other person who thinks and feels as she does, she can rest easy in terms of her own identity and move ahead in resolving conflicts between intimacy and isolation.

Streznewski's (1999) research suggests that gifted young adults need challenges and newness, opportunities to share their ideas and explore new avenues in their work, and to be able to create their own work environments in order to make all of this possible. Finding themselves in circumstances in which their needs for day-to-day stimulation are either met, or not, can be either highly fulfilling, or it can be exceptionally frustrating for the young gifted adult.

Aron (1998) suggested that this time of life is all about individuals being able to hear their own inner voice through all of the noise of the outer world and to find a way to pursue vocations that feel right to them, that call to them, and that help them discover and answer the questions that they sense they were put on earth to answer. However, in the midst of the struggle to make their way in the world—to make a life for themselves, as well as to make a living—gifted young adults may find this a daunting task.

Intellectual and imaginational intensity are particularly triggered under these circumstances. Furthermore, emotional intensity only serves to heighten a young gifted adult's responses to either the best (or the worst) of all possible situations. One phenomenon that has been emerging in the 21st century stems from the number of young gifted adults who attempt to meet their needs for challenge and newness through multi-tasking. For instance, a dynamic young woman in her late 20s with a very interesting and highly absorbing full-time job in the film industry is also partnering with a friend in a start-up company producing and marketing a new beverage product; simultaneously, she has completed the manuscript for her first novel and has an active and busy life with her equally-gifted husband (personal communication, R. Donnelly, September 13, 2007).

Sheehy (2006) described a significant portion of young adulthood as the "Trying Twenties." She suggested that this is a time when individuals are concentrating on what they feel they are "*supposed* to do" (p. 119)—i.e., according to societal norms and expectations. However, for gifted adults with high levels of intellectual and imaginational intensity, this may be further complicated in several ways. First, they are aware of all of the possibilities available to them (akin to what Toffler, 1984, called "overchoice"); second, they are concerned about what they *should* be doing in terms of using their gifts and talents productively for the betterment of society; and third, they desire to find one or more others with whom they can relate. As a result, these individuals wend their way through what seems to be a jungle of options, each with its own potential consequences.

Even with all of the challenges, many young gifted adults do make their way successfully. For instance, Noble, Robinson, and Gunderson (1993) studied young gifted adults who were radically accelerated in school. Of the individuals in their study, they found that:

Most describe themselves as relatively happy, emotionally stable, and creative, with feelings of self-worth, self-esteem, and self-efficacy, and a sense of satisfaction with their lives. Most believe strongly in the value of education, want to be successful in work which has meaning for them, and have leisure time to explore their interests; the majority also wish to find life partners and enjoy strong friendships. (p. 4)

However, these positive outcomes seem to be most applicable to young gifted adults who were offered appropriate educational interventions and who were fortunate to have the adults around them respond effectively to their intellectual intensity. For others, including those who have high levels of emotional, imaginational, sensual, and/or psychomotor intensity, it may be quite a different story. Intensity continues to have its advantages and disadvantages as adults move into their middle years.

Middle Adulthood: Approximately Ages 35 to 55 or 65

According to Erikson's theory, the middle years of adult life are a time of "generativity versus stagnation." At this phase of life, satisfaction is found through meaningful work and family involvements—both of which are venues that offer opportunities to implement and transmit our personal values and perpetuate our culture (Harder, 2002).

The concept of "generativity" was coined by Erikson and is all about passing along what we deem important for future generations—leaving the world a better place than it was when we came into it. During middle adulthood, people typically find themselves absorbed with various activities related to what might be considered their "legacy"—whether that be in the guidance they provide for their own children, in improving aspects of their profession through their work, or in volunteering to make a difference through involvement in community organizations. The focus of this phase of life is on the "big picture." Middle-aged adults are likely to take a long-range perspective—to consider societal goals, as well as their own goals in life, and how they might improve the world in whatever ways they think might be possible.

At this stage, middle-aged adults often fear inactivity and meaninglessness. There is an urgency to accomplish something worthwhile or, at the very least, to live life as fully as possible during the years that remain. Harder (2002) pointed out, "As our children leave home, or our relationships or goals change, we may be faced with major life changes—the mid-life crisis—and struggle with finding new meanings and purposes. If we don't get through this stage successfully, we can become self-absorbed and stagnate" (p. 1).

For gifted adults, the specific implications of generativity versus stagnation are two-fold. First, because of their intensity, they experience everything that others do during this phase of their lives, but at much deeper and more multifaceted levels. Therefore, they feel far greater internal pressure to change things for the better, whether that be in their own personal lives or in having a meaningful and positive impact on the world they live in—the world that today's children will inherit. Second, gifted adults typically move toward generativity at much earlier ages than the general population, and throughout the remainder of their lifespan, they show concern for promoting the well-being of future generations. A long-term pursuit of generativity can lead to a deep sense of satisfaction for these gifted adults, many of whom find their niche and can see progress from their efforts to make a difference in their world. However, as Jacobsen (1999) noted, "Although gifted adults are smart and creative, to discover and fulfill one's life mission is a painstaking task that may take many years to complete" (p. 134).

The down side of this stage of life for adults in the general population is stagnation. However, gifted adults, whose standards are typically very high, are more subject to depression than stagnation. Because their progress toward improvement and impact on the world may be far slower than what they believe should be possible, they can become desperately discouraged, mired in the morass of minutiae, wondering if anyone else will ever share their vision.

Poignantly describing the plight of gifted middle-aged adults in the workplace, Streznewski (1999) asserted that:

> *Successful institutions, both public and private, need to learn to tolerate, even encourage, the messy genius, the crabby, cranky fanatic.... The gifted among us have, more than anyone else, two qualities...their sophisticated thought processes allow them to grasp all the elements of a complex big picture, and they actually thrive on continual innovation and change.* (p. 159)

These very qualities give gifted adults an advantage when it comes to being able to continue their progress toward implementing a vision of a better future; however, these qualities are not always appreciated, nor are they supported by others who don't share their vision. Jacobsen (1999) described this as "a bittersweet experience" (p. 135), indicating that gifted adults have been preprogrammed by a world that stereotypes them—a world that no longer admires and appreciates the very qualities that were once celebrated. The result, she suggested, is that gifted adults are ill-equipped to deal with the challenges that they face; they are mired in misinformation and bereft of adequate resources to handle the reactions of those they might benefit with their vision and intuition.

Problems exist for gifted men and women alike, each in their own way. Consider these insights offered by Sheehy (2006):

> *Inside the tough-talking, hard-jogging man of 40 who is identi-fied largely by his work, there is a boy trying not to cry, "Time's running out!" A boy who often wants to say, "Hey, I'm sorry about some of the things I have to do, like kowtowing to the brass and backstabbing the young talent, like pushing memos around my desk and superfluous products into the world when I'd rather be somebody's best friend (my kids', for instance) or add just one iota of real value to the world."* (p. 167)
>
> *Inside the educated 35-year-old married woman is a young girl who remembers what it was like to win at word games or get the highest mark in the class, to control a spirited horse, or to do twenty piqué turns around the stage with her blisters raw and pounding into the bluntness of her toe shoes but it didn't matter because everyone applauded. A girl who used to have confidence and dreams and write in her diary....* (p. 166)

That young girl may have grown into her mid-30s trying to be Superwoman at home, as well as at work and in her community, while ago-nizing over her perceived failures to reach the heights she once envisioned in any of those places. The all-too-often-true clichés about the male mid-life crisis suggest that the 40-something man might quit his job, change his appearance, buy a sports car, run off with a new love, and/or join some radi-cal group—only to find that none of this satisfies the yearning in his soul.

The sense of urgency for both men and women in their middle years is very real and is exacerbated by intensity in those who are gifted. The pull of generativity becomes stronger and stronger, marked by the desire to do some-thing (anything!) worthwhile. For some gifted adults, this leads them on to new and more relevant career paths—often, second or third careers that are dramatically different from those they pursued during young adulthood. For others, it leads them toward meaningful personal renewal—educationally, spiritually, or in their relationships with friends and family. Some seek rewarding avocations that may, as time goes on, turn into vocations.

Sheehy (1995) described "the mortality crisis" during this phase of life as follows:

> *Living on the edge. That is how precarious it often feels when we come to the top of the mountain, or what seems like the top, and are startled to find ourselves looking over the edge. The view is panoramic, breath-taking. But what about the trip down? Ordinarily, a sequence of moments shifts the boundaries of our private universe gradually from the concrete concerns of young adulthood to something larger, startling, mysterious.* (p. 159)

For gifted adults, this may be an experience with the level of emotional development that Dabrowski described as "spontaneous multilevel disintegration" (Piechowski, 1997)—something that these adults may have experienced before and wonder why they are going through again. Or the catalyst for the boundaries of their universe shifting may be a dramatic event (e.g., a health challenge, a fire or serious accident, the loss of a job, or the loss of someone important to them). Regardless, the effect on gifted adults who are in their middle years is to make them stop short and take stock of their lives, asking those deep and penetrating questions about the meaning of life and about what they are meant to do (and are able to do) in the years that they have left.

Late Adulthood: Approximately Ages 55 or 65 to Death

According to Harder (2002), "Erikson felt that much of life is preparing for the middle adulthood stage, and the last stage is recovering from it" (p. 1). This stage, described as being characterized by "integrity versus despair," is supposedly one in which older adults reflect on their lives either with happiness and contentment (integrity) or focus on perceptions of failure and wonder whether it was all worth it (despair). However, the popular image of Granny in her rocking chair with her knitting and Gramps beside her with his pipe and slippers as they quietly muse about the lives they've lived simply doesn't gibe with what most gifted adults are like in their later years, especially in today's world. More likely, we'll find them running a home-based business, taking art classes, going back to school (for fun or for another degree), volunteering with a favorite organization, active in politics, and traveling to places they've always wanted to go.

As Streznewski (1999) pointed out, "The high-powered brain/mind that drives a gifted person's life does not switch to low gear simply because the body ages or some chronological milestone has been reached. The persistence of curiosity, the need for stimulation, and the drive to *do* things does not fade" (p. 236). Erikson's theory no longer seems to ring quite true for gifted adults in their later years.

Sheehy's comments bridge the gap between the standard interpretation of Erikson's theory and what we know about gifted adults and their intensity. In discussing Erikson's views on what life is like for people who are in their sixties, Sheehy (1995) said:

> *I think of integrity as the work of integration. One of the overarching desires often articulated by men and women I have interviewed in late middle age is for balance—being able to bring all the parts of one's life into harmony, as opposed to incongruity. The need becomes pressing for an emotional integration of all the different roles and the serial identities that have served us through adolescence and middlescence. It is time for coalescence. What is the essence of ourselves that we want to leave behind?* (p. 355)

This sounds much more like *generativity* than *integrity versus despair* and suggests the ways in which the intensity of older gifted adults generally is manifested.

Just as gifted children and youth do not "outgrow" their intensity, neither do adults, even into the latter years of their lives. "Rather than labeling intensity as excessive, expanded sensitivities might better be defined as a major component of artful living" (Jacobsen, 1999, p. 157). Physiological changes may affect the outward signs of some areas of intensity (psychomotor manifestations, in particular). It's not as easy to play basketball, run a 5K, or hike a steep trail as it used to be; night vision, coordination, and reaction time for driving a car become less sharp. However, the minds, emotions, and imaginations of gifted individuals in late adulthood typically remain highly active. As Sheehy (1995) noted, "All of the common denominators among 'sharp-as-a-tack' subjects tested in older age groups are by-products of a lifelong investment in mental challenge. They have above-average educations, they enjoy complex and stimulating lifestyles, and they are married to smart spouses" (p. 353). Sensual intensity may even increase during these years, especially with regard to sensitivity to touch, textures, and smells.

Many gifted individuals in late adulthood continue to seek, find, and create challenges for themselves and try to find kindred spirits. Others continue to work tirelessly, using their gifts and talents in meaningful ways toward their goals of making the world a better place. Many are lifelong learners and seekers of truth. Their lives tend to be an extension of the experiences of earlier phases, rather than a conclusion or final chapter. They desire to be active and involved as long as possible. They volunteer in schools and other organizations, join book clubs and take classes, sing in a community choir, keep up with politics and the news, and stay involved with extended family and their community. Many continue working or start second or third careers, working full or part time. Those in good health, working in their own businesses or their own endeavors (e.g., writing a novel), often work 60 hours or more per week. This is not old age as we once thought of it.

One of the notable advantages of intensity at this stage is being much more at peace with one's identity, including that of being a gifted individual with all that it implies. One gifted adult described those who are like this as being comfortable in their own skin. By this point in their lives, gifted adults have typically come to a far greater appreciation for who they are and can be more accepting of the fact that only *some* of the other people who they encounter will be like them. They typically have developed reasonably effective coping skills for dealing with their own intensity and with others' bafflement about how they differ from them. They generally continue to seek and find opportunities that connect them with others who share their interests, their passions, their characteristics, and perhaps even their self-appointed missions to change the world.

Some of the disadvantages of being an intense older adult are an extension of the issues that arose during the earlier stages of life, especially in terms of dealing with other people's lack of understanding. Sometimes these issues become more problematical again in late adulthood because of societal expectations that "senior citizens" will slow down and "just enjoy their golden years"—an image that simply is out of sync with the very nature of intense gifted adults in their later years.

Because of the ageism that is so rampant in our culture (Pipher, 2000), the intensity of older gifted adults may be totally discounted, at the very least, and misinterpreted as senility, at worst. Because of the implications of their intellectual and imaginational intensity, gifted seniors have valuable ideas and experiences to share. However, because their emotional intensity is still very much present, being dismissed and treated as if they are too old to be worthwhile contributors results in all-too-common painful (and at times enraging) experiences for them.

Strauss and Howe (1991) defined this life phase as "elderhood," describing the central role of these recurring generations throughout America's history as "stewardship." The primary focus of the elderhood generation, according to Strauss and Howe, is on "supervising, mentoring, channeling endowments, and passing on values" (p. 60). These authors provided specific examples of how this has played out since the late 16th century and is likely to be manifested on into the late 21st century. These examples clearly demonstrate the impact of gifted individuals of each elderhood generation in the past and on into the future. The role of respected "elders" has the potential for engaging the intensity of older gifted adults in far more appropriate ways than a life of either resting on their laurels or sinking into despair. Some gifted adults turn to writing memoirs or ethical wills as a way of leaving a legacy (Webb, Gore, Karnes, & McDaniel, 2004); others make efforts to reconnect with family on a deeper level than was possible when there were rigid work schedules. Family vacations and reunions become important as a way to renew social/emotional connections, as well as a way to celebrate and reinforce shared values and heal old troubles and conflicts.

Physical implications of aging do exist, and the intensity of gifted older adults tends to come into play as they deal with the issues involved in taking into consideration whatever attention their bodies demand at this time. Some of them will use their intellectual intensity to investigate everything related to whatever they are experiencing physically. Some with emotional intensity will find great satisfaction in whatever they are able to do to prolong youthful vigor; others will experience extreme frustration when they are no longer able to function at the same levels they did in their younger years. Some with imaginational intensity will over-focus on symptoms and perhaps become hypochondriacs; yet others will become very proficient in using creative visualization as an adjunct to other methods for healing.

Sheehy (1995) described a longitudinal study of women in their 70s, 80s, and 90s conducted by Cecilia Hurwich. The study found that these were women who had "mastered the art of 'letting go' of their egos gracefully so they could concentrate their attention on a few fine-tuned priorities.... Close contact with nature was important to them, as was maintaining a multigenerational network of friends. And as they grew older they found themselves more concerned with feeding the soul than the ego" (p. 414). Sheehy further mentioned that these women were not in unusually good physical condition, but that they concentrated on what they were able to do rather than what they could not. This may well reflect the benefit of older gifted adults' being able to use their intellectual and imaginational intensity in concert with their emotional intensity to develop and maintain a positive and optimistic outlook on life, regardless of their age or physical condition.

Streznewski (1999), from her interviews with older gifted adults, suggested that an active brain/mind is a significant benefit for them and that a current emphasis on "interest in life" is an important component in the health of the elderly. With the level of intensity that gifted adults take with them throughout their lifespan, interest in life (and, for that matter, curiosity about what the end of this life might be like) comes naturally.

As Jacobsen (1999) noted, "In many ways, intensity is the razor-sharp edge upon which we must balance most of our lives.... Mastering intensity is critical because it facilitates the fulfillment of our goals, enhances our relationships, and keeps the juices flowing in the right direction" (p. 308). In looking back on their lives from the perspective of decades lived, older gifted adults often find themselves assessing how and when and even if they were able to balance on that razor-sharp edge of intensity. A group of classmates gathering recently for a 50-year high school reunion was asked if their dreams and goals in life had been accomplished. The vast majority simply said "yes." However, one respondent replied:

> *There have been times in my life when everything seemed to be going dreadfully wrong, at least insofar as what my goals and dreams were at that time. However, once the dust settled on the demolition of my "best laid plans," I set off in a new direction and ended up far better off than I would've been if what I initially wanted to be had actually become a reality. As a result, I've become very philosophical and trusting; my life has already far surpassed my wildest thoughts about what it would be like.* (North Park Academy Class of 1958 Memory Book, May 10, 2008, p. 39)

Lives in Denial

Although this overview accurately describes the lifespan of gifted adults in general, we need to take a brief and somewhat distressing look at one group of these adults who may experience all of this but are in denial—denial of their intensity and, often, denial of their giftedness. Some of them spend their lives working at one menial job after another, jobs that only occasionally challenge them, living their lives on paths that may well fall far afield of what anyone who knew of their giftedness in childhood might have expected them to be doing. Some become lost in substance abuse, addictive behavior, or other ways of numbing their intensity down to a tolerable level. Some commit suicide. Others turn to a life of crime and end up in jail or prison. Some live out their lives in mental institutions. The specific reasons for this may be as complex and diverse as the gifted individuals we find in these circumstances (if we can find these individuals at all). Streznewski (1999) hypothesized, "Through early neglect or frustration, or through later choices that trap them, some gifted people defy the society which does not seem to understand or accept them. They drop out, become criminals, or give up and end it all: a tragic waste of precious lives" (p. 163).

Conclusion

Erikson's theory is a study in contrasts. Similarly, lifespan intensity is characterized by contrasts, resulting in both advantages and disadvantages. Whether or not gifted adults go through these stages at precisely the same ages or in exactly the same fashion as Erikson described for the general population, the issues are very real for them. However, each stage will probably be experienced with greater intensity. Furthermore, each of the stages may well be revisited repeatedly by adults who are gifted. Often, there is continuous disintegration and re-integration.

As a result, gifted adults are often described as "ageless." For example, their intellectual intensity often leads them down circuitous paths of analytical thinking that may be evident at any stage of life—young, middle, or later adulthood. Their emotional intensity regarding injustice on any level, from personal to global, can flare into white-hot anger at any age. Their sensual intensity can bring them to tears at the sound of beautiful music or at the sight of sunlight sparkling on a quiet lake, and their imaginational intensity can lead them to flights of fantasy that enrich their inner life, regardless of how young or old they might be. Psychomotor intensity even comes into play at any age, and the comment "You have so much energy!" is heard by gifted adults throughout their lifespan (often spoken by others who are intimidated by how much energy these individuals possess).

Despite the benefits of the work of theorists such as Dabrowski and Erikson or the writings of authors such as Streznewski, Sheehy, Jacobsen, and others as they apply to understanding gifted adults, we need to bear in mind that giftedness is "the exceptionality that is the exception" (Fiedler, 1999, p. 402). Gifted individuals of any age defy tidy classification—and also defy tidy expectations. Their individuality overrides whatever generalizations might be made about them.

If we look back at the comments quoted at the beginning of this chapter, we know that gifted individuals begin hearing remarks like these during early childhood, with the result that they often ask themselves, "What's wrong with me?" Aron (1998) described this as "a (wrong) sense of being flawed" (p. 3). Jacobsen (1999) echoed similar thoughts in her description of gifted adults, saying, "They realize they are intense, complex, and driven, but they have been taught that their strong personalities are perceived as excessive, too different from the norm, and consequently wrong" (p. 10). The "too much" comments are as familiar to gifted adults as they are to gifted youngsters—maybe even more so, since as adults, they may have become highly sensitized to criticisms heaped on their heads throughout their lives.

The five areas of overexcitability as described by Dabrowski's theory (sensual, psychomotor, intellectual, imaginational, and emotional) describe the intensity that is part and parcel of the day-to-day experiences of gifted adults. Often, this intensity causes them serious problems with others—far beyond what might have been suggested by understanding the developmental stages of Erikson's theory.

The following poem, written for a gifted adult whose intensity in all areas was profoundly evident, sums up the struggles on the journey that most gifted adults take throughout their lifespan.

Survival of Spirit
by Ellen Dove Fiedler

> *Sometimes it's just survival,*
> *And barely that, at best—*
> *One heartbeat at a time.*
> *Call it a struggle, if you will,*
> *But being in that place*
> *Feels worse than that—*
> *A hollow hole*
> *Without a sense of purpose.*

Sometimes it is a struggle—
A fight to reach beyond
The times of aching heartache,
Battling ancient demons
And those more newly born.
The site: a grey and formless place
Of lonely isolation,
Without a chart or guideposts.

For some, somehow, somewhere
From some place deep within—
A place that's been forgotten—
A tiny spark of strength ignites
Though not perceived, at first.
It's just enough to light the way
To taking one more step—
A step ahead
Onto the rocky ground.

Where does that spark come from?
A question often asked
But seldom really answered.
For those who've traveled
Rocky paths
Can't tell you how
We found our way
We only guess;
Answers still elude us.

Perhaps what really matters
Is simply that it's true
That spirit can survive.
For some, at least, the struggle
Serves to fan that spark
Into a tiny flame
That warms the soul, keeps it alive—
More prepared
For all that lies ahead

For where the path ahead may lead
Is anybody's guess
And better left unknown.
Beyond survival is a place
Where spirit truly thrives.
To live there is a dream
To bring into our
Earthly lives
So we can feel its power.

To find the source of all our power
Perhaps may be the quest
That we have set before us.
The journey is its own reward
And has its own rewards
If we will only see them—
If we can only see them
As we travel on
To find our own true path.

As this poem reflects, for gifted adults who come through what Dabrowski's theory characterizes as spontaneous multilevel disintegration, the proverbial light at the end of their dark tunnel is the next level: organized multilevel disintegration. Piechowski (1997) described these persons as follows: "Individuals are well on the road to self-actualization. They have found a way to reach their own ideals, and they are effective leaders in society. They show high levels of responsibility, authenticity, reflective judgment, empathy for others, autonomy of thought and action, self-awareness, and other attributes associated with self-actualization" (p. 374).

With all of their intensity and sensitivity in various areas, gifted adults deal with the advantages and challenges of their overexcitabilities throughout their lifespan. Our hope and our dream for them is that they come to a point in their lives of experiencing joy and self-actualization whenever, wherever, and at whatever stage of life they may find it and as often as they may find it. Through greater self-understanding and by finding kindred spirits with whom they can share life's journey, the probabilities are good that gifted adults can meet the challenges and enjoy the advantages of their intensity and be able to lead satisfying, meaningful, rich, and fulfilling lives.

Chapter 11
Annemarie Roeper: Nearly a Century with Giftedness

Michele Kane, Ed.D.

"I've been so busy living that I haven't had much time to think about dying…. I suppose I will do that one of these days."

These reflective words by well-known gifted educator and consultant Annemarie Roeper (personal communication, May, 2008) are a commentary on her current frame of mind as she nears 90 years of age. Her work with children, both at Roeper School, an independent school for gifted, and later as a private educational consultant, has influenced the lives of thousands of gifted children and their families. Annemarie's child-centered philosophy of education revolves around emotional understanding as the most essential component in understanding the complexities of the inner life of a child. Her insistence that the Self, or the soul, of the gifted child is as important as the child's cognitive abilities has changed the way that many gifted educators and counselors interact with gifted children. Her life work was honored in 1999 by the National Association for Gifted Children when she was presented with the Distinguished Service Award for 50 years of service to the gifted community.

The Roeper School, founded by Annemarie and husband George, is based on a nontraditional model in which the goal of education is to honor the Self by providing opportunities for self-actualization and inter-dependence. Such a philosophical framework, with its emphasis on social/

emotional development and community connections, is as controversial today as it was when the Roepers conceptualized it many decades ago.

The underlying principle of the school—participatory democracy—was in stark contrast to the repression that the Roepers had fled. Forced to leave Nazi Germany, George Roeper and Annemarie Bondy immigrated to America. Shortly thereafter, the pair was married. In 1941, at the invitation of family friends, they moved to Michigan and began the first Roeper School. The school became a visible and viable reminder of how compassion, concern, and empathy could replace the hatred and fear they had left behind. The path of Annemarie's life exemplifies her emotional inner world and illustrates levels of growth as described by Dabrowski's theory of positive disintegration.

As Annemarie and I talk, we sit in a garden that is a blaze of color in the hills above the San Francisco Bay area, which is home to her educational consulting practice. The steady roar of the traffic below provides an audible hum, the background to every outdoor conversation. Indoors is awash with every shade of purple imaginable; it is Annemarie's favorite color. Downstairs is the colorful playroom and conference room, an inviting environment for children. Kites dance from the ceiling, and bright pictures decorate the walls. Neatly arranged books and games invite children to explore. Upstairs, parents wait on the roomy outdoor patio or in the huge living room. Entering the front door, the visitor is led to a window wall of glass that overlooks the Bay. The scenery is dotted with mountains in the distance, the famous bridges, and an expanse of water—and as the sun sets, the view is breathtaking. Equally compelling is the collection of African Shona sculptures that are deftly arranged throughout the living room. Each sculpture calls for a careful examination, with the combination emotions carved into the stone. Bookcases line the walls in almost every room, and the alternating walls of glass, books, and stone provide a visually tempting environment that stimulates and soothes. This is the place in which Annemarie creates a sacred space where she connects with the lives of others and where she has been at home for the past eight years.

Annemarie's current journey into the way of thinking that she calls "beyond old age" is uncharted territory in the life of a gifted adult. As she grapples with effects of *ageism*, such as the impatience of some with her slower pace or being spoken about in her presence as if she is invisible, she remains a keen observer of her own life experiences. When we read her speeches, articles, and books, when we talk with her about her experiences, the words offer a glimpse into the world of this gifted exemplar, a window into a life that we can describe as intense and searching (Roeper, 1982, 1990, 1995, 2007). Annemarie recently prepared these thought-provoking remarks for a speech:

> *Maybe being beyond old forces us to really understand that the mystery is a reality. What stretches beyond the door of death is an eternity of unknown. Eternity and infinity are concepts that young children often struggle with, but soon give up because they can't find the answer. During our active lifetime, we forget about it, and get so involved with day-to-day living that we don't see the mysterious universe in which we are trying to put our feet on some kind of concrete ground. Living beyond old, with our eyes open, may force us to truly accept the reality of the infinite and eternal, as well as to continue to understand the fact that we can never really know the answer while we are on this earth.* (2006)

It's not surprising that, although she reports few thoughts about death, Annemarie has some very clear thoughts about the mystery of life. As a legendary figure in gifted education and a gifted elder, she continues to chronicle her own emotional journey and intricate inner life. She persists in blazing the trail for those who are to follow.

Years ago, Annemarie concluded that the emotions of gifted children, acting in concert with their physical and intellectual giftedness, provided the foundation for the concept of emotional giftedness (Piechowski, 1991). Decades of experiences with gifted children led her to define giftedness as "a greater degree of awareness and sensitivity and a greater ability to understand and transform perceptions into intellectual and emotional experiences" (Roeper, 1982, p. 21). This belief that "giftedness is heart and soul" is rooted in her youngest days, and it is these early experiences that shaped her thoughts, feelings, and eventually, her life work.

Clearly, Annemarie Roeper has had an impact on the field of gifted education and remains a leader in the field. In the book *Profiles of Influence in Gifted Education* (Karnes & Nugent, 2004), her contributions are noted as follows:

> *Annemarie generated an awareness among educators and parents of the gifted about the importance of the self and a child's emotions. She has shown parents and educators the importance of respecting the child's inner life and applying it to gifted education. She introduced and developed the construct of emotional giftedness.* (p. 142)

Annemarie's life story exemplifies the inner growth of an emotionally intense person as described by Dabrowski's theory of positive disintegration. The journey of her struggles and times of deep despair, yet her continuous quest for greater self-awareness and deeper self-understanding, provides a blueprint for a life of emotional and intellectual passion. Her days, which are filled with sensitivity and perceptiveness, reveal an elaborate inner life nestled in complex environmental milieus. Annemarie had to face and overcome great obstacles, such as the loss of country in World War II, her friends, home, and possessions, and her parents' school, which she loved. Yet she could still find value in such experiences—an example of uncommon resilience and an ability and desire to transcend adversity.

It often happens that extraordinary lives happen in extraordinary times; the life of Annemarie Roeper is no exception. She was the oldest child of Max and Gertrud Bondy, who were progressive German educators. In 1918, at the time of her birth, the Bondys were combining their talents to provide young students with an innovative approach to education. Max, an art historian and recent World War I veteran, believed that the world would become a better place only through humanistic education and a deep sense of community.

Annemarie's mother, Gertrud Bondy, one of the first female psychoanalysts trained by Freud, brought her new understanding about the development of the Self and the role of the unconscious to this progressive educational venture. Eventually, the couple created a boarding school for about 50 children, ages 10 to 18, in the town of Marienau, where their advanced ideas combining education and psychology flourished. In this idyllic setting of natural beauty, Annemarie and her siblings were raised within an educational community that valued the individual. These primary experiences provided the foundation for her future profession and the basis of the Roeper educational philosophy of self-actualization and interdependence.

Annemarie's earliest emotional memories are quite remarkable. She says:

> *When I was very young, I had terrible temper tantrums. And I look back at that as a good thing. It was the one way in which I could show that I had feelings. I would show myself that I was allowed to have feelings. I was very jealous of my sister and brother.* (personal communication, August 10, 2004)

Sister Ulla arrived in 1921 and brother Heinz in 1926, and they provided companionship as well as rivalry.

Annemarie remembers wishing that she could be a boy, and she often took big steps like the boys and imitated their stride:

> *As a child, probably I would define it that my Self, capital S, was having trouble allowing itself to grow. I felt that my "I" was different from other people and that I could not be a part of the real life. I felt that I was clever enough to hide this and that I was able to participate in the usual experiences. But if people really knew what I was thinking, they would know I was different, so I usually kept quiet. I began to feel that something was wrong with me. …[T]his is when my mother helped me. This is the story I've quite often told.*
>
> *This is an outside story, but it's the story of the boy who died. I was five, and he was my playmate, and I was growing up in my parents' school. After he died, the other children went wild with screaming and playing and running through the building, and they actually were very happy. I remember thinking that I couldn't identify with that and that something was wrong with me. So my mother explained to me that rather something was wrong with them and that was their way of defending themselves against this event. This let me know that I was very integrated.* (personal communication, August 10, 2004)

This initial experience of emotional sensitivity and empathy toward others is something that caused Annemarie to feel out of sync with her peers. From a young age, she described her feelings as a type of "cosmic dizziness," disquietude, and uneasiness. These unsettled feelings were her first inklings that one must learn to live with the uncertainty of the mystery of life. As the feelings became more intense and because they were not typical of the other children around her, Annemarie began to worry if something was wrong with her or if she was crazy. Later she would write, "This sensitivity and the understanding of expanded reality brings with it the need for self-protection, because the outside world does not understand and therefore often interprets these behaviors as pathological" (2004b, p. 4).

In her book *Liberating Everyday Genius*, psychologist Mary-Elaine Jacobsen (1999) echoes Annemarie's sentiments:

> *To feel like an outsider, to constantly pressure yourself to hold back*
> *your gifts in order to fit in or avoid disapproval, to erroneously*
> *believe that you are overly sensitive, compulsively perfectionistic,*
> *and blindly driven, to live without knowing the basic truths*
> *about the core of your being—too often this is the life of Everyday*
> *Geniuses who have been kept in the dark about who they are and*
> *misinformed about their differences.* (p. 17)

In spite of her worries, there was much in Annemarie's life that provided delight. Her world was filled with a profound imagination peppered with imaginary friends in a make-believe world. She spent many hours immersed in the books that filled her father's study. Reading as many books as possible, especially fiction with its world of emotions, Annemarie was filled with an overpowering love of reading that continues to this day. She also loved the fine arts, including art, architecture, and music, and delighted in all of the beauty that surrounded her. This challenge of integrating keen perceptions with personal passions would lead her to write:

> *From the beginning, the gifted show an even greater awareness of*
> *the complexities of the world, a greater desire to make sense of it*
> *all. They need to overcome the anxiety that results from this*
> *awareness by trying to bring order into the apparent chaos around*
> *them. They also have greater skills to deal with the task. In addi-*
> *tion, they experience genuine pleasure and excitement from*
> *knowledge, information, and understanding. All of this is part of*
> *the motivation for learning and the reason for the rapid growth*
> *that leads your children to acquire new skills daily.* (Roeper,
> 1998, p. 153)

Annemarie's own self-awareness and introspection eventually increased her self-understanding and led to her profound understanding of gifted individuals.

Annemarie experienced several significant emotional events during her childhood days. When she was eight, a new and very handsome older boy came to Marienau. George Roeper, age 13, came to the school; a former teacher and friend of Max Bondy recommended it to George's strict parents. Personable, affable, and a natural leader, George flourished in this new environment and soon became a favorite of the students, as well as Max and Gertrud. He also became a favorite of Annemarie, and she remembers that she *knew*, even as a young child, that she would one day marry him. A romantic relationship did evolve as Annemarie and George entered adolescence.

The pre-teen years also provoked incredible turmoil. It was during this time that her Jewish identity was revealed to her. Annemarie's parents, Max and Gertrud, wished to be assimilated into the German culture and to be known as Germans rather than as German Jews. They did not practice as religious Jews, but rather participated as mainstream Lutherans. The revelation by a classmate that Annemarie was Jewish created a great deal of inner dissonance for her. Once she learned that she was Jewish, she thought that she *should* be Jewish, and she felt that it was her responsibility to carry the Jewish identity for the entire family. This posed quite a burden as she sought to reconcile the inability of her parents to accept their Jewish heritage with her own growing sense of identity as a young Jewish woman.

In Annemarie's sixteenth year, she was involved in an incident that would change her life. Walking to a nearby village on a warm, sunny day filled with gentle breezes and swaying trees, she felt transported and transcendent. Merging with the oneness of the cosmos, she felt a deep sense of unity with all life. She was awakened from her reverie in a forceful manner. Suddenly, she became aware of people pushing, shoving, and the feeling of fear as sharp smells and shrill voices emanated from the crowd. "Heil Hitler! Heil Hitler!" echoed the nearby voices, along with a voice from the village loudspeaker. Annemarie (1985) described this life-changing event:

> *I touched the books I had just bought, pulled myself together to make myself invisible. My memory of the events ends here. I became invisible. All there was left of me was a feeling of overwhelming fear, a terrible, indefinable feeling. I was alone in the middle of a world that had become nothing but hostility, a huge angry animal. And there was no way out. It was more than a young Jewish girl in a crowd of Nazis. It was more than my inner struggle about whether or not to raise my hand also. Would they tear me to pieces if they noticed I didn't participate in the Hitler greeting or if they recognized me for who I was? Did I do it? I don't remember. My fear went beyond these concerns. I felt that I experienced a confrontation between the ultimate evil and my powerlessness and aloneness. I even recognized it as being other than evil. It was ultimate weakness being exploited. I had no inner resources to cope with this. I truly disappeared. I experienced a kind of death along with the [death of the] gentle world I had known.*

The Nazi influence increased during this turbulent time, and the school at Marienau seemed to be swallowed up by the negative atmosphere that suffused the country. Annemarie's fragile Self was battered as she felt the powerlessness of her parents in the wake of the Nazi rise to power and the general atmosphere of pervasive fear. In a personal statement created for Independent Schools, Annemarie described these times through her emotional lens:

> *In the '30s, Germany was struck with an emotional earthquake, as severe as any that have ever been experienced. The whole world rumbled and shook, and everything that was safe and certain tumbled down. Along with the bombs of World War II, the emotional edifices that had been built over the years tumbled into ruins....*
> *There was as much inner murder and death as on the outside.*

At first, her father denied that there were dangers because he had defended his country in the previous war and felt that as a veteran, he and his family would be safe. However, Gertrud soon left with Ulla and Heinz and began a new school, Les Rayons, in Switzerland. Annemarie stayed with her father at the school in Marienau so that she could complete her high school studies and graduate from there. As the peril increased and there were daily threats to their safety, it was George Roeper who secured passports for Max and Annemarie, and they fled Germany in the spring of 1937 after graduation to join Gertrud and the rest of the family in Switzerland.

As she left her beloved home and country, Annemarie noted that her sense of Self was traumatized. Confronting the ultimate evil of the Nazis was annihilating to her sense of who she was. Her Self disappeared, and she defended herself by "putting up a wall of ice" as a means of protection. One of her annual letters to friends reads:

> *Ever since I had to leave Germany in 1939, I felt that my existence had been cut into two unrelated lives: my wonderful pre-Nazi childhood in Germany in the school community founded by my parents, followed by the terrible experience shared by millions of having to leave my home, my deep roots. In one blow, our world was totally destroyed by the Nazi holocaust. I can remember today the very moment when a part of me died. I knew my heart would break if I actually felt the pain, and I felt how my ability to FEEL turned itself off. The trauma was such that my emotional life seemed to have ended.* (personal communication, August 10, 2004)

Daniels and Piechowski (this volume) describe the sensitivity of emotionally intense individuals and the resulting emotional withdrawal and protection of the Self that can happen when the Self experiences extreme pain. The injustices and discriminatory practices of the Nazis that Annemarie and her family experienced were overwhelming for someone with such extreme emotional sensitivities. Yet there is an amazing resilience in Annemarie's story. Out of her shattering experiences emerged the threads that would fill her life with meaning and purpose. Her immediate response was a lifelong commitment to education, as well as to her family. She believes that only through appropriate education can one empower individuals to take charge of their destiny rather than submit to the powerful. Annemarie and George envisioned and created a new learning community and felt that "every day that we could educate children was a triumph over the Nazis." Although the educational philosophy of her parents influenced their beliefs, it was their own personal experiences that provided the impetus for creating an educational climate where two kinds of safety—physical and emotional—were paramount.

Another key experience that shaped Annemarie's life occurred in Vienna, Austria, in the fall of 1937. Annemarie returned there from Switzerland to study medicine and to live with Pauline Feldman, the doctor who had delivered her. "Aunt" Pauline lived across the street from Sigmund Freud. Annemarie was interested in becoming a psychoanalyst like her mother. However, at age 19, she was ineligible to matriculate into the program. As Annemarie remembered:

> *Freud has been in the center of my emotional life from the very beginning, but I also had several personal experiences with him, which were very important. It was my interest in psychoanalysis that led me to study medicine. I studied medicine in 1938 in Vienna, which was interrupted by the Nazis arriving in Vienna and my having to flee a second time. I had two semesters of education in medicine and my purpose was to become a psychoanalyst. During that time, I had a 2-hour interview with Sigmund Freud and his daughter, Anna. The reason for this was that she was going to teach a course in psychoanalysis for children beginning the following March, which was for people who had a solid background in psychoanalysis. One of the conditions was that you had to be at least 21 to take this course, to have the necessary maturity. I had this interview with Sigmund and Anna in his study where*

they were asking me about my own background in psychoanalysis and my understanding of it in order to determine whether they could make an exception and have me take the course at 19. It was a very, very exciting and emotional interview for me, and at the end of it, they accepted me into the course. The course never happened, just as my becoming a doctor never happened, because the Nazis moved in and both the Freuds and I had to immediately flee the country. (Kane, 2003, p. 7)

Unfortunately, the situation in Vienna worsened, and the Nazis invaded in the spring of 1938. George got word to Annemarie about this, and she was able to flee on one of the last trains out of Vienna for Prague. She met her parents, who were visiting relatives in Prague, and returned with them to Switzerland. As the tensions in Europe increased, George was quite insistent that the family try to immigrate to the United States. An American student at the school was able to secure visas, and the entire family then headed to America. Thus, at age 20, Annemarie Roeper left behind the world of her childhood that was steeped in great natural beauty, rich cultural traditions, emotional safety, and intellectual curiosity. She was uncertain about her life in the days to come, but she knew that her life would be one that she would share with George.

Leaving Germany as a refugee in 1939, Annemarie also left behind an identity that had provided her with a sense of comfort and familiarity. Her family arrived in the United States with few personal possessions but with the quiet determination that life in America would mean creating a new school with an educational environment that reflected their humanistic views. For Annemarie, it was also a time of rebirth. Her identity began anew as she married George Roeper in New York City on April 20, 1939. George had found a spot in New Hampshire where the family began a summer camp, and eventually the Bondy family would establish a new school in Windsor, Vermont.

There were other transitions besides those of becoming assimilated into a new culture. George and Annemarie wished to create their own life as a couple and as educators without living in the shadow of Max and Gertrud. In 1941, George and Annemarie moved to the Detroit area at the behest of family friends and psychoanalysts, the Sterbas. Annemarie and George were invited to share the responsibilities as educators and administrators of the Editha Sterba Nursery School. They quickly saw the need for an elementary school and established the Roeper Grade School.

Annemarie began her career working with the youngest of children. The school was based on progressive principles passed down from Annemarie's parents—namely, the sense of community (sociology) that was so essential to Max, and the sense of self (psychology) that was so essential to Gertrud. However, George and Annemarie created their own educational philosophy, which she described as "an idealistic philosophy of life based upon self-actualization, interdependence, diversity, and human rights" (Roeper, 1991). Working together daily for the next 40 years, the couple continued to develop the school to reflect their humanistic ideals.

"At the core of Annemarie's beliefs is the unwavering conviction that emotional understanding is the key to the complex inner world of the child. Ultimately, with a learning community that fosters empathy, compassion, and appreciation for diversity, the child will flourish in a holistic manner" (Kane, 2003, p. 1). The Roepers' model places the child in the center of his or her educational experience. Annemarie observed:

> *My philosophy has always been a part of my history. I see the purpose of education, not in terms of individual children only, but in terms of understanding the world. The way I grew up was to know that I had a task to participate in my destiny, which was to leave the world a better place. As an educator, I felt a goal was to help the child become who he really is and create an environment where the Self can thrive. That's a side that educators don't see as their responsibility. I don't see education as separate from the world. To help the child follow his inner agenda so that he can change the world is the purpose of education. I did have George and always others around me who believed in our philosophy, but at times I was lonely. We just have to learn to live with the knowledge that understanding children helps us understand people, and that helps us understand the world. And we also must live with the knowledge that we really can't understand anything because we can't be all things. Living in the world and yet not of the world is what creates aliveness and loneliness.* (personal communication, July 12, 2003)

Annemarie continued to reinvent herself as a wife, an educator, an administrator, and eventually a mother. She was particularly vulnerable at this time while she was seeking to recreate her Self. Physically, the Holocaust had left her unharmed; however, the emotional and psychological toll was enormous. For Annemarie, there was a tremendous sense of survivor guilt and a feeling that to risk living with beauty and joy was to risk annihilation. Annemarie said that only later, after she had children, did she experience her love of art and art history again. She realized that her son wanted to go to an art museum, and so she allowed herself to experience the aesthetic pleasures of the museum once again in her role as a parent. She didn't believe that her Self could allow her to feel and experience the depth of delight that viewing such art treasures would bring, and she was pleased to discover that she could enjoy the experience again.

Becoming a mother and subsequent family life presented even more opportunities for intensity of experience. Son Tommy was born in 1943, son Peter in 1946, and daughter Karen in 1949. In 1946, the Roeper City and Country School moved to its present location in Bloomfield Hills, Michigan. Set on a high hill, the school was housed in the former Stephens Mansion, situated on four acres with plenty of room for children to roam and explore. Although smaller, the setting was somewhat similar to that of the school in Marienau in Germany, which was also a large dwelling with outbuildings and plenty of surrounding countryside; perhaps George and Annemarie hoped to capture the same physical setting of peace and calm. The Roeper family lived in the combination home/school for many years.

Annemarie was very protective of the time that she spent with her own children. Her growing up had meant sharing her parents with all of the other children at the boarding school, and this was a situation that she wanted to change. Although the Roeper children were blended into the larger Roeper School community, there was also a distinct Roeper family identity that Annemarie and George created as their family grew and developed. The Roeper family soon moved to a separate residence that was apart from the school, and this allowed the family the opportunity to flourish independently.

Family continues to be of central importance to Annemarie, and the recent addition of a great-grandson has been a cause for major celebration. "My family now has firm roots in America, and I am so grateful that this country has been a place where my family can carry on," says Annemarie.

A series of landmark events brought social and political changes to Roeper City and Country School. Racial integration in the 1950s was controversial but reflected the progressive philosophy of the school. Few private schools of the time welcomed the diversity that Roeper School supported. The original plan by Annemarie and George was that the school would reflect "the world in miniature." Institutional change was not easy, and at each juncture, there was a need for careful planning in the anticipation that these new ideas would become adopted seamlessly.

In 1956, a group of experts in gifted education came to Bloomfield Hills and spent a week dreaming about and designing an ideal school for gifted children. George became interested in the idea after reading a *New York Times* article. Thus, major thinkers in the field of gifted education, including Harry Passow, were invited to this event to create a model school for gifted children. The transition of Roeper School to a school for gifted involved some of the same careful planning and investment in organizational caretaking as the earlier move to racial integration. The Roeper vision, as the school focused on gifted children, was that this school was to "educate for life" rather than for college and the world of work. This educational approach evolved into the Roeper philosophy of Self-Actualization and Interdependence (SAI). Annemarie developed a document that outlined their fundamental belief—rather than developing a philosophy of education, they developed a philosophy of life (Roeper & Roeper, 1981).

This is a humanistic and child-centered approach that embodies the concept of social/emotional learning, which is the curriculum of the Self. In this nontraditional model of education, the goal is to honor the Self by providing opportunities for self-actualization and interdependence. A child-centered curriculum emphasizes emotional as well as intellectual development. In this model, the school community is of equal importance. The Self in relationship to community is a vital component educationally for the developing child. Annemarie has outlined these beliefs in her book *Educating Children for Life: The Modern Learning Community* (1990).

Other innovative approaches that the Roepers fostered were the open classroom approach and the introduction of a new administrative structure—participatory democracy. This administrative structure moved the school community from a hierarchical system to a cooperative one. Annemarie relates, "There is in society a pervasive acceptance of a hierarchy among human beings. Teachers are considered more right than children, and influential parents more right than teachers. In a structure that grows out of a deep belief in equal human rights, these unfair assumptions disappear" (Roeper, 1995, p. 109).

This approach included expanding the voting rights to members of the learning community, such as staff, students, and alumnae. In Roeper School, administrators and teachers made placement and staffing decisions jointly. They formed an administrative council that allowed for open meetings. Teacher evaluations were ongoing, and the teachers sought input from staff and specialists for the purposes of encouraging growth (Roeper, 1995). Although there were rough spots along the road, at the time of Annemarie's retirement, this philosophy seemed to be secure.

The distinction should be made between a representative democracy (in which governing is carried on by the elected leaders of the group) and a participative democracy (constituents voice opinions through voting). The Roepers used participatory democracy to provide opportunities for all voices to be heard through forums and assemblies. The expectation was that decisions would be truly made in community and that each individual had the right and responsibility to participate (Roeper, 1986). However, the practicalities of this practice caused difficulties at times for both George and Annemarie, as well as the organization, and once the Roepers left their leadership positions at the school, these practices were modified significantly.

Parent communication was always of preeminent importance at the Roeper School. There were monthly parent meetings and frequent parent newsletters, which included not only school happenings, but also information about current educational and psychological thought. Annemarie and George contributed lengthy articles based on their observations of students and the school community. Additionally, they shared material from their ongoing participation in psychoanalytic study groups.

In 1978, along with Ruthan Brodsky, George and Annemarie created a professional journal which was titled *Roeper Review*. The purpose of the journal was two-fold. The journal initially served as an extension of the parent newsletters so that the Roepers' ideas and philosophy could be communicated to others beyond the Roeper School. In this way, the commitment to gifted youth and their development was extended outside of the closed environment. The greater purpose of the journal was to encourage ideas that represented diverse perspectives and to promote professional discourse in the gifted community at large.

Annemarie's focus remained on writing about the emotional world of the gifted child, as well as aspects of their affective education. The high point for her was an issue that she co-edited with Sharon Lind which focused on the Self. This special edition illustrated Dabrowski's theory beautifully, as it described the quest for inner growth, which combines struggles of the Self along with deeper understanding of self and others (Roeper, 1998). *Roeper Review* continues today as a well-respected educational journal, maintaining its original intent as a forum for the exchange of both conventional and unconventional ideas.

For Annemarie, the decades spent creating, developing, honing, and implementing the Roeper philosophy epitomize a time of life that is typically described as the middle years. Characteristics of this phase of "generativity versus stagnation" in the lives of gifted adults include the deep need for making a difference in the world and making a lasting contribution, along with the knowledge that enduring change will result (Fiedler, this volume). Leaving an educational legacy that honors the whole child has always been a driving force behind the work of the Roepers, and their work has been noticed. According to Delisle (2000), "Through the social, educational, and political upheavals of three generations, the vision of George and Annemarie Roeper has been a constant beacon of light for the entire field of gifted child education" (p. 29).

Yet a profound concern regarding the slow progress of innovation was always in the background for Annemarie and at times led to frustration or depression. Her deep need to see the changes unfold, while at the same time feeling an urgency that information should be shared both locally and globally, became more and more important. Waiting for others to come to a new understanding and allowing for new ideas to evolve was a difficult balance for someone with the intensity of passion that Annemarie possessed.

The end of the 1970s brought significant change to Annemarie and George as they stepped into elderhood. They both received honorary doctoral degrees from Eastern Michigan University in 1978 for their contributions to the field of gifted education. Retirement from Roeper School for George in 1979 and Annemarie in 1980 meant not only a change of livelihood but also a change of venue. California became their new home, as they moved to the west coast for warmer climes and to be closer to their children who had settled there.

Annemarie quickly opened an educational consulting practice for gifted families, which has been in operation since 1983. Combining her understanding of gifted children and their families, she further shared her passion by writing three books and more than 200 articles. During this time, she continued to make presentations, give speeches, and develop ways of imparting her certainty that the emotional life of gifted children is of paramount importance.

A current project is the Annemarie Roeper Method of Qualitative Assessment, which she describes as "a method of assessment that incorporates the emotional and spiritual aspects of children into a deeper understanding of who they are" (Roeper, 2004a). This process provides an alternative method of identifying and understanding the needs of gifted children. During individual visits with both the child and the child's caregivers, the Qualitative Assessment practitioner enters into the world of the gifted child. A certification process has been developed to advance this methodology, which builds on establishing a personal relationship with a child and learning about the child's inner agenda.

In 1991, tragedy struck Annemarie and George. In late October, the Oakland Firestorm destroyed not only the Roepers' home and all of their personal possessions, but all of Annemarie's writings and speeches. It was a time of extraordinary sadness and great loss. However, several weeks later, Annemarie attended the National Association for Gifted Children annual convention. She remarked, "My NAGC plane tickets were in my purse; my work isn't over; I was meant to come." For the second time in her life, she had lost everything. She was 73 years old and needed to rebuild her life. Yet here she was at a national convention, ready to begin anew. Her growth as an individual continued as she moved through the personal and professional rebuilding process. At times, the work was arduous and difficult.

Her husband's death in 1992 was another grave loss for Annemarie. Together, they had shared in the creation of dreams and watched as these dreams materialized. Losing George meant losing the ability to discuss and confer about the issues that they both cared about so keenly. Annemarie's protector, confidant, and life partner was gone.

Clearly, Annemarie's inner work was not complete. She had been totally shattered by the experiences of leaving Germany and was still numb, even after decades of being in America. Her words are most descriptive:

> *People didn't know that I couldn't feel. And that my Self was hidden. I think my Self was hidden. It was covered up. It was really the emptiness that I felt (and I know other people feel that also) but in a way, it was really fullness. It was filled with all these emotions that were covered up. I didn't feel that I had a right to be angry about what had happened.*
>
> *It is impossible for people to see that today because I'm strong. I was not present as a Self. But everything else was there. I was head of the school. I worked with teachers, I worked with*

children, I wrote papers, and I gave speeches. But I wasn't there....
(personal communication, 2002)

After a period of time, there was a turning point, and Annemarie began to assimilate the disparate parts of her Self. From a distance, she was able to begin to experience and feel once again as her work became more accepted and more widely understood, and this acknowledgement provided a catalyst for inner change and personal growth. The old feelings of isolation and alienation that were frozen behind a wall of ice became available as the wall slowly melted. Family and friends were instrumental in helping with this transition, and they listened and provided guidance through this period of deep change. Annemarie says that at some point, the floodgates opened as she began to experience the depth of her feelings that had been disallowed. Slowly at first, and then as memories were awakened, the feelings returned with a ferocious intensity. Annemarie became more integrated in mind, body, and spirit as she was able to begin the task of experiencing her authentic Self. Phone calls and email exchanges with friends proved helpful. Working with gifted families and sharing ideas through speeches and writing provided a means of connecting outside of the Self and gave access to other levels of the inner world. Even reading works of fictions created opportunities to experience feelings vicariously through an emotional involvement with the characters in the story. The cumulative effect of this process permitted a new emotional world ready for exploration. This transformative process and resulting inner growth provides evidence of multilevelness, as Dabrowski describes it in his theory. Layers of complexity unfolded during Annemarie's journey toward self-actualization and provided times of great sorrow, as well as great joy.

Our story now wraps back to the beginning, which is "beyond old age." This developmental stage is one that Annemarie created to describe her present experiences. In her book *Gifted Grownups*, Streznewski (1999) writes, "The high-powered brain/mind that drives a gifted person's life does not switch to low gear simply because the body ages or some chronological milestone has been reached. The persistence of curiosity, the need for stimulation, and the drive to *do* things does not fade."

Annemarie, in the beyond-old-age stage, teeters between the ideas that still come fast and furious and the need to slow down those thoughts and reflect on her journey into the unknown. She remains a beacon for gifted adults as she provides us with her insights and as she portrays what life is like for a gifted adult who has embraced all that life has offered:

Living beyond old, with our eyes open, may force us to truly accept the reality of the infinite and eternal, as well as to continue to understand the fact that we can never really know the answer while we are on this earth. So, peeking around the door of death, I see the road to eternity and infinity as the reality I need to live now. From traveling miles and miles of earthly road, I will need to accept the unknown not only as the past and the present, but also as my only future. So, my conclusion is that when you reach the age beyond old, your only reality is the unknown, but this has actually always been true. We don't know the past or truly the present, we don't know whether what one feels as a Self, while we are alive, will remain as such or transform into further unknowns. Integrating these understandings as a reality may be the definition of "beyond old" age. (Roeper, 2006)

Chapter 12

Living One's Spirit Song: Transcendent Experiences in Counseling Gifted Adults

Patricia Gatto-Walden, Ph.D.

During three decades counseling gifted individuals, couples, and families, I have worked with approximately three thousand exceptional children, adolescents, and adults. In this multi-talented group, some individuals showed evidence of heightened spirituality—profound sensitivity and compassion, depth of empathy, integrity, honesty, intuitive inner guidance, living in accordance with equality and justice, and an ability to move beyond everyday reality into oneness with God, nature, the universe, or "All That Is." Their spiritual experiences were powerful ones which interested me and which I chose to examine more closely. These clients are continually working to integrate at a higher level, as described by Dabrowski's theory (Mendaglio, 2008a); clearly, they exhibit overexcitability and have experienced positive disintegration.

Their spiritual quest has been a key aspect of their lives, although it has not always been a traditional spirituality. Some of these people spoke of a meaningful intimacy with the Divine, the Almighty, the Spirit, and Universal Order, while some spoke of communication with angels, nature, animals, plants, and stars or had experiences of transcendence of an expansive universe or God. Each said that in the moment of the experience, there was a flow and ease, and that there was nothing they had to do—just simply *be*. They spoke of intrinsically knowing that a pervasive, all-encompassing *love* binds together the self to all of life and connects the self in the present and beyond. After such profound moments, they sought to re-establish the spiritual connection, wanting the flow to continue. Some were able to call forth repeated experiences through a variety of means; others could not. These enlightened moments left an undeniable positive imprint in their lives, and something in them was forever altered.

However, these people varied in the degree to which they integrated their spiritual experiences into their lives. For a few, the experiences were a cause of additional personal and social distress. In these cases, there was no one in whom they could safely confide the majesty of the experience, and they believed that this significant event must stay forever hidden away from the scrutiny of others. Those who had little prior spiritual knowledge or were uncomfortable with unusual spiritual experiences questioned their validity and wondered if the expansive experience was a figment of their imagination.

The differences between clients for whom spiritual experiences were central and those who did not mention having a spiritual encounter prompted several questions. Is communion with an all-powerful being or experiencing oneness with "All That Is" a desire common to most individuals? What are the intrinsic differences between individuals who seek and have spiritual experiences and those who seek but do not enter such expanded realms of being? What about individuals who are not searching for a spiritual dimension yet spontaneously experience spiritual moments that transform them? Is it necessary to be committed to one's spiritual development in order to grow spiritually?

The Nature of Spirituality

Volumes have been written by and about mystics, saints, spiritually enlightened persons of all traditions, and persons with heightened transpersonal awareness. Many books detail pathways toward spiritual union with the Divine, as well as charting how to live a spiritual life. Today, spirituality and its correlates—ethics and morality—are included in the literature from diverse fields—anthropology, education, leadership development, business management, philosophy, psychology, politics, physics, theology, and more. The discussion of spirituality has become commonplace in our Western world.

Incorporating spiritual development into a vast array of work milieus is likewise becoming more acceptable. Several professional organizations and journals focus on transpersonal experiences and spiritual development across the age span of diverse cultures, such as the Association for Transpersonal Psychology and the Institute of Noetic Science. Many professionals across occupations and vocations are dedicated to helping children, adolescents, and adults develop their spiritual nature (Roehlkepartain, King, Wagener, & Benson, 2006), and research has shown that children have an innate, active spiritual life and a spiritual world view (Coles, 1990; Hay & Nye, 2006; Lovecky, 1998; Reich, 2007). Conferences are dedicated to the spirituality of children (Hart, 2003), and a journal is dedicated to this field of study, the *International Journal of Children's Spirituality.*

Piechowski (2000, 2001), in his review of the research on childhood spirituality, reported that spiritual experiences are more common in childhood than in later years: "Reports show that children are capable of having genuine spiritual experiences, similar in quality to adult ones. They could occur spontaneously—in nature or at home, in church or in the car—and they had enduring significance for the person's whole life.... Childhood spiritual experiences often initiate spiritual search later in life and endow a person with strength to endure life's reverses and tragic losses" (2001, p. 9). The persistent meaning that spiritual experiences have across one's lifetime is substantiated by clients in my clinical practice, irrespective of their age.

Many psychological conceptualizations and models have addressed the nature of spirituality (Assagioli, 1965; Grof, 1976; James, 1936; Maslow, 1971), and in the last decade, the concept of "spiritual intelligence" has become prominent. Emmons (1999), studying goals and motivations, found that people who were inspired through spiritual connection gave five characteristics of spiritual intelligence: transcendence of the physical, experience of heightened states of consciousness, sanctification of everyday experience, utilization of spiritual resources to solve problems, and the capacity to be virtuous. Zohar and Marshall (2000) defined spiritual intelligence as "the intelligence with which we can place our actions and our lives in a wider, richer, meaning-giving context: the intelligence with which we can assess that one course of action or one life-path is more meaningful than another.... It is our ultimate intelligence" (p. 3). Noble (2001) defined spiritual experiences as the moment-to-moment interaction between oneself and a larger expansive reality, and she expanded on Emmons' concepts by adding two dimensions to spiritual intelligence— being conscious that physical reality is embedded in a vast multidimensional reality, and being conscious of oneself interlacing with a global community.

Of these conceptualizations, the one that I have found most useful in my counseling experience with gifted clients is Nye's (1998) concept of "relational consciousness." Nye's view bridges our understanding of how we connect with the Divine. In studying children's ways of relating to the spiritual realm, Nye delineated four dimensions: personal relationship with God, personal relationship with other people, personal relationship with Self, and personal relationship with nature and the man-made world. My clients, whether children or adults, consistently allude to one or more of Nye's four dimensions as the avenues by which they experience the Divine.

Over the years, I have seen quite a few gifted children whose parents were concerned and even alarmed by their spiritual experiences (Gatto-Walden & Piechowski, 2001, 2006). For example, one four-year-old girl saw angels at bedtime on a regular basis. Her parents feared that she was hallucinating and that something was seriously wrong with her. On mornings following such a visit from the angels, the parents reported that their daughter was exuberant and gleeful. After talking with the girl several times, I was able to assure her parents that her experiences were real and not symptomatic of a psychosis.

Another client was a 14-year-old profoundly gifted boy who was extremely emotionally sensitive and empathically connected to others without verbal discourse. He said that he felt as if he were falling apart, and he was withdrawn and depressed. He was regressing to an emotional age similar to a four-year-old and was having physical anxiety symptoms that mirrored his fellow students. He was absorbing the tremendous emotional pain and pressure—both emotionally and physically—of his classmates at his prestigious college prep school, where competition and perfectionism were common. His empathic experience of the harm that they were experiencing, as well as his personal reaction to the burdensome environment, was overwhelming him. He needed support in understanding his gift as an "empath" and instructions on how to cleanse his emotions and body of others' experiences.

Several clients communicated with nature spirits. One teenage girl cried endlessly for a tree that was going to be cut down, and she expressed that she could feel the tree's fear. Her intimate communication with nature enabled her to empathically receive the intrinsic essence of the tree and its distressed vibration in reaction to being cut down. Her parents could not soothe her fear for the tree's welfare; she wanted to lie down in front of the tree-cutting equipment to save the tree. Other clients have been empathically connected with animals and have utilized their spiritual understanding and communication by becoming animal rights activists.

Spiritually gifted children and adults often are afraid of sharing their diverse spiritual experiences for fear of judgment from others. Piechowski (2003), while discussing spiritual giftedness, said that relational consciousness in psychology has addressed only relationships with others and the relationship with oneself. The relationship with nature and with a transcendent being has been largely ignored. In my clinical practice, however, clients have repeatedly expressed all four dimensions.

Clients in my practice who are emotionally gifted and who have had ongoing spiritual experiences that continuously affect and alter their lives are, I believe, often spiritually gifted as well. These individuals, young or old, live from an internal spiritual essence that is a daily guiding force. They live authentically, with compassion for others and with utmost personal integrity. Although it can be challenging to remain open and receptive to life's unpredictable and uncontrollable moments, they are committed to trusting an ordered universe beyond themselves.

What comprises spiritual giftedness? Can we distinguish persons having spiritual experiences from those who are spiritually gifted? Is it the frequency of reaching beyond what is seen or the ease to which one can access another dimension beyond ordinary reality what is relevant? Is the transformative effect in one's life an essential component of spiritual giftedness? Is a spiritually gifted individual in an elite group of "chosen ones"? Must one live a morally exemplary life to be considered spiritually gifted? Is intellectual and emotional giftedness a prerequisite to spiritual giftedness? Do an individual's spiritual beliefs determine what spiritual giftedness is? Will being spiritually gifted look different according to one's definition and relationship with the Divine?

Throughout my practice, I have observed a capacity and predisposition to connect with the Divine in intellectually, emotionally, and spiritually gifted clients of all ages, from the very young to the elderly. Although no single age group demonstrated a higher spiritual propensity than another, I have chosen to describe here three adult clients who illustrate numerous proposed traits of spiritual giftedness. I asked each of these individuals for permission to include them in the chapter, and later I asked them to check the text of their personal narrative. The three have reflected on their story and highlighted what they believe to be significant for their character and identity development, as well as their spiritual progression.

The first client, Laura, developed an intimate relationship with God through her religious practice as a young child. Although no longer active within the church, the relationship with her "Powerful Friend" has sustained her throughout life. The second client, Charles, endured severe abuse throughout his childhood and was burdened with anxiety most of his life. He exhibited an exemplary moral and ethical character even in his early years, but his spiritual awakening occurred in his later years. The third, Suzanne, has actively pursued a relationship with the Divine within her Spirit self since her early twenties. Her inner Spirit continues to guide her daily life. A discussion incorporating Dabrowski's theory of personality development, commonalities in temperament, spiritual disposition, emotional intensity, service-oriented career choices, and dedication to living a life of heightened morality follows the narratives.

Laura

Laura, age 62, has been full of energy, love, enthusiasm, and creative expression her entire life. Having a naturally sunny disposition, she is friendly and outgoing. Throughout her life, a recurrent theme has been her desire to make others feel better, to bring them some light and joy. She is gracious in her interactions with others; however, she has difficulty reading social cues and is socially naïve. Although intimacy with others is her greatest desire, others sometimes recoil from her bubbly, emotionally intense nature. She has been told innumerable times that she is "too much" or that her enthusiasm for life must be fake. When others reject her, she feels great sorrow. In addition, when she is near someone who is despondent or anxious, she has a visceral experience of their pain and feels responsible for helping them.

Laura knows several languages and their literature, is multi-talented in the arts, music, painting, and cooking, and has two doctorates. Her profound intellectual giftedness brought her professional success, but not professional fulfillment. Throughout decades over her career, she never made a true friend. She has no long-term friends other than her husband. In spite of being a natural extrovert, she has led an isolated life. People have been put off by her intensities—intellectual, emotional, sensual, imaginational/creative—and endless energy. She has been openly insulted and overtly assaulted because of her intense, energetic, and joyful nature. Laura wrote, "I have yet to meet anyone who reflects my love-filled, open persona. I have been a target of bullies throughout my life."

Piechowski (2002) confirms that others may dislike such intensity: "It is unfortunate that the stronger these overexcitabilities are, the less peers and teachers welcome them, unless they, too, are gifted" (p. 29). Gross (1995) confirms that exceptionally gifted children are often disliked and rejected by others because of their intensity, ease of learning, and multiple talents.

Since Laura was so precocious and competent even as a young child, her mother expected her to take care of others in the family, both older and younger than she. Laura's childhood needs were left unmet, and her family has been judgmental of her throughout her life. Her siblings taunted and teased her mercilessly, which triggered a strong sorrowful response. Numerous painful family memories have brought sadness and suffering yet never have tempered her love and dedication to immediate and extended family members.

Her family abided by the Catholic Church's teachings without question. As an obedient child, she followed the rules set by the nuns, priests, and Catholic religion, as well as her parents at home. She sought to please, always wanting to be a "good girl." She wrote:

> *The Church taught me to be nice to everyone, never lie or cheat, steal, get mad, hate, or be anything but pious and humble, pure, and give everything you have to others. I believed that. It would make the world better if people acted like this. When family members were surprised that I did some of these things so ardently, I was taken aback.*

Laura knew that some of her personal values were also the principles preached by the Church (such as kindness, compassion, giving to others, humility), and she sought to live an exemplary life. However, the teachings of the Church also instilled fear of hell and a fear of what would happen if she followed her intuitive direction. In essence, she was taught to not trust her own values and morals for guidance, but rather to follow, subserviently, the rules imposed from outside authority (i.e., parents, nuns, or the Church).

Laura's lifelong personal relationship with God began in early childhood. She wrote:

> *...my mother took me to early communion services starting when I was six. There was a period of silent prayer afterwards. My mother told me to talk to Jesus, and that is what I literally did. God/Jesus was a real person to me and has continued to be since that time. I remember early on being enveloped in warmth and*

loving friendship from One who was much older, wiser, larger, kind, and interested in what I had to say. To me, God was nonjudgmental, never thought me silly or dumb, and was actually glad to hear from me. I was never afraid of God, although I wondered how such a vast and wise Entity could possibly be personally interested in me when God had so much to do. Instead, I felt deep encouragement, active listening, and empathy coming from the Source I talked to in my mind.

Many years after termination of therapy, Laura came back for additional counseling regarding an enormously difficult professional situation. My support and dedication to Laura's health and well-being were a comfort, but it was not enough. She wrote:

I sought God desperately by asking Him in my mind for solace, support, and direction. I received it in a series of clear mental pictures. There was a pastoral scene and a living space where I was sometimes held and comforted like a baby in the arms of a beneficent Being. Other times, I was a child standing close beside this large, safe Presence. When I went in my mind to this new, special place, the Being was always waiting. I could talk, express my fears and hopes, and receive nonverbal comfort. I came to call the Being "My Powerful Friend," because It was, both in deed and action. I came out of this terrifying ordeal comforted and firmly supported by what I feel is an all-encompassing, active Love who takes care of Its child.

She attained courage to follow her inner guidance and chose to leave the distressing professional circumstance by retiring.

Laura experiences her spirituality and relationship with God through three dimensions of relational consciousness. First, she has a personal dialogue and interactive communication with God, her Powerful Friend. Second, she is profoundly sensitive to others and can feel their fears or needs intuitively. Her empathy and compassionate understanding fuel her desire to help others and express her love. Third, she experiences a sense of wonder and inspiration with her garden and with the flora and fauna that surround her home. She communicates with God through nature, specifically through a loving intimacy with plants in her lush garden, which is so beautiful and bountiful that it has been the focus of local publicity.

Her relationship with God has been the foundation of her life and her daily focus, as well as the means to endure all experiences, both trials and joys. She wrote:

> *In the midst of all [of these disruptions in my life] was an empty church building with Jesus waiting for me in the tabernacle, where I was encouraged to "make visits," as we children called them, and to play the organ, all in a two-way conversation. There and inside me was a calm, safe island of retreat. It wasn't the Church, I finally realized. It was God.*

Charles

Laura's husband, Charles, is in his mid 60s and recently retired from a long and successful academic career. Throughout his childhood, Charles was abused and severely neglected. His mother overtly rejected him and let him know daily through harsh words that he was a nuisance. She lavished attention on his older brother but frequently criticized Charles with occasional slaps. His father was completely withdrawn from the family and would retreat to the couch to nap, always responding to his wife's tirades with the same words: "All I want is peace and quiet." While home, Charles remained utterly silent every day. His brother mocked and attacked him relentlessly so that he was afraid to be near him. While visiting grandparents, he was put alone in the basement, even as a young child. Regarding repeated childhood abuse, he stated, "I knew better than to complain even while very young— my mother's screaming and ranting would not stop, even if I were to speak a word or cry." In essence, throughout his young life, he pulled into a shell, took care of himself, and lived as separately as possible.

Charles attempted to remain unnoticed both at home and at school, even though he excelled academically. He appeared untouched by his mother's cruel harassment, but due to his deep emotional sensitivity, he was unable to prevent the messages of worthlessness from entering his self-concept. Subsequently, each class, assignment, and test became a means to prove his worth—or lack thereof—to himself. Charles never cared about competition with others; instead, he was on a never-ending mission to prove to himself that he was acceptable.

Due to the internalized critical voice of his mother, his scholastic accomplishments did not alter his negative self-assessment. His fear and anxiety about never being "good enough," and the internal question of whether he had anything of value to offer, lasted throughout his entire professional career, despite evidence to the contrary. Charles did not welcome recognition of his superior capabilities. He feared that any attention had strings attached of additional demands which he would be forced to meet. He assumed that he would fail to satisfy others' expectations. According to Alice Miller (1981), in order to survive repetitive criticism and ridicule, an emotionally sensitive child will put up a shield by becoming emotionally withdrawn or by separating from the emotion. Creating an inner wall of protection successfully keeps the harassment out, but it also imprisons the self within.

Despite his difficult childhood, Charles kept his strong motivation to learn. In high school, college, and graduate school, he simply could not do enough to satisfy his profound intellectual curiosity. Throughout his academic career, he received numerous prestigious awards. Once he left for college, he rarely went back to his parents' home. He was determined to live according to his own passions, values, and principles.

At the suggestion of his wife, Charles entered therapy when his father died. During the first year of counseling, he discovered how much he had been abused and severely neglected throughout his childhood. When I asked him to tell me about himself and his upbringing, he simply relayed stories without emotion. He was surprised to learn that his experiences were not normal but were abusive, and he was amazed to learn that his chronic anxiety was a symptom of Post-Traumatic Stress Disorder. As we attended to and listened to his thoughts, anxieties, and fears, his body messages and his "gut" response to the memories, he was able to recognize the extreme unmet needs of the frightened child within. The memories triggered reliving the events and resulted in panic attacks, extreme agitation, and fears. Weekly, we attended to Charles' complex inner world and to the inner child's fears and need to hide. He learned to call on a competent and safe adult part of himself—the professor—to respond to the frightened boy and protect him. Charles fought the inner battle with his anxiety in years of intense therapy.

Throughout his life, Charles freely offered compassion and kindness to others, but he needed to learn to offer himself the same thing. Being kind and compassionate to himself was unimaginable to him. Through his profound loving and steadfast partner at home—Laura—and our caring, deeply empathic, respectful, and genuine therapeutic relationship, healing began. The mantra was (and still is): *Love is the most powerful force in the universe.* Love is the healing force to alleviate self-hate, self-judgment, and self-negation.

Through therapy and his subsequent healing, Charles' gentle, loving nature began to open up, and every aspect of his life began to change. He gradually embraced his inner child and simultaneously gave free expression to his generous, tender, and kind temperament. His soft and gentle spirit had been kept hidden almost all of his life, or so he thought, by being shy and limiting his relationships to a select few. In actuality, it was impossible for Charles to hide his elevated ethical nature or his profound scholastic capability. Regardless of being the target of bullies throughout his school years, Charles never retaliated or treated others with meanness. Finally, as a professor, his heightened moral fiber demanded that he "find his voice" to stand up for students or colleagues who were being treated unjustly. He was sought out by students, junior faculty, and colleagues in need. Additionally, his lifelong passion for learning was exemplified in his teaching. Students flocked to his classes, and he was admired year after year for his teaching, as well as his research and award-winning publications. He said that the most meaningful components of his 37-year professorship were the caring relationships that he had with advisees, helping them to achieve their professional goals. Before he retired from his profession, he was awarded the highest honor attainable at a prestigious university.

Although he was an acutely sensitive and perceptive child, Charles protected himself from the onslaught of verbal ridicule by closing off his deep emotions and numbing himself. He remained hidden and thereby protected from others. Emotionally gifted individuals who were abused as children find ways to "preserve the inner core" of themselves. "There are situations which suggest that the concept of emotional giftedness should be extended to include the capacity for emotional survival against all odds" (Piechowski, 2003, p. 408).

One of the qualities found in resilient adults is that abused persons recognize, often while young, that the cruelty and neglect they experienced were unjustified (Higgins, 1994). As a result, they emotionally separate and detach from the family, thereby enabling them to survive the abuse and in later years live a life of well-being. Certainly, Charles had no intrinsic attachment to his family; instead, he strove to be as separate and independent as possible throughout his life. Being so disenfranchised by his family did not, however, protect him from the emotional pain of chronic verbal abuse and the anxiety of future attacks. Charles was resilient; despite the abuse, he was able to attain deep contentment from his personal intellectual pursuits.

Charles survived his cruel home environment through the inner knowledge that good prevailed—within him and within others. In his adult life, irrespective of how he was treated, he interacts with kindness, caring, and compassion. He gives of himself freely to those in need, not expecting any assistance in return. He believes in an order much larger than what is seen or can be scientifically tested, and he intuitively knows of his connection with an omnipotent realm through his expansive experiences with nature. He speaks often of going outside when he was young and visiting with his neighbor friend, the large dog next door. He would pet and play with the dog for hours and felt mutual love in their relationship. Simply being outside, embraced by nature, he said he was no longer alone. As soon as Charles was old enough to go by himself on a bus, he traveled across the large city to museums, where he spent endless hours lost in discovery. Through these means, Charles survived.

Charles reclaimed his life and moved from distress and fear to faith and trust, from living death to living love, from aloneness to companionship, from hiding to being open and self-respected. When talking about his spiritual birth, Charles wrote:

> *Therapy was the catalyst for my spiritual birth. The release from controlling anxiety and the surfacing of buried spirituality went hand-in-hand. The first reduction in anxiety led to a genuine spirituality—so small that I was unaware of it. However, the budding spirituality reinforced the therapeutic treatment of my anxiety to accelerate the shift from anxiety to spirituality. I had long had an intellectual knowledge of transcendence, but this knowledge could not penetrate into my emotions and relieve my panic attacks. I became consciously aware of my emerging spirituality simultaneously with the lessening grip of fear.*

For 60 years, pain and anxiety had dominated Charles' life. Finally, through the growing connection and protection that he felt in Spirit's loving presence, he developed trust both of Spirit's omnipotence and his worthiness for love.

As long as he was in the clutches of chronic fear and anxiety, Charles' profound emotional and spiritual sensitivity was blocked. However, his advanced spiritual nature shone through in his empathic response to others, as well as his just and compassionate actions. Today, Charles is able to write, "I experience my emerging spirituality as an emotional-level trust of what is. I can accept reality, including the reality of myself and the reality of my fears."

Having gained refuge in the love energy of the Divine, he has subsequently found strength and confidence in a loving self. He devotes his energy and attention to cultivating an intimate relationship with the Divine, which in turn encourages an authentic expression of his self.

Charles experiences his spirituality and relationship with God through three dimensions of relational consciousness. First, he experiences the unlimited essence of the Self, which he often experiences while writing and which leads him to previously uncharted intuitive realms and deep contentment. Second, through daily meditations, he experiences an Almighty healing force of love, which he recognizes as the presence of Great Spirit pulsating through him, protecting and guiding him. Third, he experiences moments of transcendence while working peacefully in the garden, connected intimately with Mother Earth. These spiritual experiences have been validated through his reading of American Indian traditions.

Suzanne

When she came into counseling, Suzanne was working on her Ph.D. She planned to finish her entire master's and doctoral program in four years, which she thought was ample time, even though pursuing such a program usually requires seven years. Thus far in life, Suzanne had been able to do whatever she wanted to pursue or accomplish. She would simply set her mind to it, follow through with energy and enthusiasm, and make it happen. By age 22, she was living a joyful, carefree life.

When she entered my office, she was overtly bubbly, joyful, kind, and gentle—not the typical new client. As she proceeded to tell me about herself, it became clear that Suzanne was suffering from discomfort and guilt that her life had an abundance of blessings. She did not know how to reconcile her wealth—across all aspects of her life—with the lack, pain, and hardships that other people endured. She felt unworthy of such a blessed life, certain that she was no different from the poorest individual on the street. Why was she given so much when others were destitute? Why was she healthy and strong while others were starving, weak, or physically suffering? Why had she grown up in an upper-middle class home while others did not even have shelter or clothing to keep them warm? Why was she able to breeze through school, have a swarm of good friends, and wake up joyful while others struggled with studies, were isolated or alone, and woke up desperate and depressed? Knowing deep within that she was not more worthy than the next person, she wrestled with the inequality of life. She questioned the meaning of her life, the purpose of her existence, and her relationship with "All That Is." She desperately needed to be a contributing member of humankind, a changing agent of others' pain, and a loving partner with Mother Earth. Daily, she contemplated what she must do and how she must live to be worthy of her many gifts and live a purposeful life.

Suzanne chose a field of study that connected her with the needs of the community. She became the star student in her program, receiving honors and recognition, but continued to suffer from her guilt. In therapy, we used guided visualization about what she had emotionally and physically gathered through her deep empathy to another's pain so that she would have the fortitude to once again offer her healing energy. Over time, she began to wholeheartedly embrace the bounty and majesty of her gifts. She understood that it was through her inner richness that she could be of service to others. She realized the necessity of accepting with gratitude her intellectual acuity, the depths of her emotion and empathy, her physical strength and stamina, and her spiritual attunement and vigor so that she might respond in times of others' needs. She knew that throughout her life, she would act as a healing force, be of service to others, share the energy of light and love, and actively maintain her own balance, health, and well-being.

When I contacted Suzanne to ask if she could be included in this writing, she wrote, "I think I was quite deeply attached to being recognized/standing out in some way." Her self-identity depended on her accomplishments.

> *I think it is true that "doing well" and "being liked" have often come easy for me in my life. When I think back on this dynamic, one of the challenges of this life experience is that from a young age, I came to develop my sense of self around these successes. By the time I was an adolescent/young adult, it felt almost crushing to ever have life not cooperate in supporting this perception/experience of myself. It was also challenging to be with and make sense of life experiences that were painful because they didn't fit easily with this somewhat one-sided sense of self I held.*

When one's self-identity depends on achievement and external recognition, then without the accolades, one lacks worth. This cycle of pursuing extrinsic rewards can rob the individual of time to pursue what intrinsically brings joy. With Suzanne, her self-expectation of superior achievement kept her imprisoned in her ego need. Her prayer life reflected that she must remain on top compared with others in order to maintain an internal feeling that "all is well." She said:

This motivated me to approach spirituality as a means of keeping me safe and secure, hoping that God would grant me success in my endeavors and relationships. As a child, and into my early twenties, spirituality was a place I went to for comfort, but was also closely intertwined with my desire for achievement. If things went my way, I felt "inside of the blessing," and when things didn't, I felt like I had somehow screwed up to not be meriting the blessing from Spirit that I was accustomed to.

Suzanne described how she became dependent on external cues of her worth to abate her low-grade anxiety that her everyday success would somehow evaporate. "I recall walking out in the prairie during graduate school and noticing how I was always looking for something, hoping for some mystical experience around the next bend as I'd walk in nature. There was a lack of ease and a discomfort that I was always looking to lessen."

More than a decade later, Suzanne describes her current spirituality this way:

When I consider my sense of spirituality now, it feels much softer, fuller, more fluid and open and accepting. It feels more like a natural expression and extension of who I am, and less driven out of some need to take the edge off of life. I think I've finally come to meet whatever needs I had around achieving. I feel much more content and accepting of who I am. I am as motivated as ever to be of service, but it is no longer as an apology; it just feels like a natural expression of who I am.

A spiritual principle true in Mother Nature and our human nature is balance and the harmony of life itself. Suzanne strives to live this balance, and she writes, "I'm also more aware of the need for reciprocity in life—learning and teaching, taking care of myself, offering to others, receiving from others, having friendships in which I feel 'met'—and the sustainable cycle of these things when they are approached with wisdom."

When discussing her present spiritual practices, she says that they are "ridiculously eclectic." Since having children, she is "much more flexible"—e.g., doing yoga for two minutes, listening to CDs in the car versus reading, reciting a series of "intentions, devotions, or prayers," with the two most important being "Thy will be done/May my will be yoked to God's will" and "May I cultivate an open heart in all situations and all moments." Additionally, she prays "to be open and receptive and teachable by Spirit." During coveted free moments, she practices receptive listening, journaling, reading spiritual material of all traditions, walks in nature, and reciting "energy-centering devotional prayer." She says, "most often, when I am doing counseling, teaching, holding ritual space—I also feel deeply connected to Spirit."

Suzanne experiences communion with the Divine through all four relational consciousness means: direct communication with the Divine during meditative practices, intimate relationship with and through the majesty of oneself, profound empathy and respect for others while living a life of service, and an intimate relationship with nature and the universe.

Common Traits of Three Spiritually Gifted Adults

The individuals presented above illustrate the ability to reach beyond the self and to connect with the Divine. Each is dedicated to living a courageous life of self-reflection and transformation. Daily, they strive to live in accordance with an inner barometer, which requires listening to and embracing the complex nature of their intellectual, emotional, physical, social, and spiritual selves. No longer feeling compelled to please others, they consciously choose to be open and accepting of whatever comes their way. Instead of submitting to an internalized inner authority or controlling voice, their daily goal is to simply be who they are called from within to be, moment to moment, day by day. The daily "war" within—to quiet old tapes of self-demands and judgments, and to follow inner guidance and an intuitive way of knowing—has grown easier over many months and years. The reward for their daily efforts is a life of integrity and freedom of self-expression.

All three of these individuals can be viewed through the lens of Dabrowski's (1967) theory of personality development, the theory of positive disintegration. Dabrowski describes a developmental potential to attain a personality ideal through overexcitabilities, individual values and emotional reactions, and what he calls an autonomous factor. The theory depicts the movement that one makes from an extrinsic value system, largely guided by biological impulses and social group norms (referred to as first and second factors), to an individual structure that leads to a unique personality development. Descriptions of the tenets of Dabrowski's theory can be found elsewhere (Dabrowski, 1970; Mendaglio, 2008a; Piechowski, 1979, 1986; Silverman, 1993c).

The three adults above exhibit many, if not all, of the five over-excitabilities in their everyday lives—psychomotor, sensual, intellectual, imaginational, and emotional. Life for them is vibrant in good moments and overwhelming and turbulent at more difficult times. Piechowski (1986) studied the growth of the self through one's emotional experiences and described overexcitabilities as heightened excitability imparting a different quality of experience. In later writing, he clarified, "The original meaning of overexcitability is of a heightened intensity of experiencing and an increased sensitivity to the surrounding world and to others' emotional energy fields. Overexcitability means not just more than average or 'normal' but distinctly more alive and alert. Reacting to experience is quick and strong. The perception of how everything feels, appears, and is understood differs in essence, depth, and complexity" (Piechowski, 2006, p. 34).

These intense ways of being are part of these individuals' very nature; they have experienced and expressed these intensities throughout their lives. However, the intensities were often the focus of criticism, sarcasm, and even rejection from family members, peers, and significant others. As a result, these individuals experienced the intensities as something wrong with them, something to be ashamed of, and the very things to change in order to be acceptable. How does one deal with being too different, too intense, and even unacceptable in one's very nature?

These intensities, with their heightened states of awareness and experience, while bringing a riveting depth of experience, can also feel like a curse—a differentiating and dooming force that one has no power over. Living with overexcitabilities is a two-sided coin—these characteristics exist simultaneously as strengths and also as misfortune and vulnerability.

Dabrowski's (1967) levels of personality development mirror the internal struggles of the three individuals described above, as self-review and critique continued moment to moment. At times, disapproval of self and not being able to live up to self-expectations of "what ought to be" precipitated enduring bouts of depression and anxiety, which hastened disintegration of internalized ways of being. Together in counseling, we reflected on discord within their selves and renamed their distressing experiences as the process of "death before rebirth." We worked on integrating these experiences as "seeds" for positive transformation instead of experiences that they might attempt to hide or bury.

Laura had great vacillating conflicts throughout her early and middle adult years between living following her own intuitive guidance of how she ought to live (Level III) or living with fear and remaining submissive to externalized rules (Level II). Her five overexcitabilities, years of frustrations, reflection and contemplation, journal writing, prayer, intimate communication with God, plus a supportive environment, both in her marriage and in therapy, propelled her through multilevel disintegration.

Charles' ethical and moral beliefs and internal ideology guided his everyday behavior from childhood through adulthood. Social norms were insignificant to him and thereby not attended to. He spoke of a persistent internal beckoning to "be himself" but spent most of his life imprisoned by constant anxiety. According to Dabrowski's theory, Charles has three major aspects that form developmental potential—overexcitabilities, outstanding abilities and talents, and a strong drive toward autonomous growth (Dabrowski, 1970). Charles' courage and tenacity throughout a life of physical and emotional suffering, unyielding dedication to higher-order principles, and experiencing deep contentment by being of service to others clearly depicts his multilevel personality development (Level III) through-out most of his life, and a more advanced level (Level IV) currently.

Although Suzanne has always led a blessed life as measured by worldly goods, parental love, academic success, and ample friendship, she struggled with her sense of being worthy of such gifts. Upon leaving graduate school, she continued on a path of success and achievement. At the same time, she sought to grow spiritually through the transformative love in marriage, rela-tionships with colleagues more mature in their spiritual journey, daily yoga, meditation, the practice of mindfulness, and attending silent retreats. She began to face the confines of her ego and security needs, and she reached to deeper empathic connection with others, as well as to intimate relationship with the Divine. Instead of "holding on to what is" based on a fear of loss, she opened her heart in trust to the Divine Order operating within her self and in all of life. Suzanne endured years of emotional turmoil and self-doubt as she moved from externalized security to her rich internal moral character (Level III development). At the time of this writing, it is evident that her spirituality is mature and deeply integrated. It guides her life, even in the face of numer-ous demands (children, job) throughout the day. Her development has advanced to a higher level (Level IV).

These three adults share a common character in other ways. They have a gentle and sensitive nature while prevailing with strength and tenacity in everyday life. When meeting any of them, one feels kindness, softness, competence, and a genuinely caring spirit. Although this small group of three contains both introverts and extraverts, none has a dominating presence. In their presence, one feels at ease. Although life includes stress, they live from a loving heart.

Empathy and a sense of fairness have guided their lifelong actions. Each has firm ethical and moral convictions that there is a right and just way to act. Their inner beliefs do not allow them to retaliate or hurt another human being. They live with a guiding principle that insists on equality and respect, tolerance and compassion. They believe in equality among all people and feel great personal pain in the face of another's torment. Were they to act mean or ugly to someone, they would be most unforgiving of their thoughts and behavior, since they would have breached the values that they know to be true. They maintain their own sense of justice and fairness, irrespective of what others are doing around them or to them. They have engaged in professions in which they are of service to others. Two of the three survived cruelty, abuse, or neglect, but their resilient nature prevailed. Such demonstrations of high character and morality suggest strong developmental potential (Dabrowski, 1970).

Within them, there is a deep, unmistakable reservoir of that which is beyond, limitless, and abundant. During moments of despair, sadness, or fear, they *know* that there is something better, grander, beyond what is presently seen, and to which they are intimately connected. Piechowski (2003) noted that spiritual giftedness emerges as a predisposition toward elevated states of consciousness and a facility for entering such states. Consequently, a person so endowed can carry out more extensive inner work as a process of transformation that reaches to the deepest levels of the self. In difficult moments, these individuals know that the endless supply of goodness, of love energy that is all-encompassing, is also within them. When they can access this inner sanctuary of peace and love, reaching beyond immediate concerns and fears, they enter an interior love-filled space. They describe this internal space as calm and having order, and a sense of not being alone. In other words, they possess a relational consciousness with the Divine. They fulfill Piechowski's description of emotional and spiritual giftedness with their "sense of an all-embracing connectedness" (Piechowski, 2003, p. 412).

Additionally, the three participants are profoundly intellectually gifted and display characteristics that are common for others of such advanced ability. All three felt a need to achieve throughout their lives, to do their best all of the time, and to be the best in their academic environment. Although two were motivated to compete with others, the greater competition occurred within the self. All three had the unquenchable need to achieve far-reaching, self-chosen goals. They held exceptionally high and unyielding performance expectations of themselves and spoke of their relentless self-demands, coupled with an internalized judge and jury ready to criticize any glimpse of faltering. Due to their outstanding intellectual abilities, others—family, teachers, bosses, deans, colleagues, etc.—also expected stellar academic and career performance from them.

They paired the drive and passion to achieve intellectually with physical stamina, steadfast focus, and tenacity. They had to prove their worth through accomplishments—first to themselves, and secondly to others. To be acceptable to oneself, they had to consistently achieve the highest marks and be endlessly productive. To varying degrees over lengthy periods of their lives, this productivity requirement was essential in order to feel worthwhile and to attain an inner sense of security. But today, these markers of success are faded. Instead, a fulfilling day is when they listen to the intuitive guidance within to direct the course of their day.

All three chose academic careers due to their intellectual abilities, as well as familiarity and comfort with an academic life. In this milieu, they knew the rules, and they belonged. For Charles and Laura, transition to retirement was turbulent. After Suzanne achieved tenure, proving to herself that she was academically able and thereby worthwhile, she left the university position. She pulled out of the high-pressured academic world and created her own professional quests.

Currently, focus on internal guidance aids these three individuals in making daily contemplative choices. They choose activities throughout their day based on values, desires, and passions, which in turn support their well-being. Each day, they focus on orchestrating a balanced and gratifying life.

Summary
The essence of my therapeutic work is helping clients to recognize and integrate all five domains of the self—mind, heart, body, spirit, and social aspects. It is my belief that we must listen to, respect, and honor the messages of the inner self in order to experience a state of completeness and to create stability and well-being in our everyday life. The clients described here have identified and embraced their intellectual, emotional, and spiritual

gifts, asynchronies, and overexcitabilities. Ultimately, they have discerned the wisdom within and followed internal guidance with subsequent action. They have become skilled at using their body as an accurate barometer reflecting their inner experience, and this attention to inherent experiences has helped build a sense of self-trust, intrinsic dependability, and inner balance. Ultimately, being present to the connection between themselves and the Divine (understood as Universal Order, God, Special Friend, Great Mystery, or Mother Earth, to name a few) has notably anchored their lives.

The internal experiences listed above, coupled with the individuals' high moral character and lifelong commitment to being of service, suggests a high level of personality development, as Dabrowski described it. These individuals have frequent experiences of the Divine through the four dimensions of relational consciousness described by Nye (1998). For each, spiritual communication and union provide the underpinning of their daily experience. Feeling oneness with all, encountering a pervasive loving presence, experiencing communion with Spirit—all of these experiences have transformed their understanding of life and how they live. These characteristics indicate spiritual giftedness.

These three adults are on individual spiritual paths, each unique to themselves. They live in accordance with their heartfelt desire, which in turn spurs their spiritual growth. They are choosing to follow what makes their heart and spirit sing.

Although an active pursuit of spirituality can be delayed due to trauma or survival needs, the ingredients of heightened spirituality—intense sensitivity, caring, empathy, integrity, honesty, living a life of equality and justice, being of service to others, and communion with the Divine—remain constant in their lives. They experience life's tribulations as challenges that test living a daily spiritual path. Although at times they feel emotional pain, such as anxiety, fear, sadness, or confusion, it is no longer bigger than their inner mechanism to "release" or "to let go and let God." Each has developed a means to "enter the light" and reach up to Spirit, Divine Order, or God in times of joy and gratitude, as well as during times of need. They are moving toward embracing themselves, others, and "All That Is" and uniting with an order greater than their intellectual and emotional grasp. Spiritually, as well as in everyday mundane life, the "I" begets the "We," which begets the "All"—the cycle is a continuous flow—"I," "We," "All" are One. These individuals are each committed to knowing and living this truth.

Chapter 13

What We May Be: What Dabrowski's Work Can Do for Gifted Adults

Stephanie S. Tolan, M.A.

It is never too late to be what you might have been.

This quotation, often attributed to George Eliot, might be a capsule version of what Dabrowski's theory, with its emphasis on the dynamics of human moral development, offers to gifted adults, whatever their life experience. How are we as adults to interpret the journey of our lives, our gifts, our complexities, our frustrations and failures? *And what might we be?*

To address the question of how gifted adults might use Dabrowski's legacy to help them answer these questions for themselves, let me tell some stories from the lives of gifted adults.

The first story is about my own introduction to Dabrowski. As a consultant and writer about the needs of gifted children, particularly their social and emotional needs, I first discovered the work of Dabrowski as many others in the field did, through Michael Piechowski's chapter in Colangelo and Zaffrann's (1979) *New Voices in Counseling the Gifted*, which I read sometime in the mid-80s.

I remember very well how much impact that reading had on me. Dabrowski's "overexcitabilities" were immediately recognizable, not only in the lives of the gifted children I knew, but in my own as well. Here was a theorist who made the case that the sensitivity and intensity that had been called "too much" by the adults in my early life (and so by myself ever after) were not only normal for the population of gifted and creative people, but served as a critical foundation for potential personal development. In a single afternoon, my view of my own life was turned upside down. I was here being offered an explanation that, for the first time, allowed me to accept and even value aspects of myself that had caused considerable difficulty for me and annoyance and consternation for many people in my world.

It was obvious to me that both parents and their gifted children need the affirmation that Dabrowski's work provides, and that any adults who work with these children should be aware of his work in order to understand the extraordinary levels of intensity that these children experience, the levels of intensity that influence their awareness, their view of the world, and their behavior. I immediately began to incorporate the overexcitabilities into my writing and speaking.

The result was predictable. When I shared the overexcitabilities with audiences of parents, the majority found their views of their children, their own life experiences, and the whole subject of giftedness changing as quickly as mine had. Not only did they now have a positive interpretation for a variety of sometimes odd and problematic behaviors that they had not necessarily connected to unusual intellect, but they realized that the five kinds of overexcitability showed giftedness to be a considerably broader concept than they'd previously thought. The overexcitabilities had a broadening effect on the subject of intelligence itself, just as Howard Gardner's idea of multiple intelligences had, but with a focus on development, internal processing, and experience rather than achievement. It was a huge and positive change.

However, overexcitabilities are only one aspect of Dabrowski's comprehensive view of personality and moral development. Looking more deeply into his work, I could see that his theory of positive disintegration and his delineation of what he called developmental levels were as important to understanding the possible life paths of gifted individuals as the overexcitabilities were to understanding the intensities of gifted children.

The following is a brief look at the levels of development in a lay person's language that I began to use in my talks so that the emotional difficulties and conflicts that many gifted children routinely face could be understood as an aspect of their moral and emotional development.

Table 13.1. Positive Disintegration: Levels of Development
Adapted by Stephanie Tolan

Level I – Primary Integration

Self as center of the universe. Neither empathy nor personal responsibility is available to the individual.

Level II – Unilevel Disintegration

Moral relativism; influenced by social group and mainstream values. Internal conflict is horizontal, with no mechanism for prioritizing values.

Level III – Spontaneous Multilevel Disintegration

Development of a hierarchical value system. Internal conflict is vertical between "lower" and "higher" self or personality ideal. Individual sees self as "is" and self as "ought to be."

Psychoneurosis develops (anxiety, depression, existential despair). Big questions asked: "What is my purpose?" "Is there a God?" Inability to attain certain answers creates pain and intense struggles.

Level IV – Organized Multilevel Disintegration

Development of high levels of responsibility, empathy, self-awareness. Choices more and more fit the personality ideal—powerful movement in the direction of self-actualization. Personal value system in place, superseding cultural values.

Level V – Secondary Integration

Personality ideal attained. Disintegration transcended; personal life lived in service to humanity. Behavior matches universal values and beliefs.

To move into Level III, spontaneous multilevel disintegration, requires developmental potential that is created by the presence of the overexcitabilities, especially emotional overexcitability. Dabrowski observed that many adults never achieve that third level, which is the threshold for advanced development. Those who work with gifted children and adolescents see that many of these young people routinely do reach it. It may well be that some gifted children come into the world already functioning at Level III, or they reach that stage at ages when more average children have not yet begun to develop the necessary abstract reasoning to become genuinely aware of both the nature of self and the needs of others.

In 1992, I attended the Dabrowski conference at Ashland University in Ohio, where I had an opportunity to listen to many of the major proponents of Dabrowski's work in the United States and Canada and to discuss his theories with a large group of interested people. A memory that particularly stands out from that experience is the discussion of the rarity of individual human beings who had actually achieved the fifth developmental level, that of secondary integration. Dabrowski considered that level to be so demanding that few people other than recognized masters such as Jesus and Buddha could be said to have attained it. Secondary integration seemed almost beyond human achievement. At that conference, Michael Piechowski spoke of two others who seemed to have reached that level of self-actualization: Eleanor Roosevelt and Peace Pilgrim.

I felt sure that I myself had reached Level III—spontaneous multilevel disintegration—and believed that it was the experience of disintegration that accounted for my own lifelong pattern of recurring clinical depressions. The notion that what others considered a form of mental illness was actually a process of disintegration necessary to move beyond the norms developmentally was just as affirming as the discovery that my sensitivity and intensity were a positive aspect of my being. But as intriguing as I found the subject of positive disintegration leading on to individual moral development or spiritual evolution, I remember stating clearly to several colleagues at the conference that I had no wish to move on to Level IV, much less to Level V. I was quite willing to content myself with nothing more than moments of experiencing myself as I "ought to be." It seemed to me, as I listened to discussions of the hierarchy of development, that to reach the top of the hierarchy was to give up the notion of "self" entirely. This was something that I was not ready to contemplate.

In my teens, I had attended an Episcopal school for girls and had had more than enough pressure in the direction of asceticism and selfless service. I distinctly remember thinking that Peace Pilgrim's renunciation of money, security, family, and essentially all of the comfortable and comforting aspects of 20th century American civilization was far too "saintly" for me. It was interesting to read about such people, but not the least appealing to attempt to become one.

Though I continued to speak of Dabrowski's work, sharing the above condensation of positive disintegration through the developmental levels, like most people in the gifted field, I focused my attention primarily on the overexcitabilities, which seemed to contain much more practical information for those dealing with gifted children and adolescents, making it much more likely to relate to them. After all, most people who did move into either the fourth or the fifth level of development seemed to do so as adults.

Encountering Gifted Adults

Eventually, however, I was asked to write a piece about gifted adults for the *Roeper Review.* "Discovering the Gifted Ex-Child" was published in 1994(a). Later, it was reprinted in *Advanced Development* (1996) and made available on my website, as well as on Internet reprint websites. From the time of its initial publication, the article began to bring me a steady stream of mail and email (often pages long) from adults who recognized themselves in its pages and wanted to share their stories. Some of them had only recently begun to suspect that they had been gifted children; others had been identified in school. But all of their stories included experiences of isolation, frustration, confusion, and what at best they thought of as neglect and at worst outright educational abuse. The memorable subject line of one of these emails was "Gifted Child, Broken Adult." Their needs had not been met, they wrote. What could they do now?

For the most part, they were looking for confirmation, support, and advice. Sometimes they asked for little more than a willing listener who could understand the stories they poured out and the feelings that went with them. Those with children uniformly expressed determination to somehow offer their children a better experience than they'd had themselves. They hoped that I knew of the right school or a knowledgeable counselor able to save their children the pain that they had suffered. Occasionally, someone said that in spite of a difficult childhood, she had finally found her place as a gifted adult, using her capacities in a satisfying way—but positive letters like this were extremely rare!

The fervor with which most of these correspondents described both their sense of personal recognition in reading the article and the varied emotions that accompanied that recognition (often beginning with exhilaration, gratification, and vindication, but leading on to outrage, frustration, grief, devastation, and even despair) showed evidence of the effect of their overexcitabilities. Whatever their lives had brought them, their experience of it had been deep and intense.

On the surface, most of the letters seemed unrelated to the issue of positive disintegration moving in the direction of moral development. These were mostly people focusing on the pain of their lives, their sense of having missed out on something necessary to their being. These were people who thought of themselves as victims of an unaware, uncaring system, a culture defensive and hostile to its brightest members. They were not speaking of values, or personal moral ideals, or even—usually—of a desire to be of service in the world. They seemed primarily to want from the world what they had been denied—what they felt they deserved.

Looking more deeply, however, one can find evidence of that elusive concept in Dabrowski's work—the third factor. Described as an inner drive, some difficult to define but powerful force that may help a person push through pain and frustration, through the "slings and arrows of outrageous fortune" and the disintegration of lower coping mechanisms, it is the third factor that activates the individual's innate intensity in favor of personal growth and evolution.

Each of these correspondents had somehow found and read my article, whether in the *Roeper Review*, on my website, or in a reprint database. A few had been researching articles about gifted people for help in making the right choices for their children, but the fact that they read an article about gifted adults makes it clear that there was a hook for them in the title. Even if outwardly they may have seemed to be, as Thoreau (1854/2004) put it, "living lives of quiet desperation" (p. 7), these were people who had not given up entirely. They were still longing, still searching for something better. Something was pushing them from inside to not just read about the "gifted ex-child," but to write, then, to the author, to recount their story to someone who just might offer some hope. Whenever I received such a letter, I was reminded of a fire that at first appears to have gone out—all ashes and bits of burnt wood—until someone or something stirs it. Hidden under the ashes is an ember, ready to rekindle into flame with the right combination of air and fuel.

Whether the rekindling happens or not cannot be easily predicted. But one way to encourage it could be to share with these gifted individuals Dabrowski's work, including both the overexcitabilities and the theory of positive disintegration. Discovering the overexcitabilities provides a positive interpretation of negative-seeming personality traits, and perceiving the obstacles, pains, and struggles of one's life as necessary steps in the direction of personal evolution can fundamentally change the effects of those obstacles, pains, and struggles. The additional idea of autopsychotherapy can give them hope that their ability to transform themselves and their lives does not depend on finding someone to guide them through the process.

One of these correspondents, to whom I have given the name Sarah, began her first message to me in the usual way, recounting stories of parents who didn't understand her, teachers who humiliated her, a school system that until college had little useful to offer her. But she also hinted of a spiritual journey that she had begun many years after graduating from college "as a rational nihilist" and adapting to a life as a wife and mother, writing poetry to "keep herself sane." We began a correspondence, and she allowed me to use the story of her adolescent spiritual quest in the article "Spirituality and the Highly Gifted Adolescent" (Tolan, 2000). In my response to Sarah's first message, I recommended that she read about Dabrowski's work, and she quickly became a passionate proponent of his ideas. She wrote me about the ways in which she felt that her life was a clear example of positive disintegration and movement through the levels of development.

In an effort to find something more challenging than public education, she had been sent to a Catholic school at age 13, though her family was not Catholic. By the time she graduated from high school, she had converted and was planning to become a teaching nun when she finished college. "I think," she wrote, "that might have been more the influence of the environment—Level II's willingness to accept whatever values others accept—than a really personal choice. A life of poverty, chastity, and obedience was supposed to be a high and noble calling. I may have thought that living a high and noble calling was a little like getting all A's—a way of proving my worth. And certainly a convent seemed the easiest place to live that way."

In college, she entered fully into Level III's spontaneous multilevel disintegration. The academic community's emphasis on reason and scientific materialism appealed to her intellect and quickly eroded her religious convictions. Her plan to enter the convent, and her Catholicism itself, failed to survive her sophomore year. Struggling with the big philosophical questions and her own failure to live up to the personal rules of morality that she had gleaned from the nuns, she developed a depression so deep that she seriously considered suicide in her junior year.

Looking back on her life through the lens of Dabrowski's theory, she felt that when she first wrote to me, she had been "on the cusp" between Level III and Level IV. After years of dealing with anxiety and depression, as well as several other brushes with suicide, she had begun what she thought of as a spiritual journey, trying to overcome the limits of scientific materialism and return to what she suspected had been the natural spirituality of her early childhood—a sense of utter belonging in nature and the divinity in all things. "I feel like I had a more authentic sense of self at three than I did at 30. As if I knew I belonged in the universe back then, but that awareness had been trained out of me. The other day I had a sudden sense of myself lying on my bed, pounding my pillow with both fists—I was probably only three or four—and shrieking at the top of my lungs, 'It's okay to be me! It's okay to be me!' Something very powerful in my life must have been telling me the opposite. I'm only beginning to come back to that idea now."

Having made a commitment to her own development, Sarah has continued a challenging spiritual journey, sharing her experience with me as she goes. Her most recent communication tentatively suggests that she is once more on a cusp, but "closing in on Level V, because there's hardly any conflict any more." She thinks the idea that Level V is nearly unattainable is a matter of perspective. "I guess I don't make a very good disciple," she says. "Because I have come to disagree with Dabrowski about how nearly impossible it is. Maybe the problem is that the people he believed had reached that level had chosen a path that got them famous and recognized, and he was looking for a particular *kind* of service from them. Dabrowski was Catholic, wasn't he? I think that gives his idea about the highest levels of moral development a little bit of a skew. His idea of how Level V looks seems very much like self-sacrifice, which is a really Catholic, a really Christian, idea. I believe there are people who are fully self-actualized, living in service to humanity, whose lives don't look anything like Mother Teresa or Jesus. They are *stealth* Level V people whose love, compassion, and service go under the radar. They're just quietly being what they came here to be. In *Messiah's Handbook*, Richard Bach says, 'Some say suffer, some say serve, some say detach. Who says find your highest right for yourself?'"

Sarah provides an important perspective for adults who are attempting to move through the pains, the struggles, the disintegration of their lives as deeply sensitive and intense beings toward a fulfillment of their deepest sense of self. Peace Pilgrim, one of the moral exemplars Michael Piechowski (1992) cites as an example of a person who attained Level V and the person I thought of as too saintly to imitate, suggested that the direction of what she called emotional development was from the "lower self" to the "higher self." "Your lower self sees you as the center of the universe—your higher self sees you as a cell in the body of humanity.... When you come into this world your jobs in the divine plan are there. They just need to be realized and lived" (Peace Pilgrim, 1983, pp. 10-11).

Our physical bodies have a great many cells, each with a different purpose and meaning to the whole—what Peace Pilgrim might call our body's divine plan. So it is with individual humans as cells in the body of humanity. When people asked her whether they ought to take up the life of a pilgrim in order to live the highest ideal of life, she pointed out that *she* had been called to that life, but that their task was to discover what their own purpose, their own calling, might be.

When I initially said that I didn't wish to attain the higher levels of Dabrowski's scheme of moral development, I think I was unable to fully understand what those levels meant, unable even to imagine from where I was then where I could get to be on my journey. What I knew was that I didn't want to live life the way Peace Pilgrim did, owning nothing, disconnected from family. I had not yet encountered a statement that I recently found, attributed to Ralph Waldo Emerson,[1] that "imitation is a form of suicide."

The body could not function with only blood cells, only skin cells, only brain cells. Just so, diversity is essential to the functioning of the universe. There are, indeed, universal values of love and compassion, but there are as many ways to live those values as there are individual humans. As wonderful, for instance, as the task of immune cells might be, they are only one small part of a fully functional organism.

A friend of mine who retired early in order to take on several volunteer jobs has fully chosen to live her life in service to humanity. But after Hurricane Katrina, when many people were going down to New Orleans to help, she told me that she felt guilty for not abandoning her volunteer jobs for a time and going down there, too. When we perceive a particular task as the "right thing to do" no matter who we are and no matter what else we may be doing, we are listening to external voices, not to the inner guidance of the actualized self.

Sarah's journey, though in many ways propelled by Dabrowski's theory, has taken her in a direction that she believes goes beyond how Dabrowski looked at the phenomenon of personal transformation. She says that she isn't surprised by this, nor does it in any way take away from Dabrowski's work. "It really sent me down a path I might never have found for myself. He was a visionary in his time, but it only makes sense that in our time, we may be able to transcend his vision, or at least take it to new places. Level V isn't the top of some mountain that you 'get to' like Hilary on Everest. I think it may be more like a doorway into a whole new realm. Once you find the part you came to play, the next part of the journey is the adventure of playing it."

---

1 I've been unable to verify this attribution.

Tom is another highly gifted person whose story is worth looking at through Dabrowski's lens. I met him recently in an airport as we both waited in a very crowded gate area for a delayed plane. We got to chatting, and as our conversation went beyond the question of where we were bound for that day and where we were coming from, he was led, somehow, to tell me about his education. He had begun reading long before starting school, and his first years in the system were painful and deeply frustrating. His was the classic story of the unrecognized, underachieving gifted boy, turning against a system that wasn't able to meet his needs. He had been in trouble much of the time, dabbling with drugs and committing petty crimes.

After high school, he drifted, and though he gave up drugs, he switched to alcohol. He married, had children, ended up losing his family because of his addiction, and then found Alcoholics Anonymous. "It turned me completely around," he said. "I went to college and got a degree in accounting and began to try to figure out how to live." Prior to that, he had moved from job to job and place to place, looking for a fit between himself and the world. A few years ago, he settled on an island off the coast of Georgia, where he now works for a large resort chain.

"I worked for these same people years and years ago, just after I got my degree, and it wasn't enough for me," he said. "I didn't make enough money, and there wasn't enough room for advancement. But now I love what I do." I asked him what had changed about the job. "*It* hasn't changed at all. *I* have. I don't own a lot of stuff," he said, "but I have what I need. I know what counts in life and what doesn't. Love counts. So does beauty. And connection. I'm back in touch with my kids. I had to learn to like myself first—and finally I do. I live in one of the most beautiful natural spots in the country, and I have time to enjoy it." He stopped talking for a while, staring off out the window where our plane was finally taxiing toward the gate. Then he smiled. "You know, most of my life I learned through pain and struggle. No pain, no gain, you know. But now I see that there's a lot to be learned from joy, too. Some of it you can't learn any other way." He laughed, then, as we began to gather our belongings to board the plane. "Who would have guessed, knowing me as that angry, messed up, alcoholic kid, that by the time my hair got gray, I'd have become a success?"

As I got on the plane, I thought of those letters I get from gifted adults in pain, and I thought of Dabrowski's positive disintegration. Tom, this "gifted ex-child," was an excellent example of making the choice for inner transformation. He had come through Level III and seemed well-embarked on a Level IV journey. But that last part of what he'd learned on the way seems, like Sarah's journey, to go beyond Dabrowski's theory, and it's worth remembering, even as we look to Dabrowski to offer hope to adults who do not yet feel that they have become what they could have been. Pain can knock us backwards, or it can be a spur to growth. Often, as in positive disintegration, it does first one and then the other.

But pain is not the only way that human beings grow and evolve. Joy leads to growth as well. All of us experience pain; all of us experience joy. The capacity for inner transformation depends on how we use them. As Julia Cameron (1997) has said, "Everything—all joy, all loss, all grief, all grace—is an ingredient in the greater self I am building" (pp. 38-39). The direction of personal transformation will always be uniquely individual.

From overexcitabilities to positive disintegration, to the third factor, to the awareness of moral development as an interior journey involving personal choice and the possibility of autopsychotherapy, Dabrowski offers gifted adults a way to reconfigure their experience for themselves. If they choose to do that, the particular way in which they rekindle the flame of who they can be will bring the light of their awakened awareness not just to themselves, but to the body of humanity, of which they are an integral part.

The following quotation from Osho, a Zen master, is one I use to end most of my public talks—it seems appropriate to end this chapter with it as well.

You are not accidental. Existence needs you. Without you,
something will be missing in existence, and no one can replace it.

Part Four

Current Research and Future Directions

Chapter 14

Building Firm Foundations: Research and Assessments

R. Frank Falk, Ph.D., and Nancy B. Miller, Ph.D.

Theory and research go hand in hand; each plays a part in our understanding of the social world. The relationship between theory and research is reciprocal—theory guides research, and research informs theory by providing confirming or disconfirming evidence. Today, acceptable practice calls for clinicians and teachers to use procedures that have been supported with theory and research. This chapter provides information about some of the relevant research on Dabrowski's theory, with the hope that clinicians, teachers, and parents will find it useful in understanding the characteristics of gifted and talented students.

Formal investigation into Dabrowski's theory began in 1969 with funding from the Canada Council for a large-scale research project designed to identify subjects at all levels of personality development (Dabrowski & Piechowski, 1977). Dabrowski and his University of Alberta graduate students worked to develop questionnaires, picture tests, and verbal stimuli (emotion-packed words), which were designed for administration to hundreds of subjects. Respondents completed questionnaires and provided requested information; some also wrote their autobiographies. Researchers then attempted to find and identify components of the theory—developmental potential and developmental dynamisms (moving forces of change and growth)—in these various written materials. As a clinician, Dabrowski had had many years of experience using observation and neurological

239

examinations as a way of "discriminating between higher and lower levels of development" (Dabrowski & Piechowski, 1977, p. 4). Thus, research into components of the theory began with a variety of tests, questions, and examinations, all of which contributed to the firm foundation on which the theory rests.

Briefly, we will describe two fundamental approaches to research—quantitative and qualitative—both of which were employed from the start by Dabrowski researchers. Next, we will describe the levels of development and summarize the more recent research in that area. From there, we will focus on developmental potential, specifically overexcitability, which is necessary for achieving higher levels of development. Again, we will emphasize more recent research using the latest version of the overexcitability questionnaire administered to children, adolescents, and adults.

Approaches to Research

There are two approaches to conducting research; each is based on a different view of reality. One approach takes a more objective stance, the other a more subjective point of view. The first is quantitative research, while the other is qualitative.

Quantitative Data and Analysis

Those who see research as a process of testing hypotheses are taking the objective approach. If you have ideas or hunches about how to obtain desired objectives in the classroom or how to raise successful children, you have hypotheses that could be tested. Researchers with this view see reality as something that exists apart from the observer; the scientist's job is to help us understand that reality. You might, for example, want to test the hypothesis that gifted and talented individuals will show clear signs of moral and social responsibility at higher levels of development. This is just one of the more than 70 hypotheses relating to the theory provided by Dabrowski and colleagues Andrzej Kawczak and Michael Piechowski (1970) in their book *Mental Growth through Positive Disintegration*. Conducting research in this way involves searching for patterns in the information collected, whether from a single individual, such as a life history, or from a large group of subjects, such as survey data. This kind of research is based on objective measures of variables of interest (i.e., behavior, traits, and opinions), and the data collected are numerical.

Qualitative Data and Analysis

The second approach to investigating social phenomena holds that our world is socially constructed, and each of us is creating reality daily as we give meaning to our lives. We do so by interpreting our interactions and the reactions of others, as well as the motives and desires that may be involved. A researcher using this approach might analyze interview material to discern a person's values as revealed through stated beliefs and actions.

This method was used in a recent study of the comments of Nobel Peace Prize Laureates and students attending a PeaceJam conference in Denver, Colorado (Miller, 2007). In the analysis, universal values are exemplified in a statement by the Dalai Lama, who said, "There are no national boundaries. The whole globe is becoming one body.... In these circumstances, I think war is outdated.... Destruction of your neighbor is actually destruction of yourself" (*Dalai Lama*, n.d.). A student's conventional values are reconsidered as he reflects on his PeaceJam experience: "[I learned that] we don't need to fight to settle disputes. We don't need guns, and we don't need to try and kill people" (*3 Students Learn*, n.d.).

If you take this perspective, you consider people's feelings and the meanings that they attach to them. The concerns, issues, and reactions of subjects are important and become the focus of data collection. Theory guides research in suggesting what issues should be explored, what groups should be investigated, and what questions should be asked. This research approach is called *qualitative*; it takes into account the personal or subjective experiences of subjects. It involves observations of behavior, case studies, and open-ended questions—all forms of textual data.

The research that has been done thus far using Dabrowski's theory uses both quantitative and qualitative approaches, both singly and in combination. Integrating the two perspectives provides a fuller and broader view of social and psychological concepts and processes. Findings from each approach are enriched by the insights gained from the other.

Content Analysis

Content analysis is an example of the combination of quantitative and qualitative methodology. This approach to research involves the systematic and objective study of textual content, followed by numerical analysis of the data. Information is collected by observing behavior; asking open-ended questions; or analyzing diaries, biographies, or written transcripts—any means of collecting descriptive data. Counting occurrences of particular traits or themes in the data is the final step. Researchers can use simple descriptive statistics—i.e., percentages or means—to represent the data. Researchers looking for overexcitability and distinguishing levels of development have generally used content analysis—the coding and analysis of material written by research subjects.

Levels of Development

Piechowski (2006) describes emotional development and well-being as involving: (1) awareness of oneself as an emotional being, (2) relations with others, (3) connection to the broader universe—e.g., cosmic, spiritual—and (4) an attachment to place—natural or man-made. In Dabrowski's theory, the basic requirement for emotional development is overexcitability (OE)—the innate ability of individuals to experience life with intensity and heightened sensitivity to their surroundings. Overexcitability, therefore, represents the potential or essential ingredient for advanced social and moral development.

The hallmarks of higher-level development include acting according to one's principles—for example, showing compassion, promoting peace, and campaigning for justice. Advanced development, fueled by overexcitability, involves exercising the very highest ideals humanly possible—understanding, empathy, responsibility, and universal compassion.

Early Studies and Development of Methods

Recognizing levels of development originally meant searching in autobiographical material for personality characteristics called *dynamisms*. Dynamisms are psychological processes that organize and shape personality. Examples include external and internal conflict, feelings of guilt and shame, self-awareness, self-control, and authenticity.

Dabrowski's theory of positive disintegration specifies five levels of psychological development ranging from Level I, characterized by an absence of developmental dynamisms, to Level V, in which the personality ideal, or unity with the highest universally-valued qualities, is dominant. Because of the complexity of the human psyche and its emotions, Dabrowski and his colleagues found that individuals exhibit signs of various dynamisms at different levels. Some may indicate residuals of past functioning, while others may be precursors of the level toward which one is moving (Dabrowski & Piechowski, 1977).

In 1981, University of Wisconsin professor Philip Morse, together with Michael Piechowski and David Gage, tested new instruments to assess level of emotional development as alternatives to examining autobiographies (Gage, Morse, & Piechowski, 1981). One of these instruments, called the Definition Response Instrument (DRI), consists of six themes that underlie important dynamisms. Respondents report personal experiences corresponding to the theme. Themes include: (1) susceptibility to the influence of others, (2) personal conflict, (3) inferiority, (4) dissatisfaction, (5) self-observation, and (6) personality ideal. Coders then rate subject information according to the level of development indicated. Since the introduction of the DRI, most research studies have used this questionnaire to assess Dabrowski's levels of emotional development.

In 1985, a coding system was developed that provides a more systematic and objective method of identifying these levels (Miller 1985; Miller & Silverman, 1987). Using a manual with rating criteria, coders identify themes in textual material that represent values, feelings toward self, and relations with others. Table 14.1 shows the expression of themes for each level. A summary of qualitative studies that have been conducted on levels of development can be found in Miller, 2008.

Table 14.1. Miller Assessment Coding System

Level	Values	Self	Others
I	Self-Serving	Egocentric	Superficial
II	Stereotypical	Ambivalent	Adaptive
III	Individual	Inner Conflict	Interdependent
IV	Universal	Self-Directed	Democratic
V	Transcendent	Inner Peace	Communion

Adapted from Miller & Silverman, 1987.

Quantitative Studies: Level Scores, Age, and Gender

Table 14.2 summarizes findings from 10 research studies, each using quantitative analyses of DRI questionnaire responses to examine levels of emotional development. The number of subjects in the studies range from seven to 99; the total number is 419. The ages range from 17 to 70. Although researchers have observed precursors of higher-level development in children (Dabrowski, 1964), developmental level has been reserved for assignment to adults. The average level score in the studies in Table 14.2 ranges from 1.80 to 3.55. The lowest and highest individual level scores are 1.0 and 4.5.

Table 14.2. Levels of Development in 10 DRI Studies (N=360)

Author(s)	Date	Subjects	N	Age	Average Level	Standard Deviation	Min-Max
Ammirato, S. P.	1987	Adults	60	18+	1.98	NR	NR
Beach, B. J.	1980	Lesbian and Heterosexual Women	31	17-70	1.83	.31	1.1-2.4
Bouchet, N. M.	2004	Highly Educated Adults	99	M=32	2.41*	.61	1.0-4.5
Brennan, T. P., & Piechowski, M. M.	1991	Nominated Adults	21	NR	2.66	NR	1.3-4.1
Hazell, C. G.	1984	College Students and Grads	24	17-34	2.20	.40	1.4-2.7
Hazell, C. G.	1989	College Students	61	18-38	1.80	.40	1.0-2.7
Lysy, K., & Piechowski, M. M.	1983	Graduate Students	42	M=29	2.05	NR	1.0-3.2
Miller, N. B., Silverman, L. K., & Falk, R. F.	1994	Gifted Adults	41	M=37	2.22	.50	NR
Mróz, A.	2002	Selected Adults	7	30-63	3.55	NR	3.3-3.8
Wagstaff, M.	1997	Outdoor Leaders	33	M=29	2.22	.27	1.8-2.9
NR = Not reported		M = Mean or Average			*Computer scoring		

Researchers found the highest average level scores (2.66 and 3.55) in studies specifically designed to investigate advanced development— Dabrowski's Levels III, IV, and V (Brennan & Piechowski, 1991; Mróz, 2002). In these studies, subjects were selected based on indications of personal growth—i.e., placing the needs of others above their own, exercising self-control, engaging in self-reflection, etc.

The theoretical assertion that psychological development is not age-related was supported by six separate studies (Ammirato, 1987; Beach, 1980; Bouchet, 2004; Lysy & Piechowski, 1983; Miller, Silverman, & Falk, 1994; Wagstaff, 1997). Three of these studies (Ammirato, 1987; Bouchet, 2004; Wagstaff, 1997) also found that whether one was male or female did not influence level score; however, contrary to findings of other adult developmental theories, females scored higher in the Lysy and Piechowski (1983) and Miller, Silverman, and Falk (1994) studies. This raises the question of whether the signs of emotional development, like emotional expression, represent an area in which women receive more encouragement than men in American society.

The relationship between developmental potential, designated as overexcitability (OE), and level of development was examined in four studies (Beach, 1980; Bouchet, 2004; Lysy & Piechowski, 1983; Miller, et al., 1994), and all found that the higher a person's emotional OE, the higher his or her developmental level. In addition, they found that intellectual OE (Beach, 1980; Bouchet, 2004; Lysy & Piechowski, 1983) and imaginational OE (Beach, 1980; Bouchet, 2004; Miller, et al., 1994) also correlated with emotional development. These findings support the hypothesis that emotional, intellectual, and imaginational OE are all important indicators of a person's emotional development. Although Dabrowski's theory posits that all OEs further development, the role of sensual and psychomotor overexcitability is not as clear (see Chapter 7, Jackson & Moyle, this volume).

Certain social influences also may enable personal growth. These include support of family, friends, and mentors; moral imperatives; chaos (discord, uncertainty, etc.); positive and negative states; and aspirations (Bouchet, 2004; Miller, et al., 1994). Other factors such as age, gender, family situation, and education do not appear to aid emotional development (Ammirato, 1987; Beach, 1980; Bouchet, 2004; Lysy & Piechowski, 1983; Miller, et al., 1994; Wagstaff, 1997).

Other psychological characteristics may also promote development. Jung's concept of intuition is one—as a person's intuition increases, so does the level of emotional development (Lysy & Piechowski, 1983). Two other qualities, "experienced emptiness" (Hazell, 1984, 1989) and "existential concern" (Hazell, 1984), appear to increase at Levels II and III as self-reflection becomes more a part of the personality.

In sum, the knowledge and awareness of levels of emotional development and associated variables is valuable information for counselors and instructors who deal with the cognitive and emotional struggles of clients (Beach, 1980; Wagstaff, 1997). We now move to consider qualitative studies of emotional development.

Qualitative Studies

Qualitative studies provide rich insights from textual data, as we see in the following responses from research subjects at different levels of development. Although respondents' scores tended to center around Level II, as seen in Table 14.2, it does not mean that all scores were coded at Level II. On the contrary, many scores were higher, and some were lower. And even though Level IV and V responses were rare, they were present and often occurred in response to DRI item 6, which asks respondents about desired, rather than present, qualities.

Here are brief descriptions of the different levels, followed by items of the DRI and responses that come from several previous studies, illustrating themes regarding "how one relates to others" (Miller, 1985).

At Level I, feelings toward others are superficial and competitive, lacking consideration and depth. Relationships are often based on commonality, such as belonging to a team, family, or ethnic group. Other people may be manipulated or used for one's own purposes. There is little self-reflection or recrimination. Example:

DRI Item 4:   Consider those situations which have caused you to feel frustration or anger toward yourself.

Response: Sometimes the fact that others with less intellectual preparation than myself are more successful in their jobs irritates me, but, well, I don't let it bug me for too long.

Those at developmental Level II have adaptive relationships; they try to follow social rules and expectations. However, doubt and insecurity often arise because there is no clear inner direction. Example:

DRI Item 1:   Think of times when you have been strongly affected by what others think of you or when you have compared yourself in some way to others.

Response: When I was in Superstars two years ago (an athletic event held to earn money for charity), I worried because I felt like my team was disappointed (four-man team) because I'm not very coordinated. I remember that I cried in the middle because I felt so klutzy in comparison to the true athletes on my team.

At Level III, one's feelings toward others are interdependent. Mutual respect and reciprocity characterize relationships. Example:

DRI Item 6: Think of your "ideal self" and those qualities which you think are best for an ideal life. What attributes have you dreamed of having?

Response: My ideal is to be able to help others. To accomplish this successfully, one must be accepted and trusted by others. To me, this is a tremendous challenge, one that will probably never be perfectly accomplished, but a challenge that must not be relinquished.

Relationships for those at Level IV are democratic, characterized by enduring bonds of love and friendship. Feelings toward others are characterized by empathy and compassion. Example:

DRI Item 6: Think of your "ideal self" and those qualities which you think are best for an ideal life. What attributes have you dreamed of having?

Response: I think the quality of compassion is best for an ideal life. The ability to suffer with another, to understand their perspective while honestly naming my own seems essential to building a good life. I see this attribute only being born of listening, love, a gentle yet firm discipline, an ability to wait, a curbing of untamed reactions, yet requiring that one feel strongly with others. Such compassion remembers joy and sadness in a way that helps a person connect with others rather than standing in isolation from them.

At Level V, relationships have the quality of communion. Unconditional love, empathy, responsibility, and spiritual unions are aspects of a person's relations with others. Example:

DRI Item 6: Think of your "ideal self" and those qualities which you think are best for an ideal life. What attributes have you dreamed of having?

<u>Response:</u>   To have love—not merely a feeling, but the love that is a deep, healing compassion—that reaches people and touches them and draws them into the bond of the eternal family, and opens the way in them to wholeness.

Developmental Potential

Overexcitability is a personality trait represented by intensity of feeling, sensitivity to one's environment, and passion for dreams and ideas. It takes many forms. As he observed school children in Poland, Dabrowski identified five areas of overexcitability—emotional, intellectual, imaginational, sensual, and psychomotor. Each form of OE represents heightened sensitivity in responding to stimuli—higher intensity, greater frequency, and longer duration of feeling. Overexcitability may be expressed as great joy or sadness, thirst for knowledge, inventiveness, delight in taste, or restlessness. More detailed descriptions of OE can be found in *"Mellow Out," They Say. If I Only Could* (Piechowski, 2006), "Psychomotor Overexcitability in the Gifted" (Tolan, 1994b), in several chapters in this volume, and in Mendaglio (2008a).

As described in Dabrowski's theory, overexcitability is a necessary, but not sufficient, condition for attaining higher-level development. Also important are special talents and abilities, inner processes that are conducive to development, and an encouraging environment. It is common knowledge to those in the field of gifted education that giftedness requires a social context that enables it. The same is true for emotional development; parents, childcare providers, and teachers all have an essential role in this endeavor. They have the job of providing a supportive environment, which includes a climate of affection, trust, encouragement, interest, and orderliness (Piechowski, 2008).

At school, the child with psychomotor OE, who is supercharged and energetic, needs to be able to move around the classroom, stretch, and take more frequent breaks. At home, he or she needs outlets for energy, such as outdoor activities, access to gyms or activity centers, and areas where gross motor movement is permitted. The child with high sensual OE needs an environment rich in color, sound, and texture. The natural world provides many opportunities to experience such sensations. Similarly, art museums, concert halls, and theaters also offer rich sensual experiences. Children with a vivid imagination (imaginational OE) need time to daydream, draw, write, and discover their surroundings. Children with intellectual OE need opportunities to pursue their passions for discovery through reading, computer searches, and talking to mentors. Finally, the sensitive child, the one with intense emotional OE, needs a safe environment in which to express his or her strong feelings and to maintain special friendships.

Early Studies: Development of Methods

Research on OE has gone from identifying signs of psychomotor, sensual, imaginational, intellectual, and emotional OE in autobiographical content to the development of a 46-item, open-ended questionnaire, which Piechowski (1979) used to collect data from high school students with exceptional ability. Respondents replied in writing to questionnaire items, and OE was rated as present or absent in their responses.

A few years later, Katherine Lysy collected data from graduate students (counselors and noncounselors) and discovered that some items on the OE questionnaire did not differentiate between individuals—e.g., most subjects displayed emotional OE to a particular item. By retaining only the discriminating items, Lysy and Piechowski (1983) then created a 21-item Overexcitability Questionnaire (OEQ). In this new version, they distributed items designed to elicit a particular OE randomly throughout the questionnaire, rather than grouping them by OE. Researchers welcomed this new instrument to assess OE—a trait that many believe is characteristic of gifted and talented students. The 21-item OEQ has been used in theses, dissertations, and numerous research articles. (See Silverman, 2008, for a review of these studies.)

The original scoring was conservative and did not contain sufficient sensitivity for degrees of OE. Regardless of the strength of the response or number of instances discovered, an individual only received one point for each OE. In 1982, Frank Falk, at the University of Denver, who was working with Linda Silverman and a group of graduate students to assess OE in gifted adults, introduced a new scoring system. He recommended that each instance of an OE be coded on a three-point scale as 1 (indicating mild form), 2 (indicating average strength), or 3 (very strong example). Scores obtained in this manner could indicate greater variation among subjects. This method is used today by researchers analyzing written responses to the open-ended OEQ.

Comparison of Studies: OE Profiles

Because earlier studies using the OEQ differed in the number of questions and the coding systems used, comparisons of findings were limited. One could compare OE means (average OE scores), for instance, within a study, but could not easily make comparisons across studies. Because cross-study comparisons are important sources of information about the consistency of findings, researchers looked for a new method. A well-known technique to compare dissimilar scores is to convert them to ranks. This enables one to compare the rank order of OEs both within and across studies.

The following analysis examines information from 19 studies that used the OEQ to assess overexcitability. Twelve are published articles (in gifted education, creative behavior, and psychology journals), five are dissertation studies, one is a master's thesis, and one a master's research report. Two studies required translations of the OEQ instrument. In one, the OEQ was translated into Spanish to enable responses of Venezuelan artists to be compared to American artists (Falk, Manzanero, & Miller, 1997). In another study of tenth-grade students in Turkey, the OEQ was translated into the Turkish language (Yakmaci-Guzel, 2002).

The rank order of OEs in Table 14.3 is designated so that 1 indicates the lowest ranked OE in a study and 5 the highest. To compare studies, ranks were summed across all studies to get a total ranking of OEs.

Table 14.3. Rank Order of Overexcitabilities in 19 OEQ Studies (N=1,051)

Author(s)	Date	Subjects	N	Age	P-OE Rank	S-OE Rank	M-OE Rank	T-OE Rank	E-OE Rank
Ackerman, C. M.	1997a	Tenth- and Eleventh-Grade Gifted and Non-Gifted	79	M=15.6	3	1	2	4	5
Ammirato, S. P.	1987	Adults	60	18+	2	1	3	4	5
Beach, B. J.	1980	Lesbian and Heterosexual Women	51	17-70	1	2	3	4	5
Breard, N. S.	1994	Fourth- and Fifth-Grade Gifted and Non-Gifted	117	9-12	3	1	2	4	5
Buerschen, T. M.	1995	Sixth-Grade Gifted and Non-Gifted	46	11-13	2	1	3	4	5

Author(s)	Date	Subjects	N	Age	P-OE Rank	S-OE Rank	M-OE Rank	T-OE Rank	E-OE Rank
Calic, S.	1994	Visual and Performing Artists and Grads	54	M=32.5	4	1	2	4	5
Ely, E.	1995	Junior High Creative and Gifted	76	M=13	3	1	4	2	5
Falk, R. F., Manzanero, J. B., & Miller, N. B.	1997	Venezuelan and American Artists	50	M=35.5	1	2	4	3	5
Gallagher, S. A.	1985	Sixth-Grade Gifted and Non-Gifted	24	M=11.5	2	1	3	5	4
Hazell, C. G.	1984	College Students	24	17-55	2	4	2	2	5
Jackson, S.	1995	Gifted Adolescents	10	17-19	2	1	3	5	4
Lysy, K. Z., & Piechowski, M. M.	1983	Counselors and Grads	42	M=29	1	2	4	3	5
Miller, N. B., Silverman, L. K., & Falk, R. F.	1994	Gifted Adults and Grads	83	M=32.9	1	2	4	3	5
Piechowski, M. M., & Colangelo, N.	1984	Gifted Adults, Adolescents, and Grads	119	12-59	2	1	3	4	5
Piechowski, M. M., & Cunningham, K.	1985	Artistic Adults	13	19-43	1	3	4	2	5
Piechowski, M. M., & Miller, N. B.	1995	Gifted Children	26	9-14	2	1	3	4	5
Piechowski, M. M., Silverman, L. K., & Falk, R. F.	1985	Intellectual and Artistic Adults and Grads	102	M=33	1	2	4	3	5
Schiever, S. W.	1985	Seventh- and Eighth-Grade Gifted	21	M=12.8	2	1	4	5	3
Yakmaci-Guzel, B., & Akarsu, F.	2006	Tenth-Grade Gifted and Non-Gifted	105	M=16.5	3	1	2	5	4
Sum of the Ranks (Rank Order)					38(2)	29(1)	59(3)	70(4)	90(5)
M = Mean or Average									

The total sum of ranks is as follows: Sensual = 29, Psychomotor = 38, Imaginational = 59, Intellectual = 70, Emotional = 90, even though as seen in Table 14.3, most of the studies vary somewhat from this overall order. A secondary analysis of 13 studies using the OEQ, which includes some of the same data used here, found a similar rank order of means (Ackerman, 1997b).

Many of the variations from the overall result can be accounted for by sample differences. For example, gifted samples, with superior cognitive abilities, are expected to have high intellectual OE. Likewise, artistic and creative groups should have high imaginational and sensual OE.

Emotional OE is ranked highest in 15 of the 19 studies. In the other four samples, intellectual OE is highest, including two studies composed entirely of gifted students (Jackson, 1995; Schiever, 1985) and two studies of gifted and non-gifted students (Gallagher, 1985; Yakmaci-Guzel & Akarsu, 2006).

Analysis of the OEQ-II

Although data from raters was helpful, some researches wanted a more quantitative and more easily-scored instrument. In 1996, researchers working to construct an objective format for assessing OE collected data from middle school, high school, and university students throughout the U.S. and Canada. From the nearly 1,000 subjects, they constructed a 50-item Overexcitability Questionnaire – II (OEQ-II) (Falk, Lind, Miller, Piechowski, & Silverman, 1999).

Ten items assess each OE on the OEQ-II. For example, "I love to listen to the sounds of nature" indicates sensual OE, while "I am deeply concerned about others" designates emotional OE. Items are scored by self-report on a five-point Likert scale from "not at all like me" to "very much like me." (See Falk, et al., 1999 for the development of items and results of the validation study.)

The OEQ-II provides a relatively consistent form of measurement, which allows comparison of OE means rather than ranks. To date, nine separate studies have used the OEQ-II (one study provides two sets of results—one for children and one for parents). Four of the studies were published in leading United States journals in gifted education—two in *Gifted Child Quarterly* and two in *Roeper Review.* One study was published in an international journal, two are dissertations, and two are theses. Five of the studies required translations of the OEQ-II. These include conversion into Turkish, Chinese, Korean, and Spanish. (See Falk, Yakmaci-Guzel, Chang, Pardo, and Chavez-Eakle, 2008, for a description of study characteristics.)

Table 14.4. Means of Overexcitabilities in 9 OEQ-II Studies (N=5,497)

Author(s)	Date	Subjects	N	Age	P-OE	S-OE	M-OE	T-OE	E-OE
*Bouchet, N. M., & Falk, R. F.	2001	College Students	562	M=22.3	3.45	3.22	2.80	3.30	3.72
Chang, H. J.	2001	Fifth-, Eighth-, and Eleventh-Grade Gifted and Non-Gifted	2,997	M=13	2.76	2.83	2.78	2.83	2.97
Chavez, R. A.	2004	Creative/Scientific and Other Adults	90	NR	2.87	3.71	2.52	3.48	3.25
Gross, C. M., Rinn, A. N., & Jamieson, K. M.	2007	Sixth- to Tenth-Grade Gifted	248	M=13	3.29	3.15	2.73	3.70	3.30
Moon, J. H., & Montgomery, D.	2005	High School Gifted	341	NR	3.33	3.70	3.25	3.45	3.71
Pardo, R.	2006	Eight- to 15-Year-Old Gifted and Non-Gifted	204	M=11	3.41	3.42	3.10	3.61	3.45
*Tieso, C. L.	2007a	Seven- to 15-Year-Old Gifted and Non-Gifted	486	7-15	3.49	3.16	2.88	3.39	3.25
**Tieso, C. L.	2007b	Gifted Children	143	M=10	3.48	3.23	3.10	3.34	3.22
**Tieso, C. L.	2007b	Parents of Gifted Children	161	M=34	3.25	3.39	2.14	3.71	3.46
Yakmaci-Guzel, B.	2002	Tenth-Grade Gifted and Non-Gifted	265	M=16.5	3.59	3.52	2.90	3.53	3.62
Grand Harmonic Mean					3.05	3.06	2.82	3.11	3.20
Minus and Plus 2 SE					2.79-3.31	2.78-3.34	2.54-3.10	2.83-3.39	2.90-3.50

* Means are calculated proportionately to group sizes within the study (harmonic mean)
** Means are reported separately for children and parents
M = Mean or Average
NR = Not reported

In the data shown in Table 14.4, total means for each OE were used. When only group means were reported (e.g., separate means for males and females), we calculated an overall mean, proportioning by group size. Analysis involved comparing individual study means to the grand mean or average mean of the combined studies. Meaningful differences exist when a score is two standard errors (2 SEs) above or below the grand mean.

Imaginational and emotional OE were equivalent to the grand mean in seven of the 10 sets of study scores (or 70%), thus providing the most consistent OE scores. Sensual means were equivalent to the grand mean in five studies. There was more variation in psychomotor and intellectual OE, as reported in these studies, with only four scores similar to each other and to the grand mean.

Qualitative Research

Responses to open-ended questions on the OEQ show the intensity of reactions for an individual. School counselors and teachers may obtain greater insight into a student's overexcitability, even though no specific score is obtained. Here are examples of responses of children and adults that illustrate overexcitability in replies to the stimulus questions (Ammirato, 1987; Falk, Piechowski, & Lind, 1994).

Psychomotor OE is an excess of energy. Often seen as eagerness or restlessness, those with psychomotor OE never seem to run out of energy. Examples:

OEQ #5:   When do you feel the most energy, and what do you do with it?

Girl, age 11:   I feel the most energy when I am about to go swimming, I feel as if I could go on forever and make higher limits.

OEQ #7:   How do you act when you get excited?

Adult Response: I am very verbal. If I'm angry, I rant and rave and pace. If I'm nervous, I talk about everything and especially try to make jokes about everything. If I'm happy, I also joke and laugh a lot. If I'm extremely happy-excited, I jump up and down and squeal (it's a frightening sight!).

Sensual OE is a heightened response to input from all of the senses. It may be pleasure or pain; it may be soothing or abrasive; it may be harmonious or discordant. Example:

OEQ #11:   Is taste something very special to you? Describe in what way it is special.

<u>Boy, age 9</u>:	When I taste my favorite food—lobster. It tastes luscious and juicy.
<u>Adult Response</u>:	Tasting is incredibly special. I think that it actually encompasses several sense experiences—the taste (but that experience in itself is limited to three sensations), smell (which I am acutely aware of), and in some cases, feel (texture of what is being tasted). Although taste is an experience that relates to the mouth, I find that I can feel the sensation all over my body.

Imaginational OE is obvious when the creative juices overflow. One is filled with ideas and can write or paint or conjure up images of the past and the future. Examples:

<u>OEQ #3</u>:	What are your special kinds of daydreams and fantasies?
<u>Girl, age 13</u>:	I like to dream about different countries, places that I make up, even animals that I make up. Just anything that is unusual to me.
<u>OEQ #8</u>:	How precisely can you visualize events, real or imaginary?
<u>Adult Response</u>:	I usually visualize in pictures—but my imagination is acute enough that I can "hear" conversation, feel emotional impact to a certain degree. I can almost taste or smell when fantasizing (either real or imaginary events). And touch can be sensed, but more so when remembering rather than creating situations.

Persons with intellectual OE want to know how things work and why. They are not satisfied until there is an answer for everything. They want to solve the world's problems. Mental energy abounds, and hours may be spent gathering information, trying to find solutions, and solving cryptoquips, crossword puzzles, and sudoku. Example:

OEQ #4:   What kinds of things get your mind going?

Girl, age 13:   I think I'm about the only kid who loves to ask questions. I mean, that's my life! Questions, questions, and when I finally get all those questions answered, it's put together, and it's like a puzzle and all the pieces have been put together and it looks decent.

Adult Response: New concepts of how to solve life's complex issues (good vs. evil, destruction vs. generation, self vs. significant other) as well as technological advances (biological monitoring, tissue implants, missiles/satellites for cosmic studies) are areas that truly occupy my intellectual conceptualizations.

Emotional OE is the intensity with which relationships may be felt, the joy of fulfillment, and the sorrow of loss. It is the empathy that some feel for others, the highs and lows of friendship, and the care expressed toward babies and animals. Example:

OEQ #1:   Describe how you feel when you are really high, ecstatic, or incredibly happy.

Boy, age 13:   When I feel really happy, I feel like nothing can go wrong for the rest of my life. When I am really happy, it is more so than other people I know. When I am quite happy, I am so high it seems like nothing could ever get me into a bad mood.

Adult Response: Like everything is right in the world. I feel a physical sensation, as if my heart will swell and burst with happiness. I like to take great gulps of fresh air; my eyes fill with tears.

New Approaches to Data Collection

To facilitate the collection of qualitative data, a 12-item shortened version of the 21-item OEQ, the OEQ Short Form, was created. It retains the questionnaire items with the highest correlation with the total score (Ackerman & Miller, 1997). (See Appendix A for OEQ Short Form items.) This short form is suggested for those interested in collecting examples of personal expressions of overexcitability.

The Gifted Development Center has recently begun to collect information from parents about their children's overexcitability on the OEQ-II Inventory for Parents, adapted by Helen Dudeney (Institute for the Study of Advanced Development, 2007). A child's OE profile is obtained by averaging and ranking his or her overexcitability scores. At post-test conferences with parents, counselors discuss the child's OE profile and suggest strategies for supporting the positive expression of OEs at home and at school. A similar inventory for teachers to assess their students' overexcitability is currently under development (personal communication, L. K. Silverman, August 16, 2007).

Another new version of the OEQ-II was designed as a self-rating questionnaire for younger children, the OEQ-2C (Daniels, Falk, & Piechowski, 2005), and researchers are now analyzing data from 478 children ages six to 14. Early results show the instrument to be highly reliable and theoretically valid, and they also show patterns of responses for intellectual, emotional, and psychomotor OE among gifted students that are consistent with previous findings. Gender differences found with earlier overexcitability instruments are similar in the OEQ-2C—girls have higher scores on emotional and sensual OE than boys. Future use of this new instrument may provide important information on children's intensities and sensitivities for counselors and classroom teachers.

Finally, a website designed to appeal to those who are spiritually gifted features a new method of data collection—online responses to both the DRI and the OEQ-II. The author presented preliminary findings at the annual meeting of the American Psychological Association (Apablaza, 2007).

Summary and Conclusion

Studies of Dabrowski's levels of emotional development have used both quantitative and qualitative approaches to data collection and analysis. Some research was designed to investigate higher-level development by selecting subjects who demonstrated personal growth in their lives. Other studies used undergraduate college students, graduate students in various fields, counselors, and general adult populations.

Several studies investigated the relationship between developmental potential, as indicated by overexcitability, and an individual's level of emotional development. Findings showed that emotional, intellectual, and imaginational OE predicted a person's level score—i.e., the higher the OE score, the higher the level score. Social factors also influenced a person's level score. For example, the support of family, friends, and mentors, as well as the encouragement of aspirations and morals, was associated with higher-level scores. Some psychological concepts, too, such as intuition, "experienced emptiness," and "existential concern" appeared to have a positive influence on adult emotional development scores.

Research studies of developmental potential generally have found subjects' emotional OE scores to be higher than their other OE scores on both quantitative and qualitative instruments. In a few gifted and talented samples, intellectual OE was higher. In all 19 studies using the qualitative instrument (OEQ), emotional or intellectual OE had the highest rank score. For quantitative studies using the OEQ-II, emotional, intellectual, and psychomotor shared the top two slots in most studies. Artists and highly creative samples often had higher than average means on imaginational and sensual OE.

Due to the ease of administration, scoring, and analysis, research using the OEQ-II included larger numbers of subjects than research using the OEQ. The ability to collect and analyze information more quickly is one of the attractive features of the OEQ-II. However, we believe that research using the OEQ (or the OEQ Short Form) will continue because written responses provide evidence of the nature and unique expression of overexcitability.

Five of the OEQ-II studies in our analysis are from cultures other than North American, and these represent four different languages—two of which are non-Indo-European. Despite this huge cultural gulf, results from all studies are similar. This consistency of findings provides strong cross-cultural validation for the concept of overexcitability and the adaptability of the OEQ-II instrument.

In the future, research among different populations will add to our understanding of overexcitability and to its measurement using the OEQ Short Form, 21-item OEQ, and the OEQ-II objective form. We anticipate the increased use of new instruments that assess parent and teacher reports of children's overexcitability, as well as children's self-report (OEQ-2C). New methods of collecting data, such as Internet responses, will no doubt result in the collection of even larger data sets. Thus, the future seems bright for research on overexcitability in children and adults, with new adaptations of the overexcitability questionnaire, new approaches to data collection, and objective scoring.

Finally, research on levels of development may receive renewed interest as innovative scoring methods are developed and refined (e.g., the Miller Assessment Coding System and computer-assisted analysis) and as web-based data collection reaches more subjects. With such solid foundations and progressive new approaches to research, Dabrowski's theory seems poised to take its rightful place among other major theories of personality and psychological development.

Chapter 15

Under Construction: Continued Applications of Dabrowski's Theory of Positive Disintegration with the Gifted

Susan Daniels, Ph.D.

The city of Canmore in Alberta, Canada, is surrounded by the Canadian Rockies, and on this Sunday morning, the clouds are low enough that it seems you can reach out and touch them as they swirl around the base of the mountain. It's a beautiful setting and a lovely time to be writing this last chapter. Over the last two days, I've had the good fortune to hear 17 presentations related to the work of Kazimierz Dabrowski at the Eighth International Congress of the Institute for Positive Disintegration in Human Development. Fittingly, and coincidentally, the theme of this year's congress was "Dabrowski and Gifted Education: Beyond Overexcitabilities." Several contributors to this book gave talks, and in my talk (Daniels, 2008), I provided an overview of this book. I concluded by saying, "Well, now I have to head off to write that last chapter." So I am setting about doing that with the words and images of 17 presenters swirling around in my mind as the clouds swirl outside. Apropos, one slide, presented early in the day, showed the following quote from Dabrowski:

> *The author wishes to emphasize once more his feeling that while clinical studies are quite advanced, experimental research with regard to this theory has not yet progressed enough. The author is*

*convinced that the majority of problems and hypotheses presented
here will undergo substantial modification. He will appreciate it as
an expression of the fact that the theory is "alive"....* (1970, p. xi)

Indeed, the theory is alive, well, and evolving, as the work of the authors herein indicates; it clearly has a home in the field of gifted education, and it is beginning to be more recognized in psychology. Dabrowski's work provides a theoretical base for: (1) recognizing aspects of personality development in the gifted, (2) reframing characteristics that often are viewed as annoying and troublesome in a more positive light—as essential aspects of gifted individuals' developmental potential, and (3) conducting further research related to the emotional and personality development of the gifted child. Further, the theory of positive disintegration (TDP) is a cornerstone for a new perspective on the lifespan development of gifted individuals.

We suspect, and in fact expect, that there will be an even greater surge of renewed and expanded interest in applications of TPD with the gifted—clinically, educationally, empirically, and personally. In addition to the recent publication of *Dabrowski's Theory of Positive Disintegration* (Mendaglio, 2008a), there will be a special issue of *Roeper Review* on the application of Dabrowski's work in gifted education, the publication of this book, and a possible republication of Dabrowski's original writings on TPD, which are currently available on CD via the positive disintegration website (www.positivedisintegration.com). Soon, too, the Overexcitability Questionnaire II for Children (OEQ-2C) will be published and will provide a measure for identifying the psychomotor, sensual, imaginational, intellectual, and emotional overexcitabilities of young gifted children starting at age eight, as well as a means of researching the OEs at a much earlier age than has previously been possible. As such, this will also provide additional information in the process of identifying gifted children and in understanding their emotional development and their potential for advanced development. As Falk and Miller have documented (this volume), there is a fairly large body of research in this area, yet much of it has been conducted with adolescents and adults.

Research on the theory of positive disintegration and the gifted is burgeoning worldwide, including recent research and work in progress in Mexico, Spain, Taiwan, Turkey, and the United States (Falk, Yakmaci-Guzel, Chang, Pardo, & Chavez-Eakle, 2008). In addition, interest in this work has supported a number of conferences, as well as strands within conferences. The international congress that I just attended is held in alternating years in Canada. An upcoming one-day preconference on the applications of Dabrowski's theory with the gifted will be held at the 2008 meeting of the National Association for Gifted Children (NAGC). This is the second such preconference workshop held in the last two years at NAGC, and it is likely to be continued in the future by the Counseling and Guidance Division and the Global Awareness Division. In addition, plans are underway for a symposium in the United States, alternating years with the Canadian congress. There are regular presentations on the applications of Dabrowski's work for teachers, parents, counselors, and other healthcare providers at the annual Supporting Emotional Needs of the Gifted (SENG) conference, and there are typically at least a few sessions based on Dabrowski's theory included in the conference program of the World Council for Gifted and Talented Children.

The theory also takes on new life as it is viewed in light of, and in conjunction with, other theories and perspectives. For example, Bill Tillier presented a provocative session during the first day of the congress here in Canada in which he proposed a neo-Dabrowskian and neo-Maslovian perspective on self-actualization—*multilevel actualization.* The concept of multilevel actualization provides "a new approach emphasizing a multilevel and discriminating approach to actualization" through which "multilevel analysis of the self leads to the development of a personality ideal that subsequently guides growth" (Tillier, 2008). This is an important addition to consider, as there have been earlier comparisons made between Maslow's concepts of self-actualization and Dabrowski's descriptions of the higher levels of development, yet Maslow did not account for the process of attaining self-actualization (Piechowski, 1978). In a similar vein, Sal Mendaglio (2008b) posits that TPD is poised as a personality theory for the 21st century and presents an in-depth comparison of TPD with other theoretical approaches to personality that provides a rich resource for framing future empirical investigations. Future investigations might include:

1. *Expanded cross-cultural research to verify the universality of the theory.* Research is especially needed about levels of development, as most of the existing research has focused on OEs.

2. *Continued development of a computerized coding system for scoring levels of development,* based on the work of Nicole Bouchet (2004).

3. *Furthering the study of OEs as the earliest indicators of developmental potential.* Observation and other qualitative data will provide the

groundwork for further empirical research, including application of the OEQ-2C with younger children in diverse settings and populations, further refinement of a parent checklist, and development of a teacher rating scale.

4. *Continued investigation of validity and reliability of OEQ-II and OEQ-2C.* How stable are the OEQ measures over time? For example, questions remain regarding test-retest reliability of the instruments over a period of six months, a year, five years, and so on. Regarding validity, what about predictive validity? What does it predict? Over what period of time? To what degree (i.e., what percent of the variance is accounted for)? What about concurrent validity? What other measures or behaviors does it correlate with? To what degree? With what populations?

5. *Expanded research on OEs and levels of development with diverse populations,* including people of color, older adults, those of different sexual orientation, twice exceptional individuals, and groups at different strata of socio-economic status.

6. *Further investigation of the effects of gender differences, effects across the lifespan, and family influences on the expression of OEs and level of development.* In particular, future research is needed that addresses varied aspects of giftedness in relationship to OEs and TPD—longitudinal studies and investigations related to different levels of giftedness, for example. Also, we might ask what particular aspects of each OE contribute to higher levels of emotional intelligence, moral and ethical behavior, etc. Further, we might look at how to pinpoint the potential for inner transformation in early phases of development and within unilevel elements. Additional research is also needed on OEs and family constellations by extracting and describing ways of living with intensities that families high in OEs apply.

7. *In-depth case studies of individuals—through interview and biographical analysis—at higher levels of development* (Levels IV and V).

8. *Clinical case studies from counselors, psychologists, and psychiatrists applying Dabrowski's TPD with gifted clients in therapeutic frames.* Clinical material will inform other professionals, and adults who are gifted themselves, of possible supports for living with intensity and for progressing along the difficult path of positive disintegration.

Such clinical material will also likely serve to further: (a) depathologize these intensities and sensitivities and normalize overexcitabilities as part and parcel of gifted development, and (b) tease out when and how mental health services may best be accessed and applied with the gifted.

9. *Investigation of how information and research can be applicable to counselors, clinicians, educators, and parents.* Also, consider what other groups might benefit from this information.

In the meantime, our goal in the present book has been to make highly complex material accessible without diluting its essential concepts. We also hoped to provide resources that will prompt others to conduct continued future research and to apply these concepts in the home, in the classroom, in clinical settings, and in daily life.

Our contributors hope and believe that we have shared useful information and insights for both living with and working with the intensity of the gifted. We encourage others to continue to further the important work of Kazimierz Dabrowski.

Appendix A

Overexcitability Questionnaire – Short Form (OEQ Short Form)

1. Do you ever feel really high, ecstatic, and incredibly happy? Describe your feelings.

2. What has been your experience of the most intense pleasure?

3. What are your special kinds of daydreams and fantasies?

4. What kinds of things get your mind going?

5. When do you feel the most energy, and what do you do with it?

6. How do you act when you get excited?

7. What kind of physical activity (or inactivity) gives you the most satisfaction?

8. Is taste something very special to you? Describe in what way it is special.

9. Do you ever catch yourself seeing, hearing, imagining things that aren't really there? Give examples.

10. When do you feel the greatest urge to do something?

11. If you come across a difficult idea or concept, how does it become clear to you? Describe what goes on in your head in this case.

12. Describe what you do when you are just fooling around.

Adapted from the 21-item OEQ by Ackerman & Miller, 1997.

Appendix B
Overexcitability Questionnaire – Revised (OEQ-REV)

(1997 Revision of the 21-Item OEQ)
(M. M. Piechowski, 2006)

The purpose of the revision was to restore the items tapping experience through all five senses.

1. Describe how you feel when you are extremely joyous, ecstatic, or incredibly happy.

2. What has been your experience of the most intense pleasure?

3. How vivid are your dreams, daydreams, and fantasies? Describe.

4. What kinds of things get your mind going?

5. Describe what you do when you feel full of energy.

6. What attracts you in people you like, and what in those you become close to?

7. How do you act when you get excited?

8. How well do you visualize events, people, and things—real or imaginary? Give examples.

9. What do you like to concentrate on the most?

10. What physical activity (or inactivity) gives you the most satisfaction?

11. What pleasures do you derive from looking at things?

12. What pleasures do you get from different tastes?

13. What delights you in different smells?

14. What pleasures do you experience from touching?

15. What pleasures do you experience from different sounds?

16. Do you sometimes catch yourself seeing, hearing, or imagining things that aren't really there? Give examples.

17. How do you think about your own thinking? Describe.

18. What gives you the strongest urge to do something? Please elaborate.

19. Does it sometimes appear to you that things around you have a life of their own and that animals, plants, and all things in nature have their own feelings? Give examples.

20. When you are faced with a difficult idea or concept, what do you do in order for it to become clear?

21. What do you do when you feel poetic? Describe.

22. How often do you carry on arguments in your head? What sorts of things are they about?

23. When you ask yourself, "Who am I?" what is the answer?

24. When you were young, did you have an imaginary playmate? One or several? Please describe.

References

3 Students learn lessons about peace. (n.d.). Retrieved July 22, 2007, from www.peacejam.org/news_charlotte.htm

Ackerman, C. M. (1993). *Investigating an alternate method of identifying gifted students.* Unpublished master's thesis, University of Calgary, Calgary, Alberta.

Ackerman, C. M. (1997a). Identifying gifted adolescents using personality characteristics: Dabrowski's overexcitabilities. *Roeper Review, 19,* 229-236.

Ackerman, C. M. (1997b). *A secondary analysis of research using the Overexcitability Questionnaire.* Unpublished doctoral dissertation, Texas A & M University, College Station, TX.

Ackerman, C. M., & Miller, N. B. (1997, November). *Exploring a shortened version of the Overexcitability Questionnaire.* Paper presented at the annual meeting of the National Association for Gifted Children, Little Rock, AR.

Adderholdt-Elliott, M. (1987). *Perfectionism: What's bad about being too good?* Minneapolis, MN: Free Spirit.

Adderholdt-Elliott, M., & Goldberg, J. (1999). *Perfectionism: What's bad about being too good?* (rev. ed.). Minneapolis, MN: Free Spirit.

Adelson, J. L. (2007). A "perfect" case study: Perfectionism in academically talented fourth graders. *Gifted Child Today, 30*(4), 14-20.

American Psychiatric Association. (2000). *Diagnostic and statistical manual of mental disorders* (4th ed., text revision.). Washington, DC: Author.

Ammirato, S. P. (1987). *Comparison study of instruments used to measure developmental potential according to Dabrowski's theory of emotional development.* Unpublished doctoral dissertation, University of Denver, Denver, CO.

Apablaza, K. (2007, August). *Spiritual giftedness: Issues of misdiagnosis in Indigo adults.* Paper presented at the annual meeting of the American Psychological Association, San Francisco, CA.

Aron, E. N. (1998). *The highly sensitive person.* New York: Broadway Books.

Assagioli, R. (1965). *Psychosynthesis: A manual of principles and techniques.* New York: Viking Press.

Baker, J. A. (1996). Everyday stressors of academically gifted adolescents. *The Journal of Secondary Gifted Education, 7,* 356-368.

Beach, B. J. (1980). *Lesbian and nonlesbian women: Profiles of development and self-actualization.* Unpublished doctoral dissertation, University of Iowa, Iowa City, IA.

Belenky, M. F., Clinchy, B. M., Goldberger, N. R., & Tarule, J. M. (1986). *Women's ways of knowing: The development of self, voice, and mind.* New York: Basic Books.

Blanco, J. (2003). *Stop laughing at me.* Avon, MA: Adams Media.

Bloom, B. S. (Ed.). (1985). *Developing talent in young people.* New York: Ballantine.

Bouchet, N. (2004). *To give or to take: Assessing five levels of moral emotional development.* Unpublished doctoral dissertation, University of Akron, Akron, OH.

Bouchet, N., & Falk, R. F. (2001). The relationship among giftedness, gender, and overexcitability. *Gifted Child Quarterly, 45,* 260-267.

Breard, N. S. (1994). *Exploring a different way to identify gifted African-American students.* Unpublished doctoral dissertation, University of Georgia, Athens, GA.

Brennan, T. P., & Piechowski, M. M. (1991). A developmental framework for self-actualization: Evidence from case studies. *Journal of Humanistic Psychology, 31,* 43-64.

Buerschen, T. M. (1995). *Researching an alternative assessment in the identification of gifted and talented students.* Unpublished research project, Miami University, Oxford, OH.

Buescher, T. M. (1985). A framework for understanding the social and emotional development of gifted and talented adolescents. *Roeper Review, 3*(1), 10-15.

Buescher, T. M. (1991). Gifted adolescents. In N. Colangelo & G. A. Davis (Eds.), *Handbook of gifted education* (pp. 382-401). Needham Heights, MA: Allyn & Bacon.

Burns, D. D. (1980, November). The perfectionist's script for self-defeat. *Psychology Today,* 34-52.

Calic, S. (1994). *Heightened sensitivities as an indicator of creative potential in visual and performing arts.* Unpublished doctoral dissertation, University of Georgia, Athens, GA.

Cameron, J. (1997). *Heart steps, prayers and declarations for a creative life.* New York: Jeremy P. Tarcher/Putnam.

Chamrad, D. L., & Robinson, N. M. (1986). Parenting the intellectually gifted preschool child. *Topics in Early Childhood Special Education, 6*(1), 74-87.

Chan, D. W. (2007). Positive and negative perfectionism among Chinese gifted students in Hong Kong: Their relationships to general self-efficacy and subjective well-being. *Journal for the Education of the Gifted, 31*, 77-102.

Chang, H. J. (2001). *A research on the overexcitability traits of gifted and talented students in Taiwan*. Unpublished Master's thesis, National Taiwan Normal University, Taipei.

Chavez, R. A. (2004). *Evaluación Integral de la personalidad creativa: Fenomenología clínica y genética* [Integral evaluation of the creative personality: Phenomenology, clinical and genetic]. Unpublished doctoral dissertation, National Autonomous University of Mexico, UNAM, Mexico City.

Cienin, P. (1972). *Existential thoughts and aphorisms*. London: Gryf.

Clark, B. (1988). *Growing up gifted* (3rd ed.). Columbus, OH: Charles E. Merrill.

Clarkson, P. (2003). *The therapeutic relationship*. London: Whurr.

Coles, R. (1990). *The spiritual life of children*. Boston: Houghton Mifflin.

Columbus Group. (1991, July). Unpublished transcript of the meeting of the Columbus Group, Columbus, OH.

Cornell, D. G. (1984). *Families of gifted children*. Ann Arbor, MI: UMI Research Press.

Cornell, D. G., & Grossberg, I. W. (1987). Family environment and personality adjustment in gifted program children. *Gifted Child Quarterly, 31*(2), 59-64.

Csikszentmihalyi, M. (1990). *Flow: The psychology of optimal experience*. New York: Harper & Row.

Dabrowski, K. (1964). *Positive disintegration*. Boston: Little, Brown.

Dabrowski, K. (1966). *Multilevelness of emotional and instinctive functions. Part 1: Theory and description of levels of behavior*. Lublin, Poland: Towarzystwo Naukowe Katolickiego Uniwersytetu Lubelskiego.

Dabrowski, K. (1967). *Personality-shaping through positive disintegration*. Boston: Little, Brown.

Dabrowski, K. (with Kawczak, A., & Piechowski, M. M.). (1970). *Mental growth through positive disintegration*. London: Gryf.

Dabrowski, K. (1972). *Psychoneurosis is not an illness*. London: Gryf.

Dabrowski, K. (with Kawczak, A., & Sochanska, J.). (1973). *The dynamics of concepts*. London: Gryf.

Dabrowski, K. (with Piechowski, M. M.). (1977). *Theory of levels of emotional development* (Vol. 1). Oceanside, NY: Dabor Science.

Dabrowski, K. (1996). The theory of positive disintegration. *International Journal of Psychiatry, 2*(2), 229-244.

Dabrowski, K., & Piechowski, M. M. (1977). *Theory of levels of emotional development: Vol. II—From primary integration to self-actualization.* Oceanside, NY: Dabor Science.

Dalai Lama urges teens to practice peace. (n.d.). Retrieved August 22, 2007, from www.peacejam.org/news_houstonchron.htm

Daniels, S. (2008). *Living with intensity: Applications of TPD for parents, counselors, teachers, and gifted adults.* Paper presented at the Eighth International Congress of the Institute for Positive Disintegration, Alberta.

Daniels, S., Falk, R. F., & Piechowski, M. M. (2005, July). *High intensity: Overexcitabilities in gifted children and their families.* Paper presented at the annual meeting of the Social and Emotional Needs of Gifted, Albuquerque, NM.

Davis, G., & Rimm, S. (2004). *Education of the gifted and talented* (5th ed.). Boston: Pearson.

Delisle, J. (2000). A millennial hourglass: Gifted child education's sands of time. *Gifted Child Today, 22*(6), 26-32.

Dweck, C. S. (2006). *Mindset: The new psychology of success.* New York: Random House.

Ely, E. I. (1995). *The overexcitability questionnaire: An alternative method for identifying creative giftedness in seventh grade junior high school students.* Unpublished doctoral dissertation, Kent State University, Kent, OH.

Emmons, R. A. (1999). *The psychology of ultimate concerns.* New York: Guilford.

Erikson, E. (1950). *Childhood and society.* New York: W. W. Norton.

Erikson, E. (1968). *Identity: Youth and crisis.* New York: W. W. Norton.

Everett, M. (1986). *Breaking ranks.* Philadelphia: New Society.

Falk, R. F., Lind, S., Miller, N. B., Piechowski, M. M., & Silverman, L. K. (1999). *The overexcitability questionnaire – II (OEQ-II): Manual, scoring system, and questionnaire.* Denver, CO: Institute for the Study of Advanced Development.

Falk, R. F., Manzanero, J. B., & Miller, N. B. (1997). Developmental potential in Venezuelan and American artists: A cross-cultural validity study. *Creativity Research Journal, 10*, 201-206.

Falk, R. F., Piechowski, M. M., & Lind, S. (1994). *Criteria for rating levels of intensity of overexcitabilities.* Unpublished manuscript, University of Akron, OH.

Falk, R. F., Yakmaci-Guzel, B., Chang, A. H., Pardo, R., & Chavez-Eakle, R. A. (2008). Measuring overexcitability: Replication across five countries. In S. Mendaglio (Ed.), *Dabrowski's theory of positive disintegration* (pp. 183-199). Scottsdale, AZ: Great Potential Press.

Fiedler, E. D. (1999). Gifted children: The promise of potential/the problems of potential. In V. Schwean & D. Saklofske (Eds.), *Handbook of psychosocial characteristics of exceptional children* (pp. 401-441). New York: Kluwer/Plenum.

Frank, J. (2006). *Portrait of an inspirational teacher of the gifted.* Unpublished doctoral dissertation, University of Calgary, Calgary, Alberta.

Freehill, M. F. (1961). *Gifted children: Their psychology and education.* New York: Macmillan.

Frost, R., Marten, P., Lahart, C., & Rosenblate, R. (1990). The dimensions of perfectionism. *Cognitive Therapy and Research, 14,* 449-468.

Gage, D. F., Morse, P. A., & Piechowski, M. M. (1981). Measuring levels of emotional development. *Genetic Psychology Monographs, 103,* 129-152.

Gallagher, J. J. (1990). Editorial: The public and professional perception of the emotional status of gifted children. *Journal for the Education of the Gifted, 13,* 202-211.

Gallagher, S. A. (1985). A comparison of the concept of overexcitabilities with measures of creativity and school achievement in sixth grade students. *Roeper Review, 8,* 115-119.

Gatto-Walden, P., & Piechowski, M. M. (2001). *Transpersonal knowledge and spiritually gifted children.* Paper presented at the annual meeting of the National Association for Gifted Children, Cincinnati, OH.

Gatto-Walden, P., & Piechowski, M. M. (2006). *Understanding and supporting spiritually gifted children.* Paper presented at the annual meeting of the National Association for Gifted Children, Charlotte, NC.

Gaunt, R. I. (1989). *A comparison of the perceptions of parents of highly and moderately gifted children.* Unpublished doctoral dissertation, Kent State University, Kent, OH.

Gendlin, E. (1997). *Experiencing and the creation of meaning: A philosophical and psychological approach to the subjective.* Evanston, IL: Northwestern University Press.

Goerss, J., Amend, E. R., Webb, J. T., Webb, N. E., & Beljan, P. (2006). Comments on Mika's critique of Hartnett, Nelson, and Rinn's article, "Gifted or ADHD? The Possibilities of Misdiagnosis." *Roeper Review, 28,* 249-251.

Greenspon, T. (2000). "Healthy perfectionism" is an oxymoron! Reflections on the psychology of perfectionism and the sociology of science. *The Journal of Secondary Gifted Education, 11,* 197-208.

Grimaud, H. (2006). *Wild harmonies: A life of music and wolves.* New York: Riverhead.

Grobman, J. (2006). Underachievement in exceptionally gifted adolescents and young adults: A psychiatrist's point of view. *Journal of Secondary Gifted Education, 17*(4), 199-210.

Grof, F. (1976). *Realms of the human unconscious: Observations from LSD research.* New York: E. P. Dutton.

Gross, M. (1995). *Exceptionally gifted children.* London: Routledge.

Gross, C. M., Rinn, A. N., & Jamieson, K. M. (2007). Gifted adolescents' overexcitabilities and self concepts: An analysis of gender and grade level. *Roeper Review, 29,* 240-248.

Hall, C. S, Lindzey, G., & Campbell, J. B. (1997). *Theories of personality* (4th ed.). New York, Wiley.

Hamachek, D. E. (1978). Psychodynamics of normal and neurotic perfectionism. *Psychology, 15,* 27-33.

Harder, A. (2002). *The developmental stages of Erik Erikson.* Retrieved May 21, 2008, from www.learningplaceonline.com/stages/organize/Erikson.htm

Hart, T. (2003). *The secret spiritual world of children.* Makawao, Maui, HI: Inner Ocean.

Hartnett, D. N., Nelson, J. M., & Rinn, A. N. (2004). Gifted or ADHD? The possibilities of misdiagnosis. *Roeper Review, 26,* 73-76.

Hay, D., & Nye, R. (2006). *The spirit of the child.* London: Jessica Kingsley.

Hazell, C. G. (1984). Experienced levels of emptiness and existential concern with different levels of emotional development and profiles of values. *Psychological Reports, 55,* 967-976.

Hazell, C. G. (1989). Levels of emotional development with experienced levels of emptiness and existential concern. *Psychology Reports, 64,* 835-838.

Heinigk, P. (2008, June). Soothing overexcitabilities with food. *Parenting for High Potential,* 20-22.

Hendlin, S. J. (1992). *When good enough is never enough: Escaping the perfection trap.* New York: J. P. Tarcher/Putnam.

Hewitt, P. L., & Flett, G. L. (1991a). Dimensions of perfectionism in unipolar depression. *Journal of Abnormal Psychology, 100,* 98-101.

Hewitt, P. L., & Flett, G. L. (1991b). Perfectionism in the self and social contexts: Conceptualization, assessment, and association with psychopathology. *Journal of Personality and Social Psychology, 60,* 456-470.

Higgins, G. O. (1994). *Resilient adults.* San Francisco: Jossey-Bass.

Hillesum, E. (1985). *An interrupted life: The diaries of Etty Hillesum, 1942-1943.* New York: Washington Square Press.

Hillesum, E. (1996). *An interrupted life and letters from Westerbork.* New York: Holt.

Hillesum, E. (2002). *The letters and diaries of Etty Hillesum, 1941-1943.* (complete and unabridged). Grand Rapids, MI: Eerdmans.

Hollingworth, L. S. (1926). *Gifted children: Their nature and nurture.* New York: Macmillan.

Institute for the Study of Advanced Development. (2007). *Overexcitability inventory for parents* (adapted by H. Dudeney). Denver, CO: Author.

Jackson, P. S. (1995). *Bright star: Black sky origins and manifestations of the depressed state in the lived experience of the gifted adolescent: A phenomenological study.* Unpublished master's thesis, Vermont College of Norwich University, Norwich, VT.

Jackson, P. S. (1998). Bright star – black sky: A phenomenological study of depression as a window into the psyche of the gifted adolescent. *Roeper Review, 20,* 215-221.

Jackson, P. S. (2001). *Communion: The gifted individual's deepest need.* Paper presented at the annual meeting of the National Association for Gifted Children, Cincinnati, OH.

Jackson, P. S. (2006). *Integral development and care of the gifted: Where body, mind, soul and spirit merge.* Paper presented at the annual meeting of the National Association for Gifted Children, Charlotte, NC.

Jackson, P. S. (2007). *Reaching beyond cognicentrism: Embracing integral practice in our work with gifted learners.* Paper presented at the annual meeting of the National Association for Gifted Children, Minneapolis, MN.

Jackson, P. S., (2008, in press). Integral practice and radical programming with highly gifted learners. In J. Castellano (Ed.), *A kaleidoscope of special populations in gifted education.* Waco, TX: Prufrock Press.

Jackson, P. S., & Moyle, V. F. (2005). *The narcissistic pursuit of eminence.* Paper presented at the annual meeting of the National Association for Gifted Children, Louisville, KY.

Jackson, P. S., & Moyle, V. F. (2009, in press). With Dabrowski in mind: Reinstating the outliers in support of full-spectrum development. *Roeper Review.*

Jackson, P. S., Moyle, V. F., & Piechowski, M. M. (2009). Emotional life and psychotherapy of the gifted in light of Dabrowski's theory. In L. Shavinina (Ed.), *International handbook on giftedness* (pp.439-467). New York: Springer.

Jackson, P. S., & Peterson, J. (2003). Depressive disorder in highly gifted adolescents. *The Journal of Secondary Gifted Education, 14,* 175-189.

Jacobsen, M. E. (1999). *Liberating everyday genius: A revolutionary guide for identifying and mastering your exceptional gifts.* New York: Ballantine.

James, W. (1936). *The varieties of religious experience.* New York: Modern Library.

Jamison, K. R. (2004). *Exuberance: The passion for life.* New York: Random House.

Jung, C. G. (1969). *Collected works of C.G. Jung, Vol. 11 – Psychology and religion: West and East.* Princeton, NJ: Princeton University Press.

Kane, M. M. (2003). A conversation with Annemarie Roeper: A view from the self. *Roeper Review, 26*(1), 5-11.

Karnes, F. A., & Nugent, S. A. (Eds.). (2004). *Profiles of influence in gifted education: Historical perspectives and future directions.* Waco, TX: Prufrock Press.

Karnes, F., & Oehler-Stinnet, J. (1986). Life events as stressors with gifted adolescents. *Psychology in the Schools, 23*, 406-414.

Kerr, B. A. (1991). *A handbook for counseling the gifted and talented.* Alexandria, VA: American Association for Counseling and Development.

Kline , B. E., & Meckstroth, E. A. (1985). Understanding and encouraging the exceptionally gifted. *Roeper Review, 8*, 24-30.

Kline, B. E., & Short, E. B. (1991). Changes in emotional resilience: Gifted adolescent girls. *Roeper Review, 13*, 184-187.

Kramer, H. J. (1988). Anxiety, perfectionism, and attributions for failure in gifted and non-gifted junior high school students. *Dissertation Abstracts International, 48*, 3077A. (University Microfilms No. 88-03-891).

Kurcinka, M. S. (1991). *Raising your spirited child.* New York: HarperCollins.

Larsen, R. J., & Diener, E. (1987). Affect intensity as an individual difference characteristic. *Journal of Research in Personality, 21*, 1-39.

Lash, J. P. (1982). *Love, Eleanor: Eleanor Roosevelt and her friends.* Garden City, NY: Doubleday.

Lash, J. P. (1984). *A world of love: Eleanor Roosevelt and her friends, 1943-62.* Garden City, NY: Doubleday.

Lewis, R. B., Kitano, M. K., & Lynch, E. W. (1992). Psychological intensities in gifted adults. *Roeper Review, 15*(1), 25-31.

Lind, S. (2001). Overexcitability and the gifted. *The SENG Newsletter, 1*, 3-6.

LoCicero, K. A., & Ashby, J. S. (2000). Multidimensional perfectionism in middle school aged gifted students: A comparison to peers from the general cohort. *Roeper Review, 22*, 182-185.

Lovecky, D. V. (1992). Exploring social and emotional aspects of giftedness in children. *Roeper Review, 15*(1), 18-25.

Lovecky, D. (1998). Spiritual sensitivity in gifted children. *Roeper Review, 20*, 178-183.

Lysy, K. Z., & Piechowski, M. M. (1983). Personal growth: An empirical study using Jungian and Dabrowskian measures. *Genetic Psychology Monographs, 108*, 267-320.

Manaster, G. J., & Powell, P. M. (1983). A framework for understanding gifted adolescents' psychological maladjustment. *Roeper Review, 6*, 70-73.

Maslow, A. H. (1970). *Motivation and personality* (2nd ed.). New York: Harper & Row.

Maslow, A. H. (1971). *The farther reaches of human nature.* New York: Viking Press.

Meckstroth, E. (1991). Guiding the parents of gifted children: The role of counselors and teachers. In R. M. Milgram (Ed.), *Counseling gifted and talented children: A guide for teachers, counselors, and parents.* Norwood, NJ: Ablex.

Mendaglio, S. (Ed.). (2008a). *Dabrowski's theory of positive disintegration.* Scottsdale, AZ: Great Potential Press.

Mendaglio, S. (2008b). Dabrowski's theory of positive disintegration: A personality theory for the 21st century. In S. Mendaglio (Ed.), *Dabrowski's theory of positive disintegration* (pp. 13-40). Scottsdale, AZ: Great Potential Press.

Merton, T. (1948/1998). *The seven storey mountain.* New York: Harcourt Brace.

Mika, E. (2006). Giftedness, ADHD, and overexcitabilities: The possibilities of misinformation. *Roeper Review, 28,* 237-242.

Mika, E. (2008). Dabrowski's views on authentic mental health. In S. Mendaglio (Ed.), *Dabrowski's theory of positive disintegration* (pp. 139-153). Scottsdale, AZ: Great Potential Press.

Miller, A. (1981). *Prisoners of childhood: The drama of the gifted child and the search for the true self.* New York: Basic Books.

Miller, A. (1982). *The drama of the gifted child.* New York: Basic Books.

Miller, A. (1983). *For your own good: Hidden cruelty in child-rearing and the roots of violence.* New York: Farrar, Straus, & Giroux.

Miller, A. (1991a). *Banished knowledge: Facing childhood injuries.* New York: Doubleday Anchor Books.

Miller, A. (1991b). *The untouched key: Tracing childhood trauma in creativity and destructiveness.* New York: Doubleday Anchor Books.

Miller, A. (1998). *Thou shalt not be aware.* New York: Noonday.

Miller, N. B. (1985). *A content analysis coding system.* Unpublished doctoral dissertation, University of Akron, Akron, OH.

Miller, N. B. (2007). Sources of hope: PeaceJam participants as exemplars of advanced development. *Advanced Development, 11,* 26-39.

Miller, N. B. (2008). Emotion management and emotional development: A sociological perspective. In S. Mendaglio (Ed.), *Dabrowski's theory of positive disintegration* (pp. 227-248). Scottsdale, AZ: Great Potential Press.

Miller, N. B., & Silverman, L. K. (1987). Levels of personality development. *Roeper Review, 9*(4), 221-225.

Miller, N. B., Silverman, L. K., & Falk, R. F. (1994). Emotional development, intellectual ability, and gender. *Journal for the Education of the Gifted, 18,* 20-38.

Moon, J. H., & Montgomery, D. (2005). Profiles of overexcitabilities for Korean high school gifted students according to gender and domain of study. *Journal of Gifted/Talented Education, 15,* 1-10.

Moyle, V. F. (2005). Authentic character development – Beyond nature and nurture. In N. Hafenstein, E. Kutrumbos, & J. Delisle (Eds.), *Perspectives in gifted education: Vol. 3. Complexities of emotional development, spirituality, and hope* (pp. 33-59). Denver, CO: University of Denver, Institute for the Development of Gifted Education, Ricks Center for Gifted Children.

Mróz, A. (2002). *Rozwój osoby wedlug teorii dezyntegracji pozytywnej Kazimierza Dabrowskiego* [Individual development according to Dabrowski's theory of positive disintegration]. Unpublished doctoral dissertation, Catholic University of Lublin, Lublin, Poland.

Nixon, L. F. (2008). Personality, disintegration, and reintegration in mystical lives. In S. Mendaglio (Ed.), *Dabrowski's theory of positive disintegration* (pp. 203-226). Scottsdale, AZ: Great Potential Press.

Noble, K. D. (2001). *Riding the windhorse: Spiritual intelligence and the growth of the self.* Cresskill, NJ: Hampton Press.

Noble, K. D., Robinson, N. M., & Gunderson, S. A. (1993). All rivers lead to the sea: A follow-up study of gifted young adults. *Roeper Review, 15*(3), 124-130.

Nye, R. (1998). *Psychological perspectives on children's spirituality.* Doctoral thesis, University of Nottingham, Nottingham, England.

Pacht, A. (1984). Reflections on perfectionism. *American Psychologist, 39,* 545-562.

Pardo de Santayana Sanz, R. (2006). *El alumno superdotado y sus problemas de aprendizaje: Validación del OEQ-II como prueba de diagnóstico* [The gifted student and learning disabilities: Validation of the OEQ-II as a diagnosis test]. Madrid, Spain: Universidad Complutense de Madrid.

Parker, W. D. (1997). An empirical typology of perfectionism in academically talented children. *American Educational Research Journal, 34,* 545-562.

Parker, W. D. (2000). Healthy perfectionism in the gifted. *The Journal of Secondary Gifted Education, 11,* 173-182.

Parker, W. D., & Mills, C. J. (1996). The incidence of perfectionism in gifted students. *Gifted Child Quarterly, 40,* 194-199.

Parker, W. D., & Stumpf, H. (1995). An examination of the *Multidimensional Perfectionism Scale* with a sample of academically talented children. *Journal of Psychoeducational Assessment, 13,* 372-383.

Peace Pilgrim. (1983). *Peace Pilgrim: Her life and work in her own words.* Santa Fe, NM: Ocean Tree.

Perrone, K. M., Jackson, V. Z., Wright, S. L., Ksiazak, T. M., & Perrone, P. A. (2007). Perfectionism, achievement, life satisfaction, and attributions of success among gifted adults. *Advanced Development, 11,* 106-123.

Piechowski, M. M. (1978). Self-actualization as a developmental structure: A profile of Antoine de Saint-Exupéry. *Genetic Psychology Monographs, 97,* 181-242.

Piechowski, M. M. (1979). Developmental potential. In N. Colangelo & R. T. Zaffrann (Eds.), *New voices in counseling the gifted* (pp. 25-57). Dubuque, IA: Kendall/Hunt.

Piechowski, M. M. (1986). The concept of developmental potential. *Roeper Review, 8*, 190-197.

Piechowski, M. M. (1991). Emotional development and emotional giftedness. In N. Colangelo & G. A. Davis (Eds.), *Handbook of gifted education* (pp. 285-306). Needham Heights, MA: Allyn & Bacon.

Piechowski, M. M. (1992). Giftedness for all seasons: Inner peace in time of war. In N. Colangelo, S. G. Assouline, & D. L. Ambroson (Eds.), *Talent development: Proceedings of the Henry B. and Jocelyn Wallace National Research Symposium on Talent Development* (pp. 180-203). Unionville, NY: Trillium Press.

Piechowski, M. (1997). Emotional giftedness: The measure of interpersonal intelligence. In N. Colangelo & G. A. Davis (Eds.), *Handbook of gifted education* (2nd ed., pp. 366-381). Boston: Allyn & Bacon.

Piechowski, M. M. (1999). Overexcitabilities. In M. Runco & S. Pritzker (Eds.), *Encyclopedia of creativity* (vol. 2, pp. 325-334). New York: Academic Press.

Piechowski, M. M. (2000). Childhood experiences and spiritual giftedness. *Advanced Development, 9*, 65-90.

Piechowski, M. M. (2001). Childhood spirituality. *Journal of Transpersonal Psychology, 33*, 1-15.

Piechowski, M. M. (2002). Experiencing in a higher key: Dabrowski's theory of and for the gifted. *Gifted Education Communicator, 33*(1), 28-31, 35-36.

Piechowski, M. M. (2003). Emotional and spiritual giftedness. In. N. Colangelo & G. A. Davis (Eds.), *Handbook of gifted education* (3rd ed., pp. 403-416). Boston: Allyn & Bacon.

Piechowski, M. M. (2006). *"Mellow out," they say. If I only could: Intensities and sensitivities of the young and bright.* Madison, WI: Yunasa Books.

Piechowski, M. M. (2008). Discovering Dabrowski's theory. In S. Mendaglio (Ed.), *Dabrowski's theory of positive disintegration* (pp. 41-77). Scottsdale, AZ: Great Potential Press.

Piechowski, M. M. (2009, in press). Peace Pilgrim: Exemplar of Level V. *Roeper Review.*

Piechowski, M. M., & Colangelo, N. (1984). Developmental potential of the gifted. *Gifted Child Quarterly, 28*, 80-88.

Piechowski, M. M., & Cunningham, K. (1985). Patterns of overexcitability in a group of artists. *Journal of Creative Behavior, 19*(3), 153-174.

Piechowski, M. M., & Miller, N. B. (1995). Assessing developmental potential in gifted children: A comparison of methods. *Roeper Review, 17*, 176-180.

Piechowski, M. M., Silverman, L. K., & Falk, R. F. (1985). Comparison of intellectually and artistically gifted on five dimensions of mental functioning. *Perceptual and Motor Skills, 60,* 539-549.

Piirto, J. (2004). *Understanding creativity.* Scottsdale, AZ: Great Potential Press.

Pipher, M. (2000). *Another country: Navigating the emotional terrain of our elders.* New York: Penguin.

Podvoll, E. M. (1990). *Recovering sanity.* Boston: Shambhala.

Probst, B. (2007, January/February). When your child's second exceptionality is emotional: Looking beyond psychiatric diagnosis. *2e Twice-Exceptional Newsletter, 20,* 1-24.

Reich, K. H. (2007). *Not blank slates: Recognizing children's own spiritual worldview.* Retrieved August 23, 2008, from www.spiritualdevelopmentcenter.org

Roberts, S. M., & Lovett, S. B. (1994). Examining the "F" in gifted: Academically gifted adolescents' physiological and affective responses to scholastic failure. *Journal for the Education of the Gifted, 17,* 241-259.

Robinson, N. M. (1996). Counseling agendas for gifted young people: A commentary. *Journal for the Education of the Gifted, 20,* 128-137.

Robinson, N. M., & Noble, K. D. (1991). Social-emotional development and adjustment of gifted children. In M. C. Wang, M. C. Reynolds, & H. J. Walberg (Eds.), *Handbook of special education: Research and practice, Vol. 4: Emerging programs* (pp. 57-76). New York: Pergamon Press.

Roedell, W. C. (1984). Vulnerabilities of highly gifted children. *Roeper Review, 6,* 127-130.

Roehlkepartain, E. C., King, P. E., Wagener, L., & Benson, P. L. (Eds.). (2006). *Handbook of spiritual development in childhood and adolescence.* Thousand Oaks, CA: Sage

Roeper, A. (1982). How gifted cope with their emotions. *Roeper Review, 5,* 21-24.

Roeper, A. (1985). *Images.* Unpublished manuscript.

Roeper, A. (1986). Participatory vs. hierarchical models for administration: The Roeper School experience. *Roeper Review, 9,* 4-10.

Roeper, A. (1990). *Educating children for life: The modern learning community.* Unionville, NY: Trillium.

Roeper, A. (1991). Gifted adults: Their characteristics and emotions. *Advanced Development, 3,* 85-98.

Roeper, A. (1995). *Annemarie Roeper: Selected writings and speeches.* Minneapolis, MN: Free Spirit.

Roeper, A. (1998). The "I" of the beholder: An essay on the Self, its existence and its power. *Roeper Review, 20*(3), 144-149.

Roeper, A. (2004a). The Annemarie Roeper method of qualitative assessment. *Gifted Education Communicator, 31-33.*

Roeper, A. (2004b). *My life experiences with children: Selected writings and speeches.* Denver, CO: DeLeon.

Roeper, A. (2006). *Growing old gifted.* Unpublished manuscript.

Roeper, A. (2007). *The "I" of the beholder: A guided journey to the essence of a child.* Scottsdale, AZ: Great Potential Press.

Roeper, A., & Roeper, G. (1981). *Roeper philosophy.* Unpublished manuscript.

Roosevelt, E. (1960). *You learn by living.* Philadelphia: Westminster Press.

Ross, A. O. (1979). The gifted child in the family. In N. Colangelo & R. T. Zaffrann (Eds.), *New voices in counseling the gifted* (pp. 402-407). Dubuque, IA: Kendall/Hunt.

Rush, A., & Rush, J. (1992). Peace Pilgrim: An extraordinary life. *Advanced Development, 4,* 61-74.

Salinger, M. A. (2000). *Dream catcher. A memoir.* New York: Washington Square Press.

Schetky, D. H. (1981). A psychiatrist looks at giftedness: The emotional and social development of the gifted child. *G/C/T, 18,* 2-4.

Schiever, S. W. (1985). Creative personality characteristics and dimensions of mental functioning in gifted adolescents. *Roeper Review, 7,* 223-226.

Schuler, P. A. (1997). *Characteristics and perceptions of perfectionism in gifted adolescents in a rural school environment.* Unpublished doctoral dissertation, University of Connecticut, Storrs, CT.

Schuler, P. A. (2000). Perfectionism and the gifted adolescent. *The Journal of Secondary Gifted Education, 11,* 183-196.

Sebring, A. D. (1983). Parental factors in the social and emotional adjustment of the gifted. *Roeper Review, 6,* 97-99.

Sheehy, G. (1995). *New passages: Mapping your life across time.* New York: Random House.

Sheehy, G. (2006). *Passages: Predictable crises of adult life.* New York: Ballantine Books.

Siegle, D., & Schuler, P. A. (2000). Perfectionism differences in gifted middle school students. *Roeper Review, 23,* 39-44.

Silverman, L. K. (1983). Personality development: The pursuit of excellence. *Journal for the Education of the Gifted, 6,* 5-19.

Silverman, L. K. (1993a). Counseling families. In L. K. Silverman (Ed.), *Counseling the gifted and talented* (pp. 3-28). Denver, CO: Love.

Silverman, L. K. (1993b). A developmental model for counseling the gifted. In L. K. Silverman (Ed.), *Counseling the gifted and talented* (pp. 51-75). Denver, CO: Love.

Silverman, L. K. (1993c). The gifted individual. In L. K. Silverman (Ed.), *Counseling the gifted and talented* (pp. 3-28). Denver, CO: Love.

Silverman, L. K. (1999). Perfectionism. *Gifted Education International, 13*, 216-225.

Silverman, L. K. (2008). The theory of positive disintegration in the field of gifted education. In S. Mendaglio (Ed.), *Dabrowski's theory of positive disintegration* (pp. 157-174). Scottsdale, AZ: Great Potential Press.

Silverman, L. K., & Kearney, K. (1989). Parents of the extraordinarily gifted. *Advanced Development, 1*, 41-56.

Slaney, R. B., Rice, K. G., Mobley, M., Trippi, J., & Ashby, J. S. (2001). The revised *Almost Perfect Scale. Measurement and Evaluation in Counseling and Development, 34*, 130-145.

Solow, R. E. (1995). Parents' reasoning about the social and emotional development of their intellectually gifted children. *Roeper Review, 18*(2), 142-146.

Sondergeld, T., Schultz, R. A., & Glover, L. K. (2007). The need for research replication: An example from studies of perfectionism and gifted early adolescents. *Roeper Review, 29*(5), 19-25.

Speirs Neumeister, K. L. (2004a). Factors influencing the development of perfectionism in gifted college students. *Gifted Child Quarterly, 48*, 259-274.

Speirs Neumeister, K. L. (2004b). Interpreting successes and failures: The influence of perfectionism on perspective. *Journal for the Education of the Gifted, 27*, 311-335.

Speirs Neumeister, K. L. (2004c). Understanding the relationship between perfectionism and achievement motivation in gifted college students. *Gifted Child Quarterly, 48*, 219-231.

Speirs Neumeister, K. L., Williams, K. K., & Cross, T. L. (2007). Perfectionism in gifted high-school students: Responses to academic challenge. *Roeper Review, 29*(5), 11-18.

Strauss, W., & Howe, N. (1991). *Generations: The history of America's future, 1584-2069*. New York: William Morrow.

Streznewski, M. L. (1999). *Gifted grownups: The mixed blessings of extraordinary potential*. New York: John Wiley & Sons.

Strip, C. A., & Hirsch, G. (2000). *Helping gifted children soar: A practical guide for parents and teachers*. Scottsdale, AZ: Great Potential Press.

Taylor, M. (1999). *Imaginary companions and the children who create them*. New York: Oxford University Press.

Thoreau, H. D. (1854/2004). *Walden: A fully annotated edition* (edited by Jeffrey S. Cramer). New Haven & London: Yale University Press.

Tieso, C. L. (2007a). Overexcitabilities: A new way to think about talent? *Roeper Review, 29*, 232-239.

Tieso, C. (2007b). Patterns of overexcitabilities in identified gifted students and their parents: A hierarchical model. *Gifted Child Quarterly, 51*(1), 11-22.

Tillier, B. (2008). *Introduction of the concept of multilevel actualization.* Paper presented at the Eighth International Congress of the Institute for Positive Disintegration, Alberta.

Toffler, A. (1984). *Future shock.* New York: Bantam Books.

Tolan, S. S. (1992). Only a parent: Three true stories. *Understanding Our Gifted, 4*(3), 1, 8-10.

Tolan, S. S. (1994a). Discovering the gifted ex-child. *Roeper Review, 17,* 134-138.

Tolan, S. S. (1994b). Psychomotor overexcitability in the gifted: An expanded perspective. *Advanced Development, 6,* 66-86.

Tolan, S. S. (1996). Discovering the gifted ex-child. *Advanced Development, 1*(1), 77-86.

Tolan, S. S. (2000). *Spirituality and the highly gifted adolescent.* Retrieved August 23, 2008, from www.stephanietolan.com/spirituality.htm

Tucker, B., & Hafenstein, N. L. (1997). Psychological intensities in young gifted children. *Gifted Child Quarterly, 21,* 66-75.

U.S. Department of Education. (1993). *National excellence: A case for developing America's talent* (PIP 93-1202). Washington, DC: Author.

Vandiver, B. J., & Worrell, F. C. (2002). The reliability and validity of scores on the *Almost Perfect Scale – Revised* with academically talented middle school students. *Journal of Secondary Gifted Education, 13,* 108-119.

Wagstaff, M. (1997). *Outdoor leader self-awareness and its relationship to co-leaders' perceptions of influence.* Unpublished doctoral dissertation, Oklahoma State University, Stillwater, OK.

Webb, J. T., Amend, E. R., Webb, N. E., Goerss, J., Beljan, P., & Olenchak, F. R. (2005). *Misdiagnosis and dual diagnoses of gifted children and adults: ADHD, bipolar, OCD, Asperger's, depression, and other disorders.* Scottsdale, AZ: Great Potential Press.

Webb, J. T., Gore, J. L., Amend, E. R., & DeVries, A. R. (2007). *A parent's guide to gifted children.* Scottsdale, AZ: Great Potential Press.

Webb, J. T., Gore, J. L., Karnes, F. A., & McDaniel, A. S. (2004). *Grandparents' guide to gifted children.* Scottsdale, AZ: Great Potential Press.

Webb, J. T., Meckstroth, E. A., & Tolan, S. S. (1982). *Guiding the gifted child: A practical source for parents and teachers.* Scottsdale, AZ: Great Potential Press (formerly Ohio Psychology Press).

Whitmore, J. R. (1980). *Giftedness, conflict, and underachievement.* Boston: Allyn & Bacon.

Wilber, K. (2000). *Integral psychology: Consciousness, spirit, psychology, and therapy.* Boston: Shambhala.

Witzel, J. E. (1991). *Lives of successful never-married women: Myths and realities.* Unpublished doctoral dissertation, Northwestern University, Evanston, IL.

Yakmaci-Guzel, B. (2002). *Ustun yeteneklilerin belirlenmesinde yardimci yeni bir yaklasim: Dabrowski'nin asiri dduyarlilik alanlari* [A supplementary method in the identification of gifted individuals: Dabrowski's overexcitabilities]. Unpublished doctoral dissertation, University of Istanbul, Turkey.

Yakmaci-Guzel, B., & Akarsu, F. (2006). Comparing overexcitabilities of gifted and non-gifted 10th grade students in Turkey. *High Abilities Studies, 17,* 43-56.

Zohar, D. & Marshall, I. (2000). *SQ: Connecting with our spiritual intelligence.* New York: Bloomsbury.

Author Index

289

Topic Index

About the Authors

Edward R. Amend, Psy.D., is a practicing clinical psychologist at Amend Psychological Services, P.S.C., in Lexington, Kentucky, with a satellite office in Cincinnati, Ohio. In his practice, Dr. Amend focuses on the social, emotional, and educational needs of gifted and talented youth, adults, and their families. He provides evaluations and therapy, facilitates child and parent discussion groups, and offers consultation and training for school personnel and other professionals. Dr. Amend is co-author of two award-winning books: *A Parent's Guide to Gifted Children*, and *Misdiagnosis and Dual Diagnoses of Gifted Children and Adults: ADHD, Bipolar, OCD, Asperger's, Depression, and Other Disorders*. As a strong advocate for the gifted population, Dr. Amend's service has included the Board of Directors of Supporting Emotional Needs of the Gifted, President of the Kentucky Association for Gifted Education, Chair for the National Association for Gifted Children Counseling and Guidance Division, and consultant to the Davidson Institute for Talent Development. He can be reached through www.amendpsych.com.

Susan Daniels, Ph.D., is an Associate Professor of Educational Psychology and Counseling at California State University, San Bernardino, where she also serves as Coordinator for the Gifted and Talented Education Certificate Program for K-12 teachers. During the academic year, she serves as a university-community program coordinator for developing and offering after-school enrichment in literacy and the arts. In the summers, she directs the Summer Enrichment Academy program that brings traditionally under-served and underrepresented gifted middle and high school students to campus for interdisciplinary and exploratory workshops with professors in the arts, natural sciences, social sciences, and technology. She also serves as director of Precollege Programs, an early entrance, dual-enrollment program for high-potential high school juniors and seniors. Susan is a consultant, professional development specialist, and international speaker with expertise in creativity, enrichment programming, and the social and emotional needs and development of gifted individuals. Susan may be reached through www.insightresources.org or at dr.sdaniels@insightresources.org.

R. Frank Falk, Ph.D., is the Director of Research at The Institute for the Study of Advanced Development, Denver, Colorado, and Professor Emeritus of Sociology at The University of Akron, Akron, Ohio. He has chaired the Departments of Sociology at two major universities: The University of Denver and The University of Akron. He also served as Chair of the Classical Studies, Anthropology, and Archaeology Department while at Akron and was University Vice-President of Research in 1993. He specializes in research methodology with an interest in social psychology, gifted and talented, and adult emotional development. He has authored or co-authored nine books and monographs, 12 chapters in books, 26 peer-reviewed journal articles, and delivered more than 75 presentations at professional meetings, including the National Association for Gifted Children, Social and Emotional Needs of Gifted, and the World Conference on Gifted. Since 1980, he has conducted research on the personality traits of gifted and talented students and adults using both qualitative and quantitative approaches. His most recent publications involve the measurement of overexcitabilities in Dabrowski's theory. His chapter on cross-cultural studies appears in S. Mendaglio (Ed.) *Dabrowski's Theory of Positive Disintegration.* He may be reached at rfalk@uakron.edu or www.gifteddevelopment.com.

Ellen D. Fiedler, Ph.D., Professor Emerita from the Master's degree program in gifted education at Northeastern Illinois University in Chicago, is a consultant who regularly provides professional development for school districts and other educational agencies. She obtained her Ph.D. in Counseling and Guidance from the University of Wisconsin – Madison, where she was a research assistant at the Guidance Institute for Talented Students. She has been a Gifted Program Coordinator and a State Consultant for Gifted and has provided consultation services and presentations in the United States, Canada, Australia, and Russia. She is a published author and a regular presenter at state, national, and international conferences, including the past seven World Congresses on the Gifted. She has been

Chair of the Counseling and Guidance Division of the National Association for Gifted Children (NAGC) and co-chair of the Global Awareness Division of NAGC. She lives in Michigan and is currently President of the Michigan Alliance for Gifted Education.

Patricia Gatto-Walden, Ph.D., is a nationally recognized licensed psychologist who has worked holistically with thousands of gifted and talented children, adolescents, and adults for three decades. In her adjunct consulting practice, she has helped parents, educators, and administrators understand and accept the multifaceted inner world, needs, and concerns of gifted individuals. It is Patricia's belief that home life, education, and counseling of the gifted must attend to the integration and enhancement of the mind, heart, body, spirit, and social self in order to have contentment and balance in everyday life. Additionally, her career has included graduate level counseling instruction and supervision, as well as educational administration. She has extensive experience guiding staff development seminars, program development sessions, and problem solving groups, and she has been a featured speaker at international and national gifted conferences and educational workshops. She was the co-chair of the Global Awareness Division of NAGC. Currently, she is a Senior Fellow for the Institute of Educational Advancement, which serves profoundly gifted youth through various programs, including Yunasa, a holistic summer camp. Visit www.patriciagattowaldencom.

P. Susan Jackson, M.A., R.C.C., is the Founder and Therapeutic Director of The Daimon Institute for the Highly Gifted in White Rock, British Columbia, Canada. She is also the District Coordinator of "Programs to Support Gifted and Talented Students" in Langley, British Columbia, Canada. She is a contributor to the *International Handbook on Giftedness* and the *Roeper Review* and speaks nationally and internationally on advanced development, mental health, and the highly gifted. She is the Chair-Elect for the Counseling and Guidance Division of the National Association for Gifted Children and has been researching and applying Dabrowski's theory for 12 years. Sue lives in White Rock, British Columbia, and can be reached at the Daimon Institute for the Highly Gifted through www.daimoninstitute.com.

Michele Kane, Ed.D., is an Assistant Professor in the department of Special Education and the Coordinator of the Master of Arts in Gifted Education Program at Northeastern Illinois University in Chicago. She holds advanced degrees in Counseling and Guidance, and Educational Administration. Michele is an active member of state and national gifted organizations and is currently the President-Elect of the Illinois Association for Gifted Children and the Chair-Elect of the Global Awareness Network of the National Association for Gifted Children. As a presenter for state, national, and international conferences, a major focus of Michele's work is related to emotional and spiritual giftedness and the affective aspects of educational programming for gifted students. She also provides professional development workshops for teachers, as well as seminars for parents with an emphasis on social and emotional learning. Along with her husband Dan, she is the parent of six gifted adult children.

Elizabeth Meckstroth, M.Ed., M.S.W., has served the social/emotional issues of families of gifted children since 1979. She coordinated development of Supporting Emotional Needs of the Gifted and facilitated hundreds of parent discussion groups. She assessed intelligence and personality/learning styles for hundreds of children and supported their school advocacy. Betty co-authored *Teaching Young Gifted Children in the Regular Classroom*, *Acceleration for Gifted Learners K-5*, and *Guiding the Gifted Child*, and she wrote the "Parenting" column for *Understanding Our Gifted*. She is on *The Gifted Education Communicator* Advisory Board and is a Contributing Editor for *Roeper Review*, as well as a Senior Fellow with the Institute for Educational Advancement, facilitating the Yunasa camp for highly gifted adolescents and developing a model preschool for the highly gifted. Through countless publications and presentations, she has forged awareness about highly gifted children. Betty earned an M.Ed. at the University of Dayton, a Certificate in Analytical Psychology from the C.G. Jung Institute of Chicago, and an M.S.W. from Loyola University, Chicago. She and husband Bill live blissfully in Berkeley, close to grandchildren. She can be reached at betmeck@comcast.net.

Nancy B. Miller, Ph.D., holds degrees in psychology and sociology and has received advanced training in family processes and children's psychological adjustment at the University of Virginia and the University of California, Berkeley. She is editor of *Advanced Development*, a journal on adult giftedness, and currently does research and testing at the Gifted Development Center in Denver, Colorado. She has taught at the undergraduate and graduate levels at the University of Denver and the University of Akron. From 2002 to 2006, she served as Executive Officer of Sociologist for Women in Society. She discovered Dabrowski's theory as a graduate student and has pursued an interest in the theory throughout her career. Her numerous publications focus on emotional development, gender and giftedness, women's social support and adjustment to stressful life events, and family processes. She can be reached by email at nmiller@uakron.edu, or see the website www.gifteddevelopment.com.

Vicky Frankfourth Moyle, M.A., L.P.C., L.M.H.C., holds a Master's degree in mathematics education from Indiana University and a Master's degree in counseling psychology from the University of Colorado. A teacher for more than 20 years, she has taught in Indiana, Missouri, Colorado, and Washington. Vicky is a Licensed Professional Counselor in Colorado, a Licensed Mental Health Counselor in Washington, and teaches mathematics at Bellingham Technical College. She also currently consults with the Daimon Institute for the Highly Gifted in White Rock, British Columbia. She received her certificate in Gifted Education in Missouri, where she coordinated middle school gifted programs. Current projects include co-editing the special issue on Kazimierz Dabrowski for *Roeper Review*. She is a past contributor to the *Perspectives in Gifted Education* monograph series from the University of Denver's Ricks Center for Gifted Children, and she co-authored a chapter in Larisa Shavinina's *International Handbook on Giftedness*, to be published in 2009. Vicky has presented on gifted education and gifted counseling issues at numerous conferences, including the Gifted Association of Missouri, National Association for Gifted Children, Hollingworth Center for the Highly Gifted, and International Congress on Dabrowski and the Theory for Positive Disintegration.

Michael M. Piechowski, Ph.D., author of *Mellow Out, They Say. If I Only Could: Intensities and Sensitivities of the Young and Bright,* received his M.Sc. from Adam Mickiewicz University in Poznan, his hometown in Poland. He obtained a Ph.D. in molecular biology from the University of Wisconsin – Madison. He met Dr. Kazimierz Dabrowski at the University of Alberta, Edmonton, and collaborated with him for eight years. Piechowski returned to the University of Wisconsin to obtain a Ph.D. in counseling psychology.

Subsequently, he taught at the University of Illinois, Northwestern University, and Northland College, situated on Lake Superior's Chequamegon Bay. He is a Senior Fellow of the Institute for Educational Advancement and Professor Emeritus, Northland College, Ashland, Wisconsin, where he introduced an experiential course in transpersonal psychology. He is a contributor to the *Handbook of Gifted Education* and the *Encyclopedia of Creativity.* Since 2002, he has been involved with the Yunasa summer camp for highly gifted youth, organized by the Institute for Educational Advancement. He lives in Madison, Wisconsin.

Annemarie Roeper, Ed.D., has been working for more than 70 years with gifted children and observing their rich inner lives. She is the author of several hundred articles and three books, including her latest book, *The "I" of the Beholder,* which provides readers with the results of her observations. A Holocaust survivor, she founded the Roeper School along with her husband George in 1941. This school, which has at its core an educational philosophy of self-actualization and interdependence, provides a means of educating the whole child. The Roepers also founded the respected journal the *Roeper Review,* which continues as a forum for the exchange of ideas regarding gifted education. Throughout her career, Annemarie has been an active participant in local, state, and national organizations for the gifted. She was a co-founder of the Global Awareness division of the National Association for Gifted Children and was recognized by this organization with its Distinguished Service Award. Annemarie continues her consulting work with gifted families and uses an approach that she developed and called *Qualitative Assessment.* This method of assessment is based on the inner agenda of the gifted child. Her lifework of advocacy on behalf of gifted children promises to continue into the current phase of her life, which she describes as "beyond old age."

Linda Kreger Silverman, Ph.D., is a licensed clinical and counseling psychologist who has contributed more than 300 publications to the field, including the textbook *Counseling the Gifted and Talented,* based on Dabrowski's theory, and *Upside-Down Brilliance: The Visual-Spatial Learner.* She founded and directs the Institute for the Study of Advanced Development and its subsidiary, the Gifted Development Center (www.gifteddevelopment.com), which has assessed more than 5,500 children in the last 30 years. In 2002, she established a second subsidiary,

Visual-Spatial Resource (www.VisualSpatial.org). For nine years, she served on the faculty of the University of Denver in counseling psychology and gifted education. She has been studying the psychology and education of the gifted since 1961. Silverman created the only journal on adult giftedness, *Advanced Development*, dedicated to promoting Dabrowski's theory. Co-chair of the NAGC Task Force on Assessment, she advises major test publishers, organizes symposia on assessment of the gifted, and has been instrumental in the development of extended norms for the WISC-IV.

Stephanie S. Tolan, M.A., Newbery Honor-winning author (*Surviving the Applewhites*) of more than two dozen novels for children and young adults, is also co-author of *Guiding the Gifted Child* and the author of "Is It a Cheetah?," an essay about gifted children that has been translated into more than 40 languages. She has written and spoken about the social, emotional, and spiritual needs of gifted children, adolescents, and adults for 25 years. A Senior Fellow at the Institute for Educational Advancement, she helped design Yunasa, a camp for highly gifted children and adolescents where the focus is helping unusually brilliant young people to bring balance to their lives, recognize their value to the world, and use the full range of their minds to bring joy to self and others. A gifted ex-child herself, as well as mother and grandmother of highly gifted children, she seeks to remind gifted individuals to nourish their hearts and their imaginations as well as their intellects. She can be reached through (and many of her articles on the gifted can be found on) her website: www.stephanietolan.com.